The Shell Book of
Rural Britain

The Shell Book of
Rural Britain

Keith Mossman

David & Charles Newton Abbot London
North Pomfret [Vt] Vancouver

Photographs
Copyright owners are credited in the captions.
Author and publishers thank the Museum of English Rural Life, Reading, in
particular for their help and the many credits are abbreviated to MERL.
Author and publishers are also grateful to the librarian of *The Field* for generous
help in tracing many of the photographs.

Shell U.K. Limited while sponsoring this book would point
out that the author is expressing his own views.

British Library Cataloguing in Publication Data

Mossman, Keith
    The Shell book of rural Britain.
    1. Country life – Great Britain
    I. Title
    941'.0091'734   S522.G7

    ISBN 0-7153-7394-3

First published 1978
Second impression 1978

©Keith Mossman 1978

Printed in Great Britain
at the Alden Press, Oxford
for David & Charles (Publishers) Limited
Brunel House Newton Abbot Devon

Published in the United States of America
by David & Charles Inc
North Pomfret Vermont 05053 USA

Published in Canada
by Douglas David & Charles Limited
1875 Welch Street North Vancouver BC

Contents

	Introduction	6
1	The Face of the Land	9
2	Village and Cottage	34
3	Farming	70
4	The Country Church	148
5	Communications	177
6	Six Basic Crafts	196
7	Crafts of the Coppice	243
8	The Country Garden	261
9	History in Customs	268
	Appendices	
	Sources of Information	286
	Museums	288
	A Farming Glossary	289
	Further Reading	293
	Acknowledgements	299
	Index	301

Introduction

The countryside does not bury its past with the indecent haste of the city. The city perpetually destroys as it creates, sweeping away the rubble or climbing on top of it. The tangible elements of its history may have to await the archaeologist's trowel; the Temple of Mithras can sleep unknown beneath the scurrying feet of a hundred generations of Londoners.

The countryman's material heritage has a better chance of survival. Buildings, tools and amenities change more slowly—the old is less likely to be totally destroyed, more likely pushed aside and ignored, or absorbed into the new and accepted as part of it. A townscape may indeed hold a great deal of history but, like the pages of eighteenth-century letter-writers reducing their postage, it is cross-written, with layer upon layer of messages and needs an expert to decipher it. In the countryside, where the influences of time and space and change have operated differently, the historical messages are scrawled so large that we often overlook them, or we are delighted with the page of our own time, say 'How fascinating', and fail to turn it to find out more.

Look, for instance, at a windmill, a great tower-mill against an evening sky. It is undeniably beautiful, perhaps as beautiful as any mechanical contrivance could be. But if we admire it and pass on we have not seen it. We have looked at it, yes, but to look is not to see. The windmill is there because farms around it grew corn. They probably still do, but when the mill was built it provided flour for local bakers and meal for local livestock. Like many thousands of similar mills it was essential to the life of surrounding farms and villages. It does not stand on that high ground because it shows to such advantage, but because it caught the wind and because all around there were producers and consumers who never knew our own systems of long-distance transport.

Once you start thinking about the history of the mill and you are led back to the people who served it and whom it served—to the craftsmen who made its astonishingly accurate wooden gears, and the mill-dressers who maintained the intricate channelling of its stones with such instinctive precision; to the farmers who came, pockets a-jingle with sovereigns after a good harvest, and the labourers' wives, trudging up the hill with their bags of threshed gleanings in times of bleak and bitter hardship; to the miller himself, scanning the calm sky for a sign of wind while he listened to the plaints of the baker and the distant squealing of hungry pigs, or caught by a sudden blow and wrestling with a demoniac machine as it races to destruction. It is in this way that the things which the countryside has so abundantly preserved from the past—the buildings and artefacts, the crafts born not out of theory but of experience, the foolish and trivial customs whose roots lie in our dark beginnings—these things form an historical trail, like a nature trail through a very ancient forest. In the pages that follow we pick up a few of the more obvious clues along the trail. Maybe they will remind us to look for the past as we appreciate the present, remembering that today grew out of yesterday, and that the story of yesterday's countryside is the story of the vast majority of our ancestors.

The landscape, the scenic background of country life, is as susceptible to change as the foreground details. This point needs no emphasis at the present time, with every interested individual and organisation vociferous to preserve it from the environmental pressures of a teeming population showing an increasing distaste for its own cities. The threats to the beauty and relative peace of rural areas are real enough, yet a knowledge of how that beauty came about is a partial antidote to panic and a signal of hope.

Away from the mountain and moorland areas of minimum population, rural beauty is frequently not, as is usually assumed, 'natural'. It may have resulted from an understanding use of the forces of nature, but then so does a jet plane. Our countryside is largely manmade, and no doubt many people in the past were critical of its makers. The Celts were probably furious with the Saxons who cut down the forests and established the East Anglian farmlands; the Fenlanders protested bitterly that the drainage of their swamps deprived them of fish and wildfowl; the eighteenth-century peasant watched in helpless silence as the 'Improvers' stole the common from the goose and barred him with hawthorn hedges from his traditional lands; Norfolk and Suffolk people may well have blamed the peat-diggers for leaving dirty great holes all over the place, not foreseeing the future of the Broads.

Most of the changes inspired by simple economics are now regarded as desirable. In deploring, quite rightly, the destruction of hedgerows, we forget that the new bare landscapes of arable farming are almost a return to the open lands of the past, before the familiar patchwork of fields was created. Human intervention has a way of being assimilated into the picture provided it is not too extensive or extreme. If, for instance, we continue to sterilise an area the size of Oxfordshire every ten years, by covering it with roads, we can hardly expect to preserve either the beauty or the utility of the countryside.

There is good hope that today's aberrations of planning will prove to be self-correcting, if only because lunacy is apt to be more expensive than sanity. But great changes in country life have sprung from a combination of causes over the last few decades. They become more apparent when one compares the present with the quite recent past.

The village has been an isolated unit of population throughout history, isolated and largely dependent on its own resources. Whatever aspect of country history we examine, that fact always emerges. The common bond between villages, and within the village, was agriculture. It was the undergirding of the community because most of the community was involved in it. Now modern communications have finally broken down the countryman's isolation and this in itself is a much more recent development than is generally realised. Farming, caught in a technical revolution which again is not fully realised, no longer holds the majority of countrymen in the bonds of a common interest. Rural populations today increasingly consist of migrant townspeople who must, inevitably, modify their new habitat even as they adapt to it.

The land of Britain, the stabilised front of a long battle between volcanic and seismic upheaval and the surgings of a restless sea, is one of the most marvellously varied land areas for its size in the Northern Hemisphere. Generations of unknown folk have moulded it, and if we look fairly upon their work we must admit that it was good. Now we have to steer our course between two disastrous alternatives if we are to keep it so.

We have to maintain an unrelenting grip on the allocation of land for all kinds of new urban development. Land is a strictly limited asset and the criterion of effective planning is that it should be used to the maximum wherever development is permitted. Details of architecture and siting are of secondary importance, the countryside has absorbed and mellowed many intrusions, notably the massive works of the Victorian railway engineers, which threw conservationists of the day into paroxysms of horror, but of which we are now hardly aware. It is the actual amount of land lost to non-rural development which has to be incessantly scrutinised—once lost it is irrecoverable.

We have also to take care that in our desire to protect the countryside we do not embalm it. Its viability depends, as it has always done, on work and change and growth, and even the best intentions cannot justify turning it into a place of national parks, folk museums and Best Kept Villages, all neatly wrapped in Preservation Orders. Then it would indeed be, as that inveterate townee, Sidney Smith, called it, 'a kind of healthy grave'.

1 The Face of the Land

It is said that man made the land. It is also said that God made the country and the Devil made the town. In truth, the town landscape is entirely manmade and the rural landscape much more so than is generally realised. Landscape is the totality of visible objects—hills, fields, roads, trees, houses, churches—but it is not the land. Though the landscape of Britain has been subjected to drastic and accelerating change, the land from which it springs is largely unalterable.

In moulding the face of the countryside man has been little more than a make-up artist, or at most a cosmetic surgeon. His work may be good to look upon, or it may be an abomination of desolation, but it has so far been within limits. The deep tissues of the land were laid down long before he began scratching at its skin, and it is they which, for perhaps ten thousand years in these islands, have dictated the course of his development. The proposition should be reversed—the land has made man.

The most astonishing thing about this small offshore bit of Europe is its diversity. From the old rocks of the Cornish peninsula and the deep loams of Devon, to the hill farms of Wales and the crofts of the Scottish Highlands; from the southern Downs where the first farmers settled, to the Yorkshire moors where the monks conjured the great wool industry out of a wilderness; from the sandy heaths of Norfolk where the Cokes of Holkham saw 'one blade of grass and two rabbits fighting for it', to the almost bottomless fertility of the Fens; from the abundant pastures of the high rainfall areas of the west, to the semi-Continental dryness of the East Anglian cornlands—the contrasts within a few hours of travel are difficult to parallel anywhere in the Northern Hemisphere.

The greatest influence of these differences has been on farming, and through that basic activity on other aspects of life. It is always worth remembering that the city is a product of settled agriculture. Without the marketable surplus of crops and herds to sustain it, urban civilisation could not have been born. Purely nomadic peoples, following available pasture with their flocks, never built a town. To this extent the character and productivity of agriculture dictates the course of the more sophisticated cultures that rest upon it.

The nature of land and climate also have more direct effects on the man-created environment. Buildings vary with the availability of materials. Cottages are built of stone, brick, or daub-and-wattle and roofed with tiles, stone slats, slate, or thatch because these things were near at hand. Churches are fashioned of hard limestone or honey-coloured sandstone, or flints

The Malvern Hills from near 'English Camp' (*Roy J. Westlake*)

laboriously gathered from the chalk: look at an old church and you immediately know something of local geology. Roads tended to exist only where contours and underlying soils gave some hope of their being passable in winter. Farm implements and wagons developed distinct regional forms in accordance with terrain and soils. Natural vegetation had, of course, done so from earliest times.

It is easy to see that an unspoilt village in, say, Essex (and by that we mean one in which most construction did not take place in the twentieth century) is radically different in appearance from a similar village in the Cotswolds or North Wales. This difference was not decreed by planners nor does it result from economic circumstances. It was decided long ago, in the great convulsions of the earth's crust, when Europe's fragmented north-western coastline was plunged into indecisive war with a tumultuous sea. Geologically, the British Isles came out of a very disturbed melting pot, hence their attractive lack of uniformity. In a very fundamental sense it is true that 'Time and the Ocean and some fostering star/In high cabal have made us what we are', but the time is beyond our grasp and the ocean one that no man ever saw.

A rocky chain of islets appeared above the surface of the sea in the late Cambrian Age some 500 million years ago, stretching southward from the

Brimham Rocks, near Ripon, National Trust (*Roy J. Westlake*)

Moorland near Radnor (*MERL*)

subpolar lands that joined the future Europe to the future America. These rocky peaks were the first British land and now form part of the Scottish Highlands and the Western Isles. Very ancient rocks they are, formed before the dawn of life and bearing no fossils, but the seas around them teemed with primitive creatures, sea urchins, brachiopods and trilobites, spineless and virtually brainless.

As the Cambrian Age passed slowly into the Ordovician, new types of rock formed around the first projecting peaks out of the accumulation of sediments on the seabed. Sometimes the sea would retreat and the sediments would dry and harden, then it would return and begin the deposition of a new layer. Where the sediments were of mud they accumulated where Cornwall, North Wales and the Lake District now are, and were eventually compressed into slate. Deposits of sand mixed with the shells of marine creatures became sandstone and laid the foundations of much of Shropshire and other western areas. More important still, great drifts of dead sea creatures mouldered into chalk which hardened into limestone when the sea left it exposed. The future of the land was to depend a lot on these unimaginable billions of tiny skeletons, whose calcium has been a vital element in the overlaying soils, making possible a varied natural flora and a great range of cultivated crops. From the Mendip Hills to Yorkshire and on into Scotland, the limestone built up and the western and northern parts of Britain climbed slowly out of the sea.

As yet the land was barren and tortured by incessant heavings of the earth and sudden volcanic eruptions. In Cornwall and Devon the molten magma poured out again and again, solidifying as granite outcrops, bulging through the softer sedimentary rocks into the high masses of Bodmin Moor and Dartmoor, and crumpling more of Devon into gentle valleys. Further north, the sea had laid down a level plain in Pembrokeshire, but the volcanoes dotted it with minor hills, and northward again a shattering explosion flung up Snowdon and Cader Idris from the seabed and created a whole new and impressive landscape.

By now, with at least some fairly stable land areas, the Carboniferous Age brought developments which were to effect drastically the landscape and history of the future island. Primitive plants began growing where there was water and a surface that gave them a root-hold. They were gigantic horsetails, ferns and flowerless trees, spreading dense leaf canopies over the swamps in which they grew. Perpetual summer lay over the land, a hot summer lasting for the equivalent of a million human lifespans. There was little movement in the steaming swamp-forests; the first amphibians were dragging themselves clumsily out of the water, but there were no mammals or birds. Insects were well established, and dragonflies, 3ft from wing-tip to wing-tip, were masters of the air.

All through the changeless years the vegetation of the Carboniferous jungles grew up and fell and decayed, layer upon layer compressed ever tighter, and so the coal measures were laid down. Sometimes the sea came back, weighing the stuff down under new layers of sediment, retreating and leaving coal and rock to stiffen together into their final forms. The jungle compost heaps ended as some of the richest and most accessible coal seams in Europe, and the seeds of the Industrial Revolution were sown during the long Carboniferous summer.

More features of the land were carved out in the succeeding ages. By the time the great reptiles of the Jurassic became dominant, 170 million years ago, the breaking and slipping of the young sedimentary rocks had pushed up the long ridge of the Pennines, the Malvern Hills and the mountains of South Wales. New incursions of the sea plastered the landscape with stretches of clay and there were also smaller developments of lasting significance. In what was to be Dorset, for instance, lagoons populated with vast numbers of water snails were formed. The shells of dead snails lay in deep beds and coalesced into the wonderful dark Purbeck marble, so valued by medieval churchbuilders that the Court of Purbeck Marblers, the governing body of its masons, still exists.

Much of south-east England, however, was still building below the sea,

where the skeletal remains of a myriad of sea creatures were becoming chalk. Northward the land was still linked to North America. Then the earth's crust crinkled again in a major cataclysm. Rocks were pushed together, fold upon fold, squeezing up the Alps. A scattering of volcanoes sprouted over southern Scotland. The Atlantean bridge collapsed and Britain became part of Europe. The ocean floor thrust its long-accumulated piles of chalk up into the light of day, completing an important corner of England with the softly rounded scarps of the Downs—the 'majestic chain of mountains', as Gilbert White so endearingly described the gentle protuberances.

Not that one should underestimate the importance of the Downs or of their older relatives, the limestone uplands. When man finally appeared on the scene, he found most of Europe swaddled in dense forests, with few clearings where he could take the first tentative steps in agriculture. Britain, though still part of the Continental landmass, had suffered the concentrated interplay of natural forces in a small area and offered a choice of terrain. The Downs, especially, projected treeless above the forests and their thin soil could be made to grow barley and support grazing animals. It was symbolic that the crouching skeleton of a Bronze Age man buried on Dunstable Downs was found encircled by fossilised sea urchins. If they and all their fellows had not died and been gathered up by the tidal currents of forgotten seas, the Bronze Age man would never have found a home and an ultimate resting place there.

The rough outline of the land was completed with the emergence of the southern Downs, shapely as Aphrodite, from the waves. But an immense amount of polishing and battering, erosion by frost and snow, would smooth the jagged newness of the harder rocks; soluble limestone would be dissolved by penetrating rainwater, leaving strange underground worlds like the Cheddar caves and the Yorkshire potholes. Rivers would wear away narrow valleys amid the hills and lazily change their courses on the plains, leaving belts of rich alluvial soil. The sea would continue to bite at the shoreline, sometimes regurgitating in one place land swallowed in another.

The most extensive alterations to the superficial features of the land were the results of the Ice Ages, the repeated advance and retreat of the polar ice over parts of the Northern Hemisphere. The last of them was contemporaneous with the first men, and they must have found most of Britain an inhospitable place.

Glaciers crept as far south as the London basin, scrubbing and scraping

Pew Tor, Dartmoor. The 130,000 acres of 'the last wilderness' have largely resisted settlement, and man has had little effect on the landscape (*Roy J. Westlake*)

The River Wharfe, Langstrothdale, Yorkshire (*Roy J. Westlake*)

the land with inexorable power as they came. They bulldozed sheets of soil from place to place, spreading layers of clay over chalk and often leaving it mixed with boulders collected from distant mountainsides (boulder clay is heavy land, familiar to farmers). They spread down river valleys widening narrow ones into wider troughs with curved bottoms. Equally typical of glacial activity are rock-sided river valleys where the tributary streams enter the river from a higher level, forming waterfalls. This indicates that a glacier has gouged its way along the course of the river, making it much deeper than the valleys of the tributaries which were once on the same level.

The general effect of the ice-sheets was to sandpaper away irregularities in the surface of the land, though their impression on ancient volcanic rocks was only limited. In some mountain areas, however, the enormous pressures of developing glaciers did sometimes tear away masses of the hardest rock, leaving the strange, deep, mountain lakes known as 'corries' in Scotland and 'cwms' in Wales. In their retreat the glaciers also left all sorts of stony debris, often strewn in straight lines marking the limits of their advance, or in curiously uniform hillocks such as the drumlins of the Yorkshire Dales.

A good deal of country was flooded by rivers, blocked in their lower reaches by glaciers but still channelling water from ice-free ground. The lakes so created have disappeared, for all lakes, even the deepest and most beautiful, are geologically shortlived creatures, doomed from the moment of their birth. Their feeder streams always carry in more solid matter than flows out, and they silt up. This happened with the Ice Age floodings, but they left behind many boggy patches and one major feature of the landscape.

What happened was that the rivers flowing into the Wash were dammed by the ice near their eastern outlets, and spilled over to create the Fens. This lowlying country was exactly right for a complex of shallow lakes to become a swamp, and as the ice withdrew for the last time, and reeds and other water plants luxuriated, a new type of soil began to build. The substance we call peat is produced when vegetable matter decays anaerobically, that is, without the oxygen in which the micro-organisms of normal decay are able to operate. A soil that is not waterlogged contains air, vegetable matter is pulled down into it by earthworms, transformed into humus and integrated into the soil. But where oxygen is excluded by water the process of decay reaches a certain point and then ceases, leaving the half-rotted debris to pile up and become peat. It is in fact the first stage of the coal formation that went on in the Carboniferous forests.

Where the dead vegetation is simply saturated with rainwater and lies over strata of impervious rock, as happens on the high moorlands, the resultant peat contains no calcium or mineral salts and is so poor and acid that only a limited range of plants can exist in it. All gardeners know that the peat they buy is a valuable source of humus but of no nutritive value. The Fenlands, however, were not simply a rainwater catchment, they were saturated by rivers flowing through a varied countryside, and their waters contained calcium and other minerals. The Fenland soils ended up neither acid nor alkaline, but neutral and incredibly deep and fertile. The Ice Ages and the men who drained the swamps worked unknowingly together to produce one of the most fertile patches of soil in the world.

We have not attempted a survey of British geology in these few pages: to have done so would have left us with a mass of tabulated facts and no clear reminder of what they were all about. Yet the countryside cannot be understood without bearing in mind those remoter yesterdays that made it. Without a lifetime's study one could not hope to interpret all the messages they have left scattered about, the records of violent upheavals and of slow change over times unimaginably stretched. But a backward glance such as this, a few confused glimpses of warring land and sea, earthquake and boiling rock, steaming heat and the grasp of unbroken winter, serve to remind us that man had nothing to do with the making of the land. On the contrary, the elemental forces which shaped it drew the broad outlines of future human activity.

Looking at landscape

To reconstruct in imagination the yesterdays of the countryside is relatively easy. The clues to the past that lie scattered everywhere may be interpreted with practice and lead us to an understanding of the life and work of country people in days gone by. With that understanding comes a picture of their physical background, of the landscapes which in many places and to many generations must have seemed immutable and beyond human power to change. That belief, of course, was wrong.

Looking back, we see history chiefly as a tale of accelerating change, from which the landscape, the face of the land, was not immune; in a few thousand years man has transformed its appearance. This becomes evident when we try to visualise the Britain of prehistory, or to find some tract of country that looks as it did to our Stone Age ancestors. Apart from areas like the central wastes of Dartmoor, which are so hostile that they have escaped human settlement, everything has changed, or has *been* changed, often very slowly and indirectly, by human activity.

In Tudor times it would have been easier to find landscapes that for thousands of years had been moulded only by infinitely slow pressures of nature. Not so now. We may stand on the close turf of the Downs and think that nothing here has altered since the ape-like men came shambling northward from Europe and put down roots in the shallow soil. But in fact we see a quite different landscape; the early Britons settled the long, gentle humps of the Downs and the mild north-western uplands because this was the only treeless land available to them. The Neolithic Downs were islands of open grassland poking up from dark untameable forests against which flint axes were useless. We cannot see the picture as they saw it because that background of primary vegetation has gone, but we may still deduce its existence from the way in which men kept their farms, forts, roads and trackways on the poor high chalklands and left no trace in what to us are the lush valleys.

In the same way one is tempted to explore the splendid nature reserve of Wicken Fen and think, 'This is how the fens looked before Cornelius Vermuyden set to work in the seventeenth century'. In a way it is, but it is too limited, too obviously preserved, to give a true picture of the past when, as Tennyson saw it '. . . Stretched wide and wild the waste enormous marsh'. A real understanding of the nature of this vast malarial swamp, of how much of the eastern lowlands of England it covered, of the long and sometimes desperate struggle to reclaim it, comes best from looking at the flat, controlled Fenland landscapes stretching for mile after tedious mile.

Dovedale, the Peak District. The limestone uplands present a different picture to the barren moorlands such as Dartmoor and are areas of hill farming (*Roy J. Westlake*)

Afforestation. Modern forests are criticised for their uniformity, but their scale renders them impressive and they have reversed the trend towards a treeless land (*Forestry Commission*)

The story of the Fens is to be found in these fertile and prosperous acres, where no land is wasted on village greens or roadside verges, and all too little in trees and hedges. Here one can see how the peatlands have shrunk as the water was drained out of them, leaving the waterways higher than the land they drain. It becomes more and more clearly a manmade landscape and everywhere it bears signs of the disasters that repeatedly overwhelmed those who first made it.

But if the Fenland, perhaps because it is starkly functional, is obviously manmade, the same may be said, in a greater or lesser degree, of almost every landscape in Britain. The countryside is not an artefact as a town is, nor is it a manifestation of unaided nature. At its best it is the result of co-operation between man and his environment, achieved so slowly and patiently that the whole seems more of an organic growth than a construction. Even ancient buildings are said to 'grow out of the ground', often because their builders had to use local materials which did just that. So landscapes which have escaped violent eruptions of modern technology, such as motorways and airports and all the lesser discords, tend to have an air of unaltered permanence that is deceptive.

A landscape of 'patchwork quilt' country, retaining its hedgerows studded with mature trees, heavy-foliaged in the summer sun, with field after field of growing crops or grazing cattle stretching to the horizon, looks as though it has always existed in the same state. Yet the chances are that it was fashioned some two centuries ago, when the last bout of enclosures divided up the remains of the medieval open fields and commons into private farms. Then the hawthorn hedges were planted and much of England first took on its present-day pattern. Here and there the farming landscape still shows traces of its older layout, as fragments of an original picture might be visible in an over-painted canvas. And a strange experience it is, when the oblique light of a low sun falls on an old permanent pasture, to glimpse beneath the grass the ridges and furrows of the ox-ploughed open fields where the English peasant community worked.

The facts of geology and climate have, as we have said, given this island scenery of a rare beauty and variety. This we may appreciate aesthetically and give thanks for, without worrying about the scientific whys and wherefores. Even more varied are the landscapes into which the basic scenery has been moulded, so that once the constriction of the motorway is escaped one may see a score of quite different pictures in a drive of a hundred miles—pictures that are in part the work of men and that gain in visual interest the more we know about them.

Mountain and moorland

The landscapes least changed by human activity are the high places where farming has been difficult or impossible. Man has made so much of the countryside, moulding it into a familiar pattern of field and farmstead, that areas in which climate and geology have reduced his influence offer a variety of 'noble wild prospects', as Boswell put it in an ill-fated attempt to impress Johnson with the merits of Scottish scenery.

If the convulsions of the earth's crust had been less violent, the ragged ramparts of igneous rock that stretch from northern Scotland to the Scillies, along the Atlantic side of the island, would have been covered by the sea. There would not have been the general downward tilt from west to east and the climate, like the topography, would have been much more uniform. As it is, the mountain and upland regions are the first to face the incoming Atlantic depressions and draw down upon themselves the heaviest rainfall.

Land more than 2,000ft above sea level qualifies as mountain, and agriculture carried on at heights above the 700ft level is hill farming—principally the rearing of cattle to be fattened in lowland areas, and the production of the hardy, hill breeds of sheep. These uplands are 'marginal', lying on the limits of profitable use.

Upland farming has in no way affected the scenic beauty of its special areas. The Lakeland fells, the Welsh mountains, the sweep of moor and dale in Yorkshire, have been changed hardly at all by their local populations.

The importance of the high places as unspoilt regions of recreation and escape is a consequence of modern communications and the desire of those whose lives are set in very different surroundings to reassure themselves that space and silence, peaks mirrored in still waters, and cloud shadows racing across rocky moorland are still to be found.

The factors restricting agricultural development in upland districts, the reasons for so much relatively undeveloped countryside in a small, overcrowded and intensively cultivated island, are more complex than is first apparent. Altitude, climate and geological structure have all played a part in deciding whether men have been able to wrest a living from the mountains and the moors.

The limitations of altitude are obvious, the higher one climbs above sea level the shorter the growing season, and the smaller the range of possible plantlife. New strains of grasses have helped to push the grazing potential further up mountain slopes, but in this the question of soil fertility is crucial. The heavy rainfall associated with mountain areas washes out the soil nutrients and upland pastures on the older fire-formed rocks can only be extended by the free use of lime and fertilisers. There are economic limits to the agricultural development of the hills.

The moorlands of Scotland and of the north and south-west of England show clearly that basic geology is more important than altitude in keeping to a minimum the domestication of a wild landscape. Moorland is rough ground well below the treeline. At one time many moors were probably covered with scrubby forest, the ground flora was more varied than now and heather, the most widely distributed moorland plant, was largely confined to the mountains. The moors, however, lacked natural drainage and the underlying rock held no calcium for the plants to draw upon. Dead vegetable matter accumulated in the stagnant pools and formed bogs, and the soil generally grew too acid to support a varied plantlife. Only the calcifuges or lime-haters thrived and survived. By far the most important of these is heather—a staple food for grouse and red deer and a few other indigenous species, also turned out to provide grazing for sheep. Heather is a unique example of a semi-controlled wild plant being treated almost as a crop. It is burnt off at intervals of from seven to twenty years, the old, woody growth being destroyed and replaced by succulent young growth springing from the ground.

The 130,000 acres of Dartmoor have been called 'the last wilderness'. Certainly few areas of comparable extent have changed so little at the hands of man, and the place has the qualities of moorland carried to extremes. For one thing, it is the largest unbroken mass of granite in the country, a vast slab of the rock that boiled up through the softer strata of the region and littered it with rugged outcrops that have not yet had time to mellow. Dartmoor is the source of all the major rivers of Devon, a monstrous stone roof from which the rains are shed. Its highest point, High Willhays, is very nearly the highest in England south of the Pennines, being robbed of this distinction only by the eastern scarp of the Black Mountains where they cross the Welsh border into Herefordshire.

The desolation of Dartmoor contrasts starkly with upland pastures in the Peak District of Derbyshire at a similar height. Here the underlying rock is limestone, and excellent grass comes from its inexhaustible minerals and good drainage. Reclamation of moorland is going on somewhere all the time, a nibbling away at the edges, even of Dartmoor, but these particular wild places will never be involved in the changes which create new landscapes in more fertile areas; they may of course be ruined by industrial and technological development, or by the pressure of mobile hordes vainly seeking solitude, but that is a problem peculiar to our own time.

The West Country moors have changed in one respect over the last 3,000 years. In the late Stone Age they must have been quite populous—by the standards of the time. They are littered with stone hut circles, menhirs of standing stones, and barrows or burial mounds. Apart from the availability of stone, and that a stubbornly untractable sort, it is difficult to see why the sites were so popular. Admittedly, Exmoor, which has been described as the feminine companion to Dartmoor's brutal masculinity, is crossed by river valleys and sheltered coombs, but the Neolithic people preferred the hard heart of Dartmoor and the windy boulder-strewn wastes of Bodmin. The Cornish moor has in fact more reminders of prehistoric settlement than any other spot in England.

Few people since the Stone Age settlers have chosen to make their homes on the high moorland and theirs was no doubt a choice between evils. Only on high ground, whether on the moors or the kindly turf of the downland, were they clear of the menacing, almost universal forest.

The Downs

The chalk downland of the southern half of England is undramatic country; variations on a theme of rounded green hills; benign forms many times repeated in many countries with only minor differences. Yet the downland has always acted as a powerful stimulant of the imagination and all that has been written about it, even the most simply descriptive of guidebooks, is permeated with a sense of the past. Not the historical past, but very remote ages and things we accept easily until we try to imagine them. In Kent and Surrey, Sussex, Hampshire, Wiltshire, Dorset and Berkshire, the Downs are as familiar as the backyard, as unnoticed as the sky. But when one thinks about them they are hard to believe.

Gilbert White saw the South Downs—a mere projection from the main chalk mass further west—as a chain of majestic mountains. For Kipling their bare summits were peopled with unseen presences, things from the forgotten morning of mankind that touched him in the dark and cried as they passed. Perhaps it is a dangerous exercise to let one's imagination loose on the Downs, or perhaps it is the only way to know them.

Their long gestation and precipitate birth are surely the strangest way imaginable of turning the ocean itself into dry land. For time beyond reckoning the tiny sea creatures that are the Downs lived and took their food from organisms more primitive than they. As they died, myriads of them every moment of the day and night throughout the slow millennia, their skeletal remnants sank in an endless slow rain from the light and swarming life near the surface to the darkness of the seabed. There they lay, accumulating in depth until the earth heaved and pushed them up again in great, soft, white, rounded blobs.

The downland has changed since the first men picked their way across the waterlogged valley that is now the English Channel and cultivated its meagre soil. For one thing, they are much drier: rainfall in the south of England is lower than in pre-Roman times, and there appear to have been downland springs which have long ceased to flow. Water supply would have been an important element in permanent settlement, in view of early man's fear of the well-watered lowland regions. The dewponds which relied on the condensation of atmospheric moisture were an ingenious later amenity for the benefit of livestock.

The Downs are by nature treeless, their only indigenous tree species being the juniper and, possibly, the yew. Where chalk hills have become naturally well wooded, as in the magnificent beechwoods of the Chilterns, their claim to be truly downland may be rejected by the purists. Isolated tree clumps such as the Sussex 'hangers' are usually planted in handy pockets of clay or greensand.

One feature of the chalk country makes it worthy of close study. It is in some places undergoing basic ecological change as a result of a decline in downland sheep flocks and the introduction of myxomatosis. The short, close turf of the Downs was produced by the continuous nibbling of generations of sheep who, as on the limestone Cotswolds, trimmed the grass, manured it and eliminated much coarser herbage. When their numbers fell the rabbits were allowed to multiply in the way that rabbits do and they carried on the work, though much less competently. When the rabbits were virtually wiped out by myxomatosis, the seedlings of a wider and untypical flora, no longer in danger of having their heads bitten off, began creeping up the slopes. Areas of scrub have been spreading and, if the spread were to become general, a major characteristic of downland, its dwarf vegetation and windswept openness, would be endangered.

Hedgerows

Before the enclosures the typical picture of a peasant village was one where those who worked the land lived close together, surrounded by open arable strips and unfenced commons where stock was herded. To our way of thinking all the cultivated areas would have had a flat, bare look, and this disappeared only with the last great rush of enclosures towards the end of the eighteenth century. With the enclosures came boundaries to farm and field and the isolated farmhouse on its own land. The boundaries were, and legally still are, mainly ditches, but alongside them hedges were planted as permanent stock-proof fences. Where stone was plentiful, dry-stone walls were the alternative, and in parts of the West Country earthen banks or 'baulks'. But over much of the land, hedgerows, mostly planted some 200 years ago, have become a 'natural' part of the scene.

Changes in farming practice created them, and now changes threaten to destroy them. Mechanised farming cannot operate efficiently in very small fields, and every year more than 2,000 miles of hedge are grubbed up and the ditches levelled to give elbow room to ever more massive machinery. Fortunately the process is slowing down, there are signs of a return to traditional mixed farming, away from continuous grain growing and prairie farming, even in predominantly cereal areas.

The ecological consequences of hedge-grubbing are becoming better appreciated by farmers and others. The value of windbreaks on soils liable to 'blow' is obvious, as is the effect of the policy on wildlife to anyone who stops to think. The hedgerow is vital to birds, small mammals and many plants—just how vital is shown by the figures. There are still some 600,000 miles of hedges in Britain, and if they average only 2ft in width they cover an area greater than all the officially designated nature reserves.

Admittedly, hedges occupy potentially productive land, but without them the countryside would look strangely bleak. The open fields of the medieval peasants also looked that way, but all around them were the great woodlands which we have since destroyed. For us it is mainly the hedgerows which give such an appearance of luxuriant growth to the varied country southwards from the Midlands plain across the Thames valley to the upsurge of the Downs.

The visual impact of this growth is pointed out by the late H. E. Bates, in an essay written in 1939 and published in *The English Countryside*.

Other countries can produce fields, a wealth of trees beside which our own appear often very ordinary. But no other country can produce anything which, like stitchery, binds together the varying patterns of the landscape in such a way that the pattern is made infinitely more beautiful. If this seems extravagant, try to consider the English landscape without the hedge. It would not be the English landscape.

The simile of the patchwork quilt is relevant when one takes a vertical view, or looks at an aerial photograph: then the patches show up, no two identical in size or shape, hardly two alike in shade of colour. Boundaries followed roads and lanes, or ditches that had to go with the lie of the land to take the drainage water: there are no uniform blocks or straight lines. But the patchwork image is less obvious when the view is oblique, as from a hillside looking across a wide valley. The picture then, especially in summer, is often of a lightly wooded area, with the fields as mere clearings among the hedgerow trees. It is the quantity of hedgerow timber that brings a heavy-foliaged lushness to the summer landscape.

Our hedges are in some measure the last great monument to the passing of the English peasantry; more were planted in the eighteenth-century enclosures than at any other time. They were mainly of hawthorn or quickset, the first name deriving from the Old English *haw*, 'a hedge', the second expressing the ease with which it is propagated and grown. It is by nature a small, tough, thorny tree, the May tree whose foam of white blossom, enveloped in its drowsy yet oddly disturbing scent, is a symbol of early summer. As a hedging plant it has the virtue of prickliness and the ability to survive continual cutting back.

The hawthorn was familiar to the countryman long before its seedlings were grown in millions to mark the new boundaries. The peasant poet, John Clare, who witnessed the last days of the peasantry, saw it growing to full stature on the commonlands before the enclosers 'stole the common from the goose'.

> Ye injur'd fields, ye once were gay
> When Nature's hand displayed
> Long waving rows of willows grey
> And clumps of hawthorn shade.
> But now, alas, your hawthorn bowers
> All desolate we see!
> The spoilers' axe their shade devours
> And cuts down every tree . . .

More than that, the berries from the hawthorns which shaded the commoners' livestock were the raw materials of the hedges which excluded them for ever from their traditional grazing. The lives of the peasants, whose scrawny cattle roamed the wastes, were no doubt hard and meagre, but they had a certain independence and the loss of that independence comes to mind whenever one looks at a hawthorn hedge.

Hedges have changed their make-up over the years. They began as double rows of hawthorn seedlings, occasionally interplanted with ash or other saplings. Regular trimming made them effectively impenetrable, and the most skilled form of trimming was that known as laying or layering. This craft is mentioned elsewhere in the book, but its origins give us another odd little sidelight on rural history.

It was foxhunting that produced the beautifully kept hedges of the nineteenth century. Organised hunting began in the Midlands—specifically in Leicestershire—about 1770, shortly before the extensive commons of the area were taken over by the new race of farmers and enclosed. The very people who had enjoyed uninterrupted gallops over the commoners' heaths and grazing lands had covered them with obstructive hedges. Business had clashed with pleasure; the only solution was to ensure that the obstacles were kept within bounds and jumpable. Hence the meticulously layered hedge, uniform in height and spread and, as it turned out, the most effective stock fencing until the invention of barbed wire.

Another consequence of foxhunting and improved farming was the planting of artificial 'covers'. They may still be seen on the ground and even picked out on Ordnance Survey maps, predominantly in the Midlands. Not only John Clare's 'hawthorn bowers' but great stretches of gorse and scrub fell to the improvers' zeal and the cleared land went under the plough. It was then realised that, in destroying these natural sanctuaries, the foxes had been evicted along with the peasants and steps were taken to restore their proper environment. Copses, spinneys and gorse patches were planted on the new farms, to the benefit of various creatures, including game birds, and to the landscape, but primarily inspired by solicitude for foxes.

The composition of hedgerows changes with time as different plants establish themselves within the shelter of the original planting. With the original hawthorn will grow up blackberry, wild rose, elder, viburnum, honeysuckle, wild clematis, holly, hazel, spindleberry and other shrubs and climbers. In times of depression and neglect these extras can swiftly turn a hedge into a rampant mess, but they certainly make it more interesting.

Among hedgerow trees will be found oak, elm, ash, willow, sycamore, crab-apple and maple. Mostly they are natural colonists like the smaller species, the seeds being carried by birds, rodents, or the wind; while the elm, the typical hedgerow tree of East Anglia, spreads widely by means of suckers. Conifers are rare in hedges, though on light soils the Scots pine has been used as the main hedging plant.

The value of hedgerow timber cannot be ignored when the economics of hedges are under discussion. The world price of hardwoods grows faster than the trees themselves, and the Forestry Commission has this to say:

> Elm is probably the most important hedgerow timber in England. The common English elm usually produces large and well-formed butts, requires little attention, and reproduces readily from suckers in the hedge at no cost. The timber retains a high value for furniture. It is often insufficiently appreciated that a great volume of hardwood timber is to be found in hedgerows.

Apart from their economic worth we have the ironic fact that in the end our hedges may owe their preservation to the machine. The cost of keeping them trimmed had damned them almost as completely as the inconvenience of small fields, until the advent of the mechanical hedge-cutter made their retention possible under modern conditions. Now the scream of the circular saw on its long, groping, hydraulically operated arm is a familiar winter sound in the countryside. The casual observer may deplore the quality of the work, the skilled hedger of old would have been speechless with horror at the sight of the uneven, splintered finish, but the machine does in hours what the handworker will do in weeks, and this more than anything has reprieved the hedge.

Long may it survive, rough or tidy, a thing of beauty, a sanctuary and a living memorial to a social revolution.

The rebirth of forests

Little is left of the natural woodlands that once covered much of the land. Their destruction was perhaps the greatest change wrought by man in the island's landscape, a slow transformation from isolated clearances in the forest to isolated patches of forest in a largely cultivated terrain.

The word 'forest' is derived from the Latin *forestem sylvam*, 'the wood outside', applied by the Normans to the wild country of mixed woodland, heath and scrub beyond the boundaries of the feudal village. The haunt of wolf, wild boar and outlaws disowned by the community, these unsettled areas were steadily shrinking in Norman times and many were preserved as royal hunting forests or 'chases' to guarantee the monarch and the nobility adequate scope for their favourite recreation. Forest law was exercised with extreme severity, poaching being punished by death or mutilation, but commoners often retained certain rights in the royal forests, including the gathering of reeds for thatching, the collection of firewood by cutting such boughs as they could reach 'by hook or by crook' and the right of turbary, or cutting turves for fuel. The last was an extremely destructive activity, preventing natural regeneration by the digging up of tree seedlings.

Naturally regenerated beechwood. Local furniture industries were founded on such woods and the craftsmen who worked in them (*Forestry Commission*)

Common rights are still maintained in the New Forest, made a royal forest in 1079 and the largest surviving area of medieval woodland. It probably bears a fair resemblance to the ancient hunting grounds when they were first designated—a varied environment of tree cover and open glades, shrub growth, ponds and grazing areas. The typical forest was not a uniform mass of trees, though the tree canopy in the Sussex oak forests and the Chiltern beechwoods must have been quite dense. Purely coniferous forests were unknown in England.

Parts of many royal hunting forests are to be found in the south and the Midlands—Epping, which has an area of 9 square miles, Bernwood, near Aylesbury, Rockingham, not far from Stamford and Cannock Chase in Staffordshire. That existing forests are often the remnants of much greater is shown by the frequency with which town or village names ending in 'ley', 'a clearing or grazing ground in a wood', occur near their boundaries. An example is Bletchley, in the vicinity of Whaddon Chase.

Despite the conservation imposed by kingly sport, forests dwindled apace from the time of the Tudors. The oaks of the Sussex Weald fed the furnaces of the ironmasters and glassblowers, and by the seventeenth century the Navy Secretary, Mr Pepys, was expressing concern about the supply of timber for shipbuilding. A little later, in his fascinating guidebook, *A Tour Through the Whole of Great Britain*, Defoe several times refers to the destruction of woodlands, and John Evelyn began preaching the novel idea that you must plant trees if you want to continue felling them.

Nevertheless, Britain became steadily more treeless throughout the eighteenth century. Iron-smelting moved northwards from Sussex and Hampshire and coal replaced charcoal, but otherwise the new industrialism demanded more and more timber for building, pit props, canal works and other purposes. By the beginning of the nineteenth century woodlands had shrunk to an estimated 5 per cent of the total land area.

It comes almost as a shock to realise that this particular low point was reached nearly two centuries ago and that since then things have actually improved. Many factors contributed to the slow improvement. The eighteenth century saw a great flurry of tree-planting by landowners for purely aesthetic reasons. Landscape gardeners like 'Capability' Brown planted on a scale never seen before. Then came the effects of the enclosures; the peasants' rough grazings—the 'wastes' as they were called—were fenced and cleared of their scrub and spinneys, leaving bare ground for the plough. Later, however, the hawthorn hedges, that enclosed and divided the new farms, became a vast nursery for seedling trees, and the landowners, worried by the lack of natural shelter for foxes and game, planted the little copses and coverts which now add so much to many an otherwise featureless landscape.

Timber began to be thought of as a longterm crop. Natural regeneration was fostered in private woodlands, more care was taken of the many coppices from which came hurdles, tool handles, walking sticks, clog soles and other products in enormous quantities. Local timber supplies became important to many industries, the furniture-makers of High Wycombe, for instance, depending on a continuous flow of chair legs and other parts from the 'bodgers' who worked in the beechwoods, turning beautifully finished components on their primitive pole lathes.

New species of trees were introduced and established. Britain had only one native conifer, the Scots pine, and relied on imports of softwoods from Canada, Russia and the Baltic states. Modern conifer plantings are mainly of comparative newcomers, the Douglas fir, the European larch, the Norway and Sitka spruces.

The Forestry Commission

The shrinkage of the woodlands, arrested during the nineteenth century, was abruptly resumed during World War I. The cutting off of imports and the consequent shortage of simple and vital things like pit props led to the founding of the Forestry Commission in 1919. Its task was to advise and assist private landowners in afforestation schemes and to acquire and plant with trees land unsuitable for agriculture—uplands and lower mountain slopes, infertile sands and even areas of industrial waste such as tips and slag heaps.

The success of the Commission has been remarkable. It has a million acres under supervision and itself owns three million acres of forest. Much of its land is open to the public, including the seven National Forest Parks. Among these are Snowdonia, the ancient Forest of Dean in Gloucestershire and the Queen Elizabeth Forest Park, wonderfully sited between Loch Lomond and the Trossachs.

The Commission is often criticised for the sombre uniformity of its great conifer plantings, and of course these forests cannot compare for beauty, and as wildlife habitats, with mixed or deciduous woodlands. Yet it must be remembered that the success of the Commission is measured in terms of commercial production of timber treated as a crop to be reaped and planted again. Everything else—the attention now being given to hardwoods, the reclamation of scarred and useless landscapes, the impressive forest drives—are by way of a bonus.

What matters most is that the woodlands have climbed back to nearly 9 per cent of the land area, reversing a trend that had continued since the Iron Age Britons first tried their axes on the ocean of trees lapping their downland settlements. It is good news, for a treeless land is but a few steps away from becoming a desert.

Fens and Broads

Ways in which human activity has affected the eastern lowlands from the Wash provide an interesting contrast. On one hand an enormous marsh has been dried out, on the other large areas of dry land have been flooded.

As we have seen, the Fens were created by slow-moving rivers which got lost on their way to the sea. They ran into a great shallow basin of boulder clay, and here, 130 million years ago, began the accumulation of rotting plants, of vast reed beds, of teeming aquatic and semi-aquatic life. Here and there outcrops of clay projected above the mush, rare firm footholds, like the Isle of Ely. The eventual human population adapted to its peculiar environment, living by fishing and wildfowling and was very isolated. The impenetrability of the Fens became clear to the Normans when the Lincolnshire landowner, Hereward, fought a guerilla campaign against them, based upon Ely.

The Romans made half-hearted attempts to cut drainage channels in the Fens, but the first serious attempt at reclamation began in 1629, when the Earl of Bedford started a massive programme with the Dutchman, Cornelius Vermuyden, as consultant. The old Bedford river was dug between Erith and Denver, 21 miles long and 70ft wide. The new Bedford, 100ft wide, was added later, running parallel to the first cut. As the water was carried away and the land dried, a system of drainage channels developed over widening areas. Soon luxuriant crops of wheat, hemp and flax grew on the reclaimed land and cattle fattened on the new pastures.

The apparent success of the Bedford scheme proved illusory and the waters regained much of their lost territory as the Fenmen had always predicted. Fen soils are of two kinds; near the sea they consist of marine silt, but inland the clay is overlaid by a great depth of uniquely fertile peat. The physical properties of peat change with its moisture content—every gardener knows that wet peat shrinks when it dries. As the Fenland peat dried, the land sank lower and lower until it was below the levels of the dykes and drains. The banks of the new cuts were built up until their waters flowed above the surrounding land which could no longer drain naturally into them. By 1700 much of the reclaimed land had reverted to marsh, and eels and tench swam over the new pastures.

Once it was realised that the Fens would not drain naturally, the work proceeded again on a sounder basis. Since water could not flow uphill from the land to the main drainage channels, it must be pumped up, and again the experience of the Dutch served as a model. Windmill pumps protected the newly drained areas and continued to do so until steam and diesel pumps successively replaced them. Now the work is done by large automatic electric pumps.

The modern Fenland is scenically unattractive, without ancient villages or mature woodland. There are no greens or wide roadside verges, the land is too precious to be wasted. Sugar beet, potatoes and other vegetables, cereals, soft fruit—these are the objects of interest in Fenland scenery, and few areas can show crops to equal them. The banks of the many waterways support a rich variety of plant species, and in the nature reserves of Wicken and Woodwalton one may see the last of the great wilderness of waters. There, too, attempts are being made to re-establish two famous former inhabitants of the Fens, the Large Copper and Swallowtail butterflies.

One thought pervades this featureless, prosperous landscape; it is artificially created, and without constant care would revert to its natural type. Some of it started to do so in the floods that followed the bitter winter of 1947 and months of effort were needed to restore the position.

The peat is still shrinking and the level of the land slowly falls. Old gateposts appear to lift themselves out of the ground until they totter and fall. In Holme Fen stands the Holme Post, an iron pillar driven right through the peat into the clay below. In the middle of the last century the top was level with the surface, today it is more than 12ft above it.

Along the middle reaches of three sluggish East Anglian rivers, the Bure, the Yare and the Waveney, stretch the shallow lakes of the Broads. Crowded with holiday craft in summer, they have in winter a sullen wildness, a desolation of grey water and dead reeds under a limitless sky. Then it is easy to believe that here is a scene unchanged from the remote past.

But the Broads are manmade as surely as the Fenland farms. Not by design, for their makers, exercising a legal right to dig peat for fuel, had no intention of leaving large stretches of land permanently under water. The same result has, of course, been achieved elsewhere by the excavators of sand and gravel, as anyone approaching London by the Eastern Region line to Liverpool Street can hardly fail to notice. We may hope that in time many of these waterfilled craters will mellow into miniature lake areas.

However, the Broads will always have a special place among holes in the ground. They show how an entire landscape may be radically changed by a sparse peasant population doing a normal job of work for a few centuries.

There are said to be twelve large Broads and twenty-four small ones, mostly in Norfolk though Suffolk has a few. Each Broad is supposed to lie in a different parish which, however improbable it now is, would accord with the distribution of the original diggings.

The natural life of the region is now threatened by pollution and deoxygenation of the water. It would be a tragedy were the peat-diggers' ponds to become nothing more than sterile boating pools, for they have long been an exception to many of man's hideous list of environmental accidents.

2 Village and Cottage

The village

Until about 1850 more British people lived in the country than in towns, which meant that they lived in villages. For almost the whole of our history the village has been the normal community for most of the population and this is emphasised by the persistence of villages on the same sites and often under the same names for more than a thousand years.

The Roman 'villas', or the farm settlements of the wealthy, were strung thinly along the military highways, but the Anglo-Saxon villages which followed them sprang up everywhere over the succeeding centuries. Not only were most of our villages in existence when the Domesday Book was compiled in 1086, many of them were already ancient. The new colonists, the Saxons, Jutes and Norwegians, came with sharp axes and cultivated clearings spread through the lowland forests everywhere south of Northumberland.

By the time of the Norman Conquest the general pattern of almost self-supporting villages was established, ready to be extended and formalised by feudalism. Villages acquired churches and manor houses or castles. Around each community lay the open fields, great patchworks of rectangular strips of arable land and vast commons or 'wastes' on which cattle were herded. No hedges and rough tracks for roads—unless a Roman highway still survived—but the shape of the village itself would closely resemble the oldest part of the same village today.

Except in the upland areas, the mountains and the moorland, nowhere can one drive more than a few miles without coming to a village. It may be quite large, with shops and modern houses, or it may consist of a dozen cottages, a nameboard and a church. The plan of the old village, disregarding new developments and council estates, nearly always falls into one of three categories. It may be haphazard—more a planlessness than a plan—with little groups of dwellings dotted here and there for specific reasons. Perhaps it is on high ground near the church, because this site has been immune to flooding, or beside a stream which once provided a good water supply, or along a track which led to the peasants' open fields but now merely leads back to the village centre. It takes some time to sort out the growth patterns of such a village.

The other categories of village, however, are immediately recognisable types and the reasons for their oft-repeated patterns tell us something of their past. They are known as 'green' villages, and linear or 'street' villages.

The village in autumn (*BTA*)

The shape of the village

Green villages

The clustered houses round the village green form such a universally accepted picture of the traditional English scene that it must have a strong factual origin. As, of course, it has. England has thousands of green villages displaying every possible variation of buildings surrounding a piece of common land. Outside the encircling houses the common land has been gone for at least 150 years, but the publicly owned patch in the heart of the built-up area has survived. The question is, why was it there in the first place?

The village pond. A campaign is now under way to preserve it for environmental reasons, but not long ago it was an essential filling station for horses, cattle and steam engines (*MERL*)

Green villages are commonest in the eastern half of England, though the Devon village with houses facing on to a small square seems to have come from the same mould. The Saxon settlers probably designed their villages for defence as did the prehistoric builders of fortified encampments and hillforts—a perimeter of huts enclosing an area into which flocks and herds could be driven for safety. Defence against whom or what? The comparison with the Voortrekkers' *laager*, or the circle of covered wagons under Red Indian attack, is natural and it may indeed be that the most peaceful of rural scenes owes its layout to tribal warfare and pillage. Another explanation, however, seems more likely. The green village was planned to protect the community's livestock from animal predators at night, just as in African villages where the same pattern has evolved. Here the circle of huts forms a compound with only one or two openings. Through these the cattle are driven at night and the openings closed. The Saxon farmers did not have to contend with lions, but every settlement was initially surrounded by forest and the wolf was common throughout Britain. In daylight the stock could be guarded while they grazed and at night they would be driven into the protected sleeping ground in the village centre.

Once the general shape of the village was established there would have been little reason to change it in later centuries when wild beasts were only a folk memory and the central common was used for small livestock like goats and geese—as it still is in some places—or as a sports ground. The hewn timber huts of the Saxons gave way to the peasants' cotts and the picturesque cottages which still fringe many a green, but there was no urge to replan the original site.

The shape of the green village varies with the size and shape of the green itself. One of the most photographed of its kind, Finchingfield, in Essex, has a wide, roughly triangular green with irregularly grouped, whitewashed cottages reflected in the village pond. Matfield, Kent, has a more definitely triangular green, and Stamfordham, Northumberland, a long rectangular one, but the square or broad rectangle is the most usual. Sometimes the green has been partially swallowed up by a school or some other parish building, sometimes it has almost disappeared. At the other extreme a large village may have several greens and of these Clavering, again in Essex, is a remarkable example. It has no less than seven, comprising Hill Green, Sticklings Green, Starlings Green, Roast Green, Deers Green, Sheepcote Green and Bird Green. Two of them are typical green hamlets and could well have started as independent settlements in close proximity, but the rest have no sizeable patch of common land, only extra wide verges. The division of a parish in this way may have resulted from the sharing of the land between several manors: in the case of Clavering six manor houses are extant.

The well at Avebury, Wiltshire. Many villages had no piped water until after World War II—and some villagers thought it an inferior product (*MERL*)

Houses facing a green are usually of the typical local cottage type and purely residential. One rarely finds a farmhouse among them, even though there is nothing but farmland beyond them. In the north-east, however, it was found in a detailed study of green villages that many houses fringing the greens had once been farmsteads and still retained yards and outbuildings. At one time most of them would have been the homes of peasant farmers, but with the enclosures they would have been left with nothing but grazing rights on the green itself, and only one or two houses in the village became residences of the new large-scale farmers.

One almost universal feature of the green is the well or pump, now a quaint survival, but once an important part of the community's water supply. Many villages were, until quite recently, dependent on wells for drinking water and only the larger properties boasted a well of their own. The cottagers filled their buckets at the pump, which might or might not be within easy walking distance, and when mains supplies were at last available some of the older generation were reluctant to change over to 'piped stuff'.

Another common feature of the green is the village pond, now thought of as a wildlife habitat and an environmental asset. In the past this too existed for a purely practical reason; to water stock grazing the green and horses passing through the village. It is still sometimes known as the horsepond, and iron horses as well as flesh and blood ones were frequently watered there. Up to about 1950, when the combine-harvester ousted the steam threshing tackle, the latter could often be seen drawn up by the pond, suction hose dangling in the water and the engine turning gently as it satisfied its thirst on the way to another job. Today, a campaign is being waged to save our remaining village ponds, fast being silted up, used as rubbish tips and sterilised by the seepage of herbicides and pesticides from the land. Those who in childhood have sprawled beside a pond and watched, fascinated, the up-and-down wrigglings of 'pollywogs', the stir of a fish under the flowering island of water crowsfoot and the skimming flash of dragonflies over the surface, can but hope that so much of beauty and interest will not be allowed to perish.

Street villages

Although the beautiful green villages of England go back to very primitive beginnings, they are not necessarily older than those built as a single long street. An early life of St Cuthbert describes a fire in a seventh-century village which was threatened with complete destruction as the flames spread along its single street.

Many old villages such as Staplehurst, Kent, and Long Melford, Suffolk, are built on this simple pattern, though in most cases there has now been expansion at right angles to the main road. The mark of the true street village is that the oldest houses are all sited along the highway as a simple ribbon development, with newer roads and houses further back. Sometimes the one-time street village may have become a town and lost its original shape entirely. This is the case in Windsor, Berkshire, which, despite its castle and its borough charter, was still a village of a thousand souls when the cartographer John Norden drew a plan of it in the seventeenth century. It was then a long ribbon of buildings on both sides of the road with nothing but fields behind them. It had been a borough since the thirteenth century and so must have been a typical street village for a long time before its expansion in other directions began.

Many street villages are based on the sites of Roman roads, and these were possibly still in existence as metalled highways when the villages were founded. The attraction of having a dry, firm track between the two rows of dwellings may have been a strong argument in districts where a wide enclosed green was unnecessary, and once settlement along the verges of a road had started it progressed like all ribbon development by continuing to extend in the same line.

The larger street villages sometimes went in for road-widening operations, not, as with us today, to accommodate through-traffic, but to allow more space for trading. Markets and fairs were held in the street where no green was available, and lack of space seems to have led to the houses being set further and further back during successive rebuildings. The exceptionally wide main street of Marlborough, Wiltshire, is indicative of its former importance as a market, while Moreton-in-Marsh, Gloucestershire, originally a true street village built along a Roman road, has widened out to enclose strips of green.

Siting of villages

The reasons for preferring a particular site are not often apparent. It must be remembered that when our oldest villages were born the inhabitants saw a countryside vastly different to our own.

A powerful factor must often have been the ease with which the natural woodland could be cleared and cultivation started, and many placenames enshrine the name of the person who first made a field or a farm there. When one has to start by felling trees it is natural to look around for a clearing or open space in the forest cover to lessen one's labours. Other things like water supply being equal, the suitability of the site for cultivation must often have been a decisive factor.

Fenland villages were sited on islands before the Fens were drained, limited to such humps of land as were permanently above the waters. Other settlements were founded on streams which were once navigable and so had a ready-made means of transport when the primitive tracks were impassable. Many of the finest Cotswold villages, like Bourton-on-the-Water, are sited on small, but once navigable, rivers.

Lost villages

It is a strange thought that in this heavily populated island, villages have been permanently abandoned and, like Pickworth in Rutland, have left no trace except for a fragment of the church.

The fact that a great many thriving villages were left to moulder back into the land in the Middle Ages is a tribute to the potency of the bubonic plague virus when it arrived in the fourteenth century. In Lincolnshire alone, for instance, the sites of 150 medieval villages have been located, and that they no longer exist is mainly attributable to the Black Death.

Up to the first outbreak of the plague in 1348, the population of the southern half of England had increased rapidly and, except for undrained fens, infertile moorlands and the royal forests, most of the land was under cultivation. The number of villages multiplied accordingly and coincided with a great era of church building. But the Black Death slew between a third and a half of the population in the more densely peopled regions, and numbers of villages and their surrounding fields were deserted. Once the number of able-bodied survivors fell below the minimum needed to carry on some kind of cultivation and bury the dead, they were forced to leave their homes and fields and join another community—peasant farming was a communal activity, and once the community was weakened beyond a certain point it ceased to be a productive unit and the village had then lost the fundamental reason for its existence.

Some of the depopulated villages were later re-occupied, but others never recovered and, in eastern England and the Midlands, disappeared under grass as the profitable sheep filched more and more land from the peasant farmer.

The sheep or, rather, their wealthy owners, did in fact add significantly to the number of deserted villages after the worst ravages of the Black Death had passed. The mixed farming of the peasants had been, in its primitive way, intensive. But with fewer men to work the land and with the manorial system breaking up, the flockmasters began to seize and enclose the abandoned fields for grazing. Unfortunately, the derelict lands were not enough for them, and over a period of more than two centuries the ultimate tragedy of the Highland clearances was foreshadowed in many parts of England. In Northumberland the sites of some 160 deserted villages are known, and the disappearance of most of them may be blamed more on the sheepfarmers than on the plague.

Ingarsby, Leicestershire, is still visible as a number of oblong humps that were once cottages; it once belonged to the Abbey of Leicester, and in 1469 the abbot drove out the inhabitants and converted the manor to a sheep and cattle run. Near Stockerston, in the same county, lies Holy Oak Farm, marking the site of a village that once bore that name. In 1406, Sir Robert Brudenell evicted the villagers to add more acres to his grazing. It was reported that the villagers were idle or had either perished or departed. Sir

Site of deserted village, Lower Ditchford, Gloucester. Hundreds were abandoned during the Black Death and many were never reoccupied (*Cambridge University Collection*)

Robert, one of the Brudenells of Deene, came of a family with an insatiable land-hunger—well into the sixteenth century they were still grabbing land by every conceivable means, to enlarge their deerparks.

The latest villages to vanish fell victim to another fad of the landed gentry, though their inhabitants were resettled, usually not too far from their former homes. These obliterations occurred in the eighteenth century when the surroundings of the burgeoning Palladian mansions were being ever more ambitiously landscaped. Proud owners were advised that a particular village spoilt the view from the great house, so the village was demolished and rebuilt in a position of decent obscurity.

The rebuilding was sometimes ambitious and reflected the landowner's 'advanced' ideas. The small Dorset town of Milton Abbas had developed close to a Benedictine monastery and was very ancient when the Earl of Dorchester bought it, with the whole abbey estate, in 1752. He built his new house on the site of the ruined abbey and, as the town was in the way, demolished it. The replacement village was equipped with church and almshouses, and the cottages were built in pairs separated by plots of land bearing chestnut trees. Often, however, there was what seems to us

The village shop in the 1920s (*MERL*)

inexcusable destruction. Sir Gilbert Heathcote wiped out the medieval Rutland village of Normanton and its church to enlarge his park and, although he replaced both, the new church was located inside the park and not in the village.

Much field work remains to be done in identifying sites of lost villages, and anyone prepared to investigate patterns of flattish humps and sunken strips in waste corners of the countryside may discover them to be all that is left of streets and homes. The best companion in such explorations is *Lost Villages of England*, by M. W. Beresford.

The village store

In most villages in 1900 one would have found that cottages' front parlours had become shops. The status of the occupants was in no way lowered by the fact, it was indeed established by the mere possession of a front parlour, and a selection of goods might be crammed into the window in place of the usual pot plants. There might even be a proud notice over the front door to the effect that the premises were 'Licensed to Sell Tobacco'.

Today, things are sadly reversed. Every village has private dwellings converted from former shops and sometimes the last grocer has gone the way of the village craftsmen and services. They are usually remembered by the housenames—'Saddlers', 'Cobblers', 'The Forge', 'The Wheelhouse'—but the village stores have mostly sunk without trace.

Village baker's cart. The bread was probably baked in brick ovens heated by faggots from local hedges—as it still was in the 1930s within 40 miles of London (*MERL*)

Modern transport and the evolution of the village from a self-contained, locally employed community into a rural residential area, has inevitably taken away the trade of its shopkeepers. Like other independent traders they face the competition of supermarkets and chain stores now that a car-owning population has easy access to nearby towns. The pity of it is that even those who do the bulk of their shopping out of the village still need a local shop at times, but the local shop cannot survive on occasional and emergency custom.

The village trader still keeps going in remoter and more isolated places, not only because of their greater distance from large centres, but because the village is still a community. The attitude of mind that kept trade within the village was summed up by Ernest Pulbrook in *English Country Life and Work*. 'It is unwritten law that he who lives by the district must help the district to live in return.' Today, too few villagers live by the district and those who merely live *in* it feel no such constraint. The bonds of mutual obligation have fallen away from the commuter village.

For the one third of the rural population which has no cars the closure of village shops is a disaster, coinciding as it does with the collapse of public transport in the country. The bus was probably the most effective agent in ending the isolation of the village, but despite the rural bus services of the 1930s, when services were incomparably better than now, village folk retained the habit of shopping near home for everyday needs. Since then, both the village store and the country bus have fallen victim to the car.

Village trade used to include a strong element of barter in the days when money was a scarce commodity. Part-payment with garden produce or a few jars of honey still goes on, but things used to be organised on a more formal basis by means of the contra account. For trade between traders a three months' account was very convenient when practised in a close-knit circle with that mixture of mutual trust in general and a suspicious haggling over detail that were typical of the countryman's transactions. The farmer would pay for a quarter's bread by supplying the baker with faggots to heat his brick oven; the blacksmith would set the cost of shoeing the butcher's cob against the price of several Sunday dinners; the undertaker might find his grocery bill settled by a timely demise in the grocer's family.

A lot of fun has been had at the expense of the traditional village store and its stock-in-trade and memories of the sort of shop that was common up to 1939 are of a comprehensive if slightly disorganised service. There was seldom any attempt at display, but the scene changed with the seasons. Packets of seeds and a few garden tools in spring gave way to assorted boxes and punnets of summer fruit and vegetables brought in by customers. There were butterfly nets and bamboo fishing rods for the children, crates of ginger pop, flypapers, cheeses and sides of bacon shrouded in muslin. Frozen foods were unknown, but a limited selection of ices was usually available.

By October, pairs of wellingtons and galoshes were dangling in inconvenient places, firelighters and 'pimps' (bundles of chopped kindling wood), shining new paraffin lamps and hurricane lanterns and the appearance of Lightning Cough Cures and bottles of liniment among the weird medley of human and animal medicines, all told of the approach of winter. Fireworks were there long before the fifth of November, in trays labelled Halfpenny, Penny and Twopence, and out of school hours a

Carrier's cart in Oxfordshire, c. 1874. For many villages it remained a vital link with town and railhead until 1914 or later (*MERL*)

wrangling group of small customers was always to be found poring over them, deriving as much pleasure from the purchase as from the eventual explosions.

Within a month the firework trays were full of Christmas cards, the price tags not much altered. The scent of the shop changed subtly with the arrival of extra oranges and boxes of dessert apples. Boxes of crackers, cottonwool snowballs, bundles of multi-coloured strips for making paper chains, Chinese lanterns, coloured candles, and other festive material spilled confusingly over the normal merchandise. The small clearings usually found on the counter vanished under pot-bellied jars of ginger in syrup, pressed tongue in flat glass containers, bowls of mixed nuts, Bath chaps wearing paper frills, bottles of non-alcoholic ginger wine, and other ephemeral goodies. Christmas trees propped against the doorpost entangled the unwary in the winter dusk. And then, as always, given time and a willingness to help in the search, one had a good chance of finding the items that one sought.

That was one great strength of the village store. Its stock inventory was based on the principle that you never knew what daft things people might want and that anything non-perishable was a longterm investment. It might lie buried for years and be rediscovered only by the combined efforts of customer and shopkeeper, but its presence was properly regarded as a boost for the latter's reputation.

The quality of the shop's eatables was often such as to be unknown to the present generation. Bacon joints held up for your inspection before being rashered scrumpy-thin or gluttonous-thick as you desired; great wedges of Cheddar cheese dividing under the cutting-wire; boxes of plump raisins and hemispheres of candied peel, each holding its lens-shaped block of sugar; bins of butter beans, split peas for pease puddings and oatmeal for porridge, fine, medium and coarse, according to whether you were prepared to cook it for an hour or for half the day and most of the night; ramparts of biscuit tins bearing the labels of a vast selection. All to be weighed before your very eyes, some things in bags of thick blue paper, others in thinner bags carrying the proprietor's name, and a folded bag placed beneath the weights on the scale pan as a demonstration of perfect equity.

The old-style village shop belongs to the past as irrevocably as does the windmill. The village is still by rights the territory of the small trader and he may yet again regain his position by adapting to modern needs. Just so long as the adaptation is not too complete and the shop has some appeal for those to whom the package provides no alibi for the contents, and to whom promotion is no substitute for service. Whatever its deficiencies, the village store never gave its customers the feeling of being a tolerated nuisance.

The pub

It goes without saying that the village inn is not what it was. Also, one fears that it never has been. It is said to have been ruined by modern decor, the telly, too many female customers and keg beers. Chesterton thought it was deteriorating eighty years ago. Charles Kingsley in the 1850s encouraged his parishioners to play cricket on Sundays rather than endanger their souls in the alehouse, and in 1829 William Cobbett was telling the labouring classes that only by brewing and drinking their beer at home could they escape being poisoned by noxious chemicals at the hands of unscrupulous landlords.

Country pubs are much scarcer than they used to be; in many villages up to half of them have ceased to trade within living memory, though they were in the past grossly over-supplied with hospitality. Almost anywhere one may encounter a well pickled ancient mourning the days when every seventh house was a pub, and one can only assume that their hosts emulated the Chinese laundrymen and lived by drinking one another's ale.

The pub's local trade declined with improved transport to neighbouring

The 'Who'd Have Thought It' inn, Milton Combe, Devon (*Roy J. Westlake*)

towns. For the Victorian village labourer it offered the only escape from the grind of work and the inadequacies of home (for his womenfolk there was virtually no escape at all), but when first the bicycle and then the motor bus came within his reach other forms of relaxation became possible.

The modern pub catering for the motorist is in the main stream of tradition. The inn, the house offering shelter and hospitality, grew out of travellers' needs. There may have been many fewer people on the roads of the past but the arduous and hazardous nature of journeying made a good inn and an honest innkeeper doubly important.

Inns of the Middle Ages took over the work of succouring the wayfarer from the monastic orders—many were started by the monasteries themselves as a source of revenue. This first phase of organised innkeeping was supported by the pilgrim traffic. Shrines were everywhere the main tourist attraction and the financial blessings of every holy relic fell not only upon the town that owned them but on the inns strung along the routes that led there.

The late eighteenth century saw more people travelling and a great

A drink outside the pub in Somerset, c 1912 (*MERL*)

The New Inn, Stratton, Cornwall, 1880 (*MERL*)

advance in the quality of inns. Canal inns, with their associated stables, were established in lonely places that could not otherwise have hoped for a decent pub. On the improved roads the advent of the stage coach, and the development of the coaching inn as an integral part of the service, did a great deal to raise standards generally. Some of these hostelries were, by contemporary reckoning, large and luxurious. They were not confined to major towns, a small village was a likely site if it stood in the right position on the highway for a changing post. That, of course, was the point about coaching inns—they were creations of the trunk route. Today you will find a 'Waggon and Horses' almost anywhere, while a 'Coach and Horses' will probably be on a main road.

Which brings us to the question of inn signs. Tracing their origins is a fine sport provided you are not, as Mathew Arnold put it, hot for certainties in this our life.

The most interesting thing is that they are the last survival of a once universal custom, when most of the population were illiterate merchants and craftsmen and even private dwellings had to identify themselves by distinctive and easily recognisable signs. The fact was given legal expression in a charter granted to Londoners by Charles I: 'To expose and hang in and over the streets signs and posts of signs affixed to their houses and shops for the better finding out such citizens dwellings, shops, arts or occupations.' In the village, where everybody's business was known to everybody else, signs were less necessary, but inns were compelled by law to exhibit them for the benefit of travellers. Anyone selling ale or wine without publicly announcing his trade could have his stock confiscated. No under-the-counter stuff was tolerated.

The earliest inn sign was probably a green bush or a bunch of leaves on a pole. It may have originated with the Roman sign for a wine shop—the vine leaves that were the symbol of Bacchus. Since then almost every bird and beast, real and mythological, a host of common objects and the names and insignia of the great and famous, often combined in bizarre and apparently pointless ways, have been used. The subject offers material for a lifetime's research or an excuse for on-the-spot investigation of every unusual case.

Pub signs, like placenames, have a wonderful capacity for changing themselves over the centuries while retaining obvious similarities. For instance, there are many Blue Boars, and the blue boar is the armorial badge of the earls of Oxford, none of whom seems to have been important enough to justify this widespread memorial. But the badge of Richard III was the white boar, and although his subjects may have called him 'the Hog' in private, many prudent landlords blazoned their loyalty by operating under his symbol. Then Richard went down at Bosworth and on the morrow of the battle they were faced with the cost of repainting the signs to demonstrate allegiance to Henry VII. Mercifully, it was recalled that the Earl of Oxford was a stout supporter of Henry and, overnight, hundreds of White Boars simply turned Blue. More difficult to elucidate are cases like that of the Andrew Mac, wearing the sign of a splendid Highlander. At some time in the past an artist must have misunderstood his instructions, for the inn had previously been named after a ship of the line, the *Andromache*.

The bar, by the way, was a Tudor invention and at first quite unlike its modern version. Known as the buttery bar, it was a service hatch through which drinks were passed to the customers. It was an inhospitable arrangement and obviously intended to be slammed shut if they became rowdy.

The Victorian village

The nineteenth-century village lasted until the war of 1914, and some of its essential features persisted for much longer. It is near enough to us in time, and yet far enough in experience, to carry a guarantee of nostalgia; we see it always in the sunlight of a great and settled calm.

There is some truth in the vision, for in this period the village attained a perfect balance between the isolation of the past and the total assimilation into the uniformly urban civilisation which it now faces. Although isolation had ended with the railway, better roads, the postal service, newspapers, and the telegraph, the Victorian and Edwardian village managed to keep something inherited from its youth in the Middle Ages; it remained a community.

It was socially more static than the towns, despite the growing discontent of the under-privileged labourers, and even those who had long ceased to bless the squire and his relations still tended to keep their proper stations. But they were a community because of a common interest in the land—except in mining or quarrying villages everyone's life was somehow affected by agriculture and its ancillary trades. The farmer was the first to feel the effects of a bad season or poor prices. The landlord would be forced to reduce or forgo his rent; the farmworker would be stood off to exist on the edge of starvation; the saddler would sit idle while harness was patched with string; the parson would ponder the yield of his glebe land and the meagreness of his Easter offering. Conversely, in prosperous times there would be a general improvement, however inequitable its effects.

This common dependence on the land, this shared experience of prosperity and woe, had been, throughout its long selfcontained existence, the binding force of the village community. It was essentially the cohesion of work, of making a living, and the village maintained it almost up to our own day.

By the 1870s, however, there were innumerable reports of large families living in cottages with one bedroom reached only by a ladder, of whole streets with livingroom floors of beaten earth, and of forms of sanitation that must have been as distressing to the passing traveller as to the inhabitants. Complaints of contaminated water supplies were naturally very common. Shallow wells became polluted with drainage water; there were too few wells and their situation was often worse than inconvenient, it was not unknown for the main village water supply to be in the churchyard. Cholera and typhoid were fairly frequent visitors, and the incidence of all types of infectious disease was increased by the over-population characteristic of nineteenth-century villages.

Yet it cannot be denied that the villager, despite extreme poverty, was better off than the urban industrial worker. There was fresh air and an open sky, and a countryside which was very lovely and better cared for than it had ever been. The fields, the parks, even the gardens of the often deplorable cottages, evoked an admiration more sound than the romanticism of the town-based rustic poets.

Today and tomorrow

The village has a past longer than that of our most ancient cities; has it a future? As a collection of dwellings, obviously yes. Nearly all villages, whether they have changed much or little, whether they have suffered from the developer or have escaped him, now have a prosperous look about them. No cottage lies derelict, the greens are mown, many are plainly entrants for the Best Kept Village competition. But what of the village as a community?

The farming revolution which, in the span of a lifetime, reduced the number of men and women working on the land by nearly nine-tenths, also transformed the village. Workers were sucked into the towns and townspeople took over their cottages. The weekenders, the retired and the commuters have spread in widening circles through the villages around every major city, inevitably destroying the basis of common interest in work which made the old village a community. However conscientious the new-style villagers in the preservation of their surroundings, however enthusiastically they support local organisations and activities, the village and the land must often be peripheral matters to them rather than the central all-absorbing objects of concern they were to their predecessors. And the village is no more likely to remain a true community than any random slice of a suburb.

A recent study has suggested that the village will survive as a viable and vital place only if it provides local work for a substantial part of its population. If the work has some association with agriculture—fruit and vegetable processing, wallboard manufacture from straw, and so on—much of the character of the old village could be retained.

The name of the place

Placenames have been described as encapsulated history, but extracting the history from the capsule is often far from easy. The difficulties in the tracing of origins, and the weirdly unexpected explanations that emerge, make this form of countryside detection especially interesting. Along with map and guidebook should go the appropriate county volume of the English Place Names Society or one of the two major reference works, *The Concise Oxford Dictionary of English Place Names* or *The Names of Towns and Cities in Britain*. On coming to an oddly named place the terrain may be inspected for a possible explanation, a local shopkeeper asked if he can account for it, and a few guesses made before looking up the known facts. Both local opinion and visitors' guesswork are usually wrong.

Many names are Anglo Saxon to start with, and that is not the same thing as being English. On top of this they may have been modified by successive invasions; in the north-east by the Scandinavians, in southern and central England by Norman-French and Latin influences and everywhere to the west by the Celtic tongues, Welsh, Gaelic, and Cornish.

An attempt to interpret a name in terms of modern language will succeed only by the merest fluke, a fact which early antiquarians failed to appreciate. That rare old character, John Aubrey, believed that Slaughterford in Wiltshire was named after a ford where the Danes had been massacred in battle. He was strengthened in his belief by the fact that the plant called Danewort grew in the district and, according to seventeenth-century superstition, it flourished only where Danish blood had been shed. Later research proved that the Old English name of the village was *Slathorn-ford*, the ford where the sloe or blackthorn tree grew.

A further lesson may be found in this business of 'slaughter'. In Surrey there is a place called Slaughterwick, 'the place or premises of the sloe tree', the suffix *wick* or *wich* meaning a group of buildings. But in Gloucestershire there is another Slaughterford, and this has nothing to do with sloe trees. It is the ford of the *slohtre*, the slough or muddy place. The reader may care to elucidate for himself the naming of those lovely Cotswold villages, Upper and Lower Slaughter, but he will have noted that at least two quite different Old English words have been transformed into 'slaughter', the meaning of which word today has no linguistic association with either.

Compound names

Equally confusing are those impressive duplex and multiple names like Houghton Conquest and Ashby-de-la-Zouch. Here the place bears the name of a sometime lord of the manor, and this may have been modernised, Anglicised, or simplified. Stansted Mountfitchet, in Essex, scene of a recent battle over an airport, was the manor of Norman lords from Montfiquet. Sydenham Damerel, in Devon, was given to John D'Albemarle in the thirteenth century. Aspley Guise, Bedfordshire, is 'the aspen-tree clearing of Anselm de Gyse'. The incredibly named Berrick Salome, Oxfordshire, is 'the barley farm of Almaric de Suleham'. No doubt the name came strangely to the English peasant, but Salome, about whom the priest had told him, was a fair approximation.

The word 'stoke' appears in many manorial placenames, meaning 'the special property of'. Thus Stoke Poges became the property of Robert le Pugeis in 1255. The Essex village of Layer Marney, however, was already named after a stream called the Layer when a Norman lord from Marigny was given possession of it. Kingston Bagpuize in Berkshire was the King's Farm (*ton*) when it went to a Norman from Becquepuis.

Many compound names reflect the temporal standing of the Church. There are some forty places bearing names like Bishop's Stortford or Bishopton (bishop's farm). Another score are typified by Abbot's Ripton or Abbotsford. Monkton (monk's farm) occurs in Kent, Devon and Ayrshire, and monks turn up in many other ways. Ecclesiastical associations are often expressed in Latin. *Monachorum* is 'of the monks', *Episcopi* is 'of the bishop', and the exceptional *Fratrum*, as in the Dorset village of Toller Fratrum is 'of the brethren'. Latin elements occur for other reasons, *magnum* and *parva* replacing great and little, for instance. Sometimes a part-Latin name relapsed into the vernacular. The charming Hertfordshire village of Brent Pelham was once Burnt Pelham, then the more dignified Pelham Combusta, but at some stage both the Latin and the memory of an ancient disaster seem to have faded. A few miles from Brent Pelham is Wendens Ambo, a sore puzzle to the stranger. '*Ambo*' is Latin for 'both' and long ago existed both Great and Little Wenden, now merged.

But it is hard to understand why the Somerset town of Weston should have substituted *super Mare* for 'on sea'. Especially as now, with the abandonment of classical education, it is only a matter of time before everyone assumes it to have some reference to an exceptional female horse.

English names

No absolutely reliable rules in the interpretation of placenames can be laid down and, as the few examples given are enough to show, the original versions may become something radically different. But certain constituents of names are used so often, and so many of them obviously fit the place in question, that they may be accepted as the basics of placename detection.

This is no place for the whole fascinating list, only for a sample of those most commonly met with.

–ton, as in Linton, is about the most popular ending. It normally means a farm or medieval village. It does not mean a 'town' in the modern sense though both derive from the Old English *tun*.

–ham, as in Newnham, usually means a meadow or grazing ground. It may also mean a home; *–hampton* indicated a home farm.

–chester or *–cester*, as in Cirencester, applies to a fortified place. It is Anglicised Latin for a Roman *castra* or encampment.

–stow, as in Morwenstow, indicates either a holy place or a place of meeting. In the former case it is usually preceded by the name of a saint. Morwenstow, the Cornish coastal village made famous by the Reverend Stephen Hawker, is the holy place of St Morwenna. Wistanstow in Shropshire is the *stow* of St Wystan, otherwise unknown, except that one of our greatest modern poets, Wystan Hugh Auden, was given his name.

–worth signifies an enclosure, Oakworth in Yorkshire being 'an enclosure of oak trees'. Sometimes it appears as *–worthy*, and Woolfardisworthy in Devon, the enclosure of one Wulfheard, is the longest one-word placename in England. The Sussex town of Worthing was nobody's enclosure but the settlement of a Saxon tribe called the Wurthingas.

—*port* does not necessarily indicate a port in the modern sense. There are several Newports, for instance, far from sea or river. It refers to a gate and therefore to a walled township. It often means a place important enough to hold a market or fair. The word Chipping in names such as Chipping Norton and Chipping Barnet has the same message; buying and selling or 'cheaping' was carried on there. The appellation may have been thought undignified, for Blandford Forum in Dorset was Cheping Blaneford in the thirteenth century. Both forms mean 'having a market' but the English was supplanted by Latin.

—*hurst*, —*den* and —*ley* occur as endings to hundreds of names in the Weald of Kent and Sussex. There has been argument over whether they represent woodland or pasture, —*hurst* may mean a wooded area, —*den* a valley, and —*ley* is still used by farmers to described temporary grassland. In fact, placenames in the Weald which include these words all seem to have the same origin; they record the penetration of the Anglo-Saxons into the dense forests, the clearing of land for grazing and the founding of settlements.

Norse and Celtic influence

The Danes and Norwegians gained no such permanent footing as did the Saxons, but in the area of the Danelaw, roughly north and east of a line from London to Chester, they established distinctive placenames.

The end syllable —*by* is the Viking word for a village and is found all over this part of the country. Derby is 'the village with a deerpark'. Whenby, in the North Riding of Yorkshire, appears to be 'the village owned by women'.

The word —*thorp* is a common element of names from the Midlands northwards. It implies a subsidiary settlement, an offshoot of a larger Viking colony. Thus Scotton Thorpe, Yorkshire, was a hamlet attached to the village of Scotton, and Easthorpe and Westhorpe, Nottinghamshire, were eastern and western 'suburbs' of Southwell.

Other Scandinavian components are common in North Country and Midland names. A valley is —*dal* (dale or —*gill*, a hill is —*fell*, a brook is —*beck*, and —*thwaite* means 'a clearing in the forest'. Nordic personal names and even nicknames are also perpetuated. Bromkinsthorpe, Leicestershire, is the hamlet of Brunskinn, the brown-skinned person.

Travelling southward from Northern England along the Welsh Marches, the remnants of Celtic names are found in the English counties of Herefordshire and Shropshire. In Cornwall the Celtic influence is much stronger, producing names quite unlike others in the West Country and explaining why Cornishmen speak of crossing the Tamar into England.

> By Tre, Ros, Pol, Lan, Caer and Pen
> You may know the most Cornishmen

And the most Cornish placenames. One soon notices that the generally descriptive parts of these names come at the beginning and not at the end as in Anglo-Saxon names. *Tre* means a farmstead, the equivalent of the Old English *–ton. Pen* is a headland; Penzance is 'holy headland' and the old name for Land's End was Penwith, 'cape seen from afar'. Omitted from the ancient rhyme is *Bod,* 'the house'. Bodmin is the house of the monks, reminding us that an important monastery was once sited there. Cornwall was a great haven for saints when Christian communities elsewhere were suffering the fury of the Norsemen. Saints' names abound in placenames, often not easily identifiable. St Perran, for instance, turns up repeatedly, as in Perranporth, 'the port of St Perran'. Mevagissey is 'the church of St Mew'.

Scottish names

Many of them are basically Gaelic with Scandinavian additions, the Viking invaders leaving their imprint on the Celtic originals as the Normans did on Anglo-Saxon names in England.

This shows more clearly the further north one goes. Shetland was a Viking colony and has a purely Viking name. Orkney had the Gaelic name of *Orc*, but the Norse termination *–ey*, meaning island, was added to it instead of the Gaelic for island, which is *–innis*. Sutherland has a Viking name, 'the south land', which it was to the Vikings on Orkney and the Shetlands.

Cape Wrath, apparently so well named, is another example of a misleading modernisation. Its true name is *Hvarf*, Norwegian for 'the turning of the coast'. Dingwall recalls the Norse custom of holding community assemblies on particular areas of open ground. Like Thingwall in Cheshire and Tynwald in the Isle of Man, it means 'field of assembly'.

Not many saints are commemorated in Scottish placenames, though one well known one, Tobermory, is 'the well of St Mary'. A curious case is that of the Hebridean island of St Kilda, apparently named after a saint unknown to the hagiographers. St Kilda in fact never existed. He (or she) was created by a misreading of the Norse name *Skildar*, or 'shields'. The distant outline of the island's hills suggested to the approaching Vikings the convex outlines of their shields.

The opening syllable *Pit–*, as in Pitlochry, occurs in scores of Scottish names. It pre-dates the Normans and may have come from those mysterious people, the Picts. It is generally interpreted as 'the portion of', designating a piece of land. Pitmaduthy in Ross-shire, for example, is 'Macduff's piece'. A slight variant is found in such names as Pettymuck in Aberdeenshire—'the portion of the pigs'.

A few Anglo-Saxon elements will be found in names in southern

Scotland. Edinburgh has the familiar Old English ending *–burgh*, 'a fortified town'. Modern English occurs in the Highlands in Fort William, Fort George and Fort Augustus, but these are relics of an army of occupation. The last commemorates William Augustus, Duke of Cumberland, alias 'Stinking Billy'.

Welsh names

Placenames in Wales are predominantly Celtic with bits of English and Norse. They are less varied in origin than those in England and suggest a nation that, despite the wars along the Marches and the Severn from Roman times onwards, remained more homogeneous than the English mixture of warring tribes and races.

The opening syllable *llan*, a church, may be used in conjunction with a saint's name like the Old English *–stow*, a holy place. It is used so frequently that other distinguishing features are sometimes added to the name to prevent confusion between the many places with churches dedicated to the same saint, so building up long, compound words. Thus Llanfairfechan is 'little church of St Mary' and Llanfair-ar-y-Bryn 'St Mary's church on the cliff'. And of course there is the one that got completely out of control.

In Anglesey there is one of the few places to attract tourists solely by its name. But the truth about

Llanfairpwllgyngyllgogerychwyrndrobwlllandysiliogogogoch

is that the last forty letters have no right to be there. The true name is Llanfairpwllgwyngyll—long enough in all conscience for a small place—meaning 'the church of St Mary near the pool of the white hazel'. When some local patriot set about expanding it in the nineteenth century he inserted a middle portion meaning 'near the fierce whirlpool', a reference to the Menai Straits, and added to that the name of another village, not even in Anglesey but in Cardiganshire, which derived its name from a cave (*gogo*). The longest placename in Britain is a splendid and profitable forgery.

Two common prefixes are *Pont–*, 'bridge', and *Aber–*, 'mouth of the river'. Aberaeron is unusual in commemorating a Celtic deity. It marks the mouth of the river, named after the goddess of battle. Most of the Welsh counties have Celtic names, but Flint is exceptional in meaning what it says in contemporary English—the county of hard rock.

Rhyl is a hybrid, being simply the English 'hill' preceded by the Welsh definite article, *yr*, making it 'the hill'. Pontypool is another straightforward combination, *Pont* (Welsh) and pool (English)—'the bridge over the pool'. But on the whole English was no more effective than Norse in displacing Welsh names, and even the singularly beautiful county of Pembroke, so popular with the English that it has been called 'little England beyond

Wales', has a purely Celtic name meaning 'end land'. The similarity to Land's End is appropriate, for like the Cornish peninsula it is washed by the warm Atlantic Drift.

Wales is a mountainous country and most of the hill-names are Celtic. Among the elements most commonly met with are *bron* ('round hill or breast'), *carreg* ('rock'), *cefn* ('ridge'), *glyder* ('heap'), *mynydd* ('mountain'), and *pen* ('summit'). Snowdon has an English name ('snow hill'), but should properly be known by the Welsh *Eryri*. This may mean 'height of the eagles', but a more prosaic explanation is probable. It appears to mean 'tiles on the roof'.

The cottages

The cottage typifies the countryman's home because a majority of countrymen have always lived in it. By an 'unspoilt' village we usually mean one in which most of the smaller dwellings are built in the traditional style of the area and have not been submerged in modern housing development. The manor houses, farmhouses and parsonages may be equally important, but it is a sound instinct which assesses a village in terms of its cottages. Once they are dominated by modern buildings in completely different styles, the character of the village is permanently changed.

Many cottages give an impression of great age, especially those exhibiting ancient and blackened timbers inside or out. Old they may indeed be, but as a rule they are many centuries younger than, say, the parish church. The oldest small dwellings in any village rarely date back further than the late sixteenth century and most of them will be of later origin. There are, of course, some exceptional survivals, but small, cheap buildings lapse into ruin and disappear, though their successors may be erected on the same sites. The larger and more costly a building the more likely were succeeding generations of occupants to possess the will and the means to keep it in repair.

The traditional cottage of today, however, is a recapitulation, almost a repetition of those of the past. Things changed little and slowly in cottage-building, and the worst nineteenth-century specimens must have differed hardly at all in essentials from the average of Tudor times. Even the lovingly modernised cottage has in its very walls the story of its own and its ancestors' primitive past.

The timber frame

It goes without saying that until recently cottages had to be constructed of local materials. In building as in most things the village must fend for itself. In hill districts there was stone but not always the skills to use it. Everywhere in the lowlands was timber, straw, clay and frequently chalk.

Timber-framed cottage, stripped down for restoration. Elizabethan door with decorated spandrels, and moulded roof beams, probably Flemish (*Suzanne Beedell*)

These are still the basic constructional materials of cottages in the greater part of England, though much less so in Scotland and Wales.

The medieval peasant's hut which evolved into the cottage is often referred to as a hovel. In the strict sense it certainly was, for 'hovel' derives from the Anglo-Saxon *hof*, 'a house', and no doubt it was equally so in the accepted sense of being crude, cramped and very nasty. Incidentally, a 'hovel' in East Anglia has come to mean a barn, and not a mean or squalid one but the lofty steel-girdered Dutch variety.

The peasant's hut was a tent-like structure, usually single-roomed and made of poles covered with straw or turf. It developed into a cottage form which was still primitive but held the possibility of further advance.

The cruck cottage

This simple hut is made by sticking two rows of poles into the ground some way apart and bringing each opposing pair together at the ridge to form a row of inverted Vs. The sides are then covered with laths or branches and finished with a layer of thatch or turf. The ends are filled with more poles and branches covered with mud ('daub and wattle') and you have a shelter of sorts. Nomadic herdsmen probably used it before settled agricultural communities began, and woodland workers like chair-leg bodgers and the makers of clog soles were still using this basic design for their temporary huts up to seventy years ago. More remarkable, cottages built on the principle of the cruck—the crotch or forked branch—are still in existence, though very few are left.

The cruck method affected cottage-building for a thousand years or more because of its strength and durability. So long as you had strong poles leaning inwards and joined at the ridge pole the thing could not possibly collapse. There was no question of the weight of the roof causing the walls to bulge outwards because walls and roof were one. The more weight you piled on the inverted Vs, straw, turf or any other material, the more solidly the framework held together.

The disadvantages are obvious. There are no vertical walls on the longest sides, the walls slope inwards from ground level, greatly reducing headroom. Most people with old timbered cottages are familiar with the problems of the bedroom in which the walls begin their inward slope about 3ft from the floor; the cruck building has no upper storey because the apex of the triangular section is too narrow.

The builders realised how restricted the interior was, with the walls sloping in from the ground to the ridge, and sought to enlarge the living space by converting the shape from an inverted V into a sort of arch, with the sides drawing in slowly at first and then more sharply above head-height. But they still thought it essential to preserve the cruck principle of timbers that ran in one piece from ground to ridge. So, like the shipbuilders, they began to use curved branches, matching them as best they could and splitting those thick enough down the centre to give identical pairs.

The cottage assumed its present shape when timber uprights were used to erect vertical walls, the tops of the uprights being joined by a longitudinal 'plate' from which separated roof timbers led up to the ridge. Tie beams extended from wall to wall at plate level, preventing the walls being pushed outwards by the thrust of the roof timbers, and these timbers were themselves held in position by simple trusses. Yet, even after the frame had proved its complete stability and much larger houses were being built in this way, the obsession with the cruck continued, a pair of ground-to-ridge timbers being used at each end of the building or at the end of each bay in a longer cottage. The feature is still found in seventeenth-century cottages.

The size of cottages

The early cottage we have been describing was a one-room affair and the distance between the end crucks was invariably 16ft. This is the 'bay' referred to above, and the length of a bay became universally adopted and remained so, cottages being enlarged by adding additional bays to their length or a lean-to structure at the side where there was a vertical wall of sufficient height.

Why the length of 16ft should have been so widely adopted for the one-room dwelling is a matter of conjecture, that it was so is shown by the number of existing cottages with plans based upon it. The accepted explanation is that like other fundamental measurements it was based upon the ox. Just as the furlong is the 'furrow-long' that the ox-team could plough before it rested at the headland, just as the rod, pole or perch is the length of an ox-goad, so, it is suggested, the 16ft bay was the right size for stalling two yoke of oxen—four animals whose housing was probably as important as that of their owner and his family. Buildings are easier to erect when one keeps to a standard size.

Certainly the 'bay' was a recognised unit in medieval days, though now it applies to a section of a barn or factory without regard to dimensions. But in the past it was actually used as a measure of bulk in the case of hay, and the medieval property tax known as 'gavelage' or gable tax was apparently based on the space enclosed between gables, in other words, so much per bay.

The single-bay cottage did not go out with the Middle Ages. In the seventeenth century Bishop Hall could still write of a house, 'Of one bay's breadth, God wot! a silly cote . . .'. As late as 1884 single-room cottages were being reported to a commission on working-class housing. But the timber-framed house developed far beyond its humble beginnings into the elaboration of Tudor times, into manor and farmhouse, into projecting upper storeys and all the variations of 'black-and-white' and 'half-timbered' domestic architecture which, like the simplest cottage, is one with the rural background.

Daub-and-wattle

Building materials are heavy to transport and the countryman's home, like much else in his life, had in the past to be fashioned from what lay near at hand. This is worth emphasising again, because if you examine the materials used in a really old cottage they give the impression of being very local indeed.

There is little sawn or prepared timber except for floorboards, and even they are likely to be of irregular width. Other timbers are roughly trimmed, often crooked, and sometimes apparently cut from the nearest hedgerow and used with the bark on. This is particularly so with roof timbers under thatch, which often look quite inadequate but rarely need renewing. If these makeshift timbers escape woodworm, they become steel-hard in the course of time.

The stuff used for filling the walls was also obtained from as near the site as possible. Close to most cottages of this type is a small pond, or a tradition of one in the past. It may have served the customary use of watering stock, but primarily it provided the walls of the cottage. Hazel rods were fixed between the timber studding, and a mixture of wet clay and chopped straw or straw chaff spread over them. According to some builders, cow manure was also added to the mixture, but they are always vague as to the reason for this. It might be that the final outer coating, a plaster of lime or crushed chalk, was tinted with cow manure to produce a warmer colouring. (The Ministry of Agriculture once recommended that asbestos roofs on new farm buildings should be sprayed with liquid cow manure to encourage the growth of mosses and lichens and simulate natural weathering, but that is a different matter.)

The clay and straw mix, or unbaked brick, is used worldwide for building, especially in areas of low rainfall. In Britain it must be protected by wide eaves, which is why thatch is as technically right for these cottages as it is aesthetically. A rain-soaked wall never dries out and eventually begins to disintegrate. The saying that the house lasts as long as the roof is quoted elsewhere (see Thatching, p233) and in Devon, where the typical 'cob' cottage has walls entirely of clay mixture, with no framing, the saying is that cob must have a good hat and shoes. The walls must stand on a stone footing to stop them returning to the earth from whence they came, and the spreading eaves shelter them from all but the most fiercely driven rains.

There is something immensely comforting and protective about the look of a low-roofed thatched cottage; it appeals to a primitive urge to seek shelter from a hostile outer world—mainly because it was designed to shelter itself from destruction by the elements.

Pargetting

The exterior of the clay-walled cottage, whether timber-framed or built of clay alone like the Devon cob, had to be protected on the exterior by a plaster which offered at least some resistance to penetration by water. From the late seventeenth century onwards, a mixture of lime, fine sand and bullocks' hair was used and this provided a rendering that did not crack easily and gave a smooth enduring surface. Great care was taken in the preparation of the plaster, the materials—with or without an added mixture of cow manure and the liquid drainage from stables—being 'worked up' very thoroughly. The toughness of the old plasterwork is sometimes demonstrated by comparison with its modern equivalent on a renovated cottage. The new cement plaster, usually on an expanding metal base, frequently shows cracks after a few years, while undisturbed parts of the original coating have matured over a couple of centuries into a sort of resilient hide.

Over much of East Anglia timber-framed cottages have been completely plastered, the timbers themselves being covered. Not all, of course, for in Essex and Suffolk much fine exterior timbering is visible, but it does seem that in this part of the world, as in the West Country, there has been a predilection for the unbroken wall surface, dazzlingly white and once whitewashed every year, practically as a social obligation. An increasing number of colour-washed cottages are now appearing, but Britain is not a Mediterranean country and the contrasts of shadow and white walls are perhaps better suited to our kindly sunlight than a confusion of colour.

The impulse to decorate the plain whiteness in some way has, however, always been strong in East Anglia, where it has found expression in the ornamental patterning of plasterwork known as pargetting. The origin of the word is obscure, but in the same area a chimney is said to be 'parged' when its interior brickwork is plastered.

The more intricate pargetting, such as the figures on the gables of the Sun Inn at Saffron Walden, was usually reserved for town houses and the larger country homes. Cottage decoration took the form of a simple motif of scallops or half-circles enclosed in a square or rectangular panel marked by double lines. An entire wall might be covered with these decorative panels, or they might be used here and there to relieve the monotony of large plain surfaces. It has been said that the art of pargetting has been lost, but this is not so. Many village builders still practice it and almost insist on doing so

Pargetting (*Suzanne Beedell*)

whenever the chance occurs. The result may not be as attractive or as longlasting as older examples, but that is due more to the nature of modern quick-drying plasters than to any loss of skill by the plasterer.

Brickwork

Bricks were at one time expensive and scarce. Like stone, they could only be transported in quantity by water which limited their distribution before the canal systems of the eighteenth century. In Tudor times, when they began to be used to a limited extent in domestic architecture, they were mainly an imported prestige product. The mass-produced brick which, in the nineteenth century, housed, or at least contained, the urban poor at negligible cost, was not available when the older parts of the villages were built. The probable consequences if it had been are frightful to contemplate.

Brickwork in the larger Tudor houses was often used as infilling for timbered walls, always an attractive combination and especially so where the 'herringbone' pattern was employed. Chimneys on the more prestigious Tudor houses are among the earliest examples of truly decorative brickwork. It was the chimney, too, that occasioned the first real use of brickwork in the cottage.

The 'silly cote' of the medieval peasant had no chimney. The fire was built on a stone hearth and the smoke either escaped or failed to escape through a hole in the roof. When ceilings came into fashion, a hole was made in the ceiling and a hood or canopy fitted round it to collect the smoke and lead it into the space under the roof which acted as a 'smoke chamber' and from which it could drift out through the hole at its leisure. This arrangement was still in use in the seventeenth century, the development of the chimney with its open hearth and massive breast, which adds so much to the interior of the cottage, is less a sign of extreme antiquity than a splendid modern improvement.

The stone-built cottage

Stone was not much used in the earlier cottages, even in the mountain and moorland areas where the stone-walled type now predominates. Timber and mud were so much quicker and easier to handle, and so much of the land was covered with forest that the timber-framed structure was the easier option.

The use of dressed stone in small buildings was very rare before the seventeenth century, the masons from Norman times onwards being occupied with more important buildings such as churches. Stone cottages eventually predominated in those parts of western and northern Britain, from Cornwall to the Scottish Highlands, where easily worked stone was available. Sooner or later a plentiful supply of a local material always

Village cricket team, before 1914 (*MERL*)

The team off for a match (*MERL*)

dictated the style of building and the crafts of the builders; churches in limestone and sandstone districts are adorned with the work of the mason, those in East Anglia with the work of the woodcarver. At the lower end of the building scale the same local trends are obvious, though it was a long time before anyone qualified to call himself a mason could be bothered with cottages.

The first cottage-builders to use stone were in fact not masons at all but the craftsmen who built, and whose successors still build, dry-stone walling. The walls of these primitive cottages were some 2ft thick and composed of stones fitted together without mortar. Individual stones were often much larger than those employed in walls, there was indeed a preference for really hefty boulders, but they were fitted together with the same consummate skill. A few cottages of this type are still to be found in the Highlands and Islands of Scotland; there were once many of them in parts of Yorkshire, and in Cornwall where the broken out crops of granite were just waiting to be used.

With the wider use of dressed stone from the seventeenth century onwards the entirely stone-built village began to appear and in some places, notably in the Cotswolds, a style of cottage architecture quite different to the timber-and-clay product evolved from the use of a different material.

The walls of stone cottages are thick, but frequently not as solid as they appear. They were sometimes built with a central cavity filled with rubble and small stones and, as there was usually no foundation, the problem of 'rising damp' has persisted. The builders did not suffer the constraints of those who used clay; they had no fear of their walls crumbling in the wet and placed less emphasis on 'hat and shoes' than the cob and daub-and-wattle men. They used increasing amounts of stone, replacing thatch with stone slates or 'slats' and covering earthen floors with flagstones.

The stone-slated roof is as perfect for a cottage in its way as the thatched one. Even when new it has a certain mellowness about it and when encrusted with moss and lichen it reinforces the impression that a traditional cottage always manages to convey—that, with a modicum of human guidance, it has, Topsy-like, just growed.

Modern dwellings, however well designed and built, invariably stand out, unassimilated, in a village of old cottages. Not because of their newness or their architectural style, but because they are built of alien materials. The preservation of ancient cottages is very worthwhile from everyone's point of view, the occupant's no less than the interested traveller's. These words are being written—with an electric typewriter, not with a quill pen—between walls of mud and poles under a roof of wheat straw. The cottage has adapted itself to the needs of some ten generations and with a little care will survive to serve ten more.

3 Farming

Historical ups and downs

Agriculture, the growing of crops and the tending of livestock, is the business of the countryside. The fact that it is our largest industry, one of our most productive in terms of output per man, and the one most essential to our survival, is better understood from reading statistics than from direct observation. This book, however, is about looking at the countryside, not about statistics, and the work of the farmer and farmworker has shaped the countryside we know, and been shaped by it in turn, in a way that could apply to no other industry.

Farming is a commercial enterprise but it is unique in being unable to control completely its cycle of production. Despite all its technical advances, nature holds an overriding power of veto. There is a story of a London-based company which acquired an Australian sheep station. The price of wool rose sharply and a cable was sent from head office saying 'Start shearing'. The reply was immediate, 'Cannot shear. Lambing.' Management cabled again, 'Stop lambing. Start shearing.'

To say that farming is a business is true; to say that it is a business like any other business is manifestly absurd. No other business expects to be disrupted by the whims of the climate or the sudden eruption of a virus. Nobody who has seen field after field of corn lying twisted and sodden like storm-wrack on the beach, or has watched bulldozers digging the grave of a life's work in building a herd, is going to believe that one.

Environmental forces affect the farming business more subtly than this. They have laid down rules for it ever since the first Stone Age men scratched at the turf of the high downland in order to sow seed. It is the experience of thousands of years which has established that the eastern half of Britain, with its low rainfall, is best for cereals, and the wetter west for dairying because of its abundant grass and mild winters. It has also kept most crops to the lowland farms and left the hills to livestock-rearing. The predominance of a crop in any particular area is seldom due to chance. Soil and climate established hop gardens in Kent and Hereford, early potatoes in Cornwall and Pembrokeshire, fruit in Cambridgeshire and the Vale of Evesham. New techniques now permit the penetration of crops into non-traditional areas, but broadly speaking the farmer has succeeded by sticking to nature's guidelines.

The diversity of the island's climate and geological structure has created the same variety in farming that it has in scenery. Even in the great corn-growing areas there is no real 'prairie farming', no vast tracts of

A Cotswold Farm by Stanley Spencer (*Tate Gallery*)

monoculture. One may pass through a wonderful variety of farming landscapes in a tour of rural Britain and most of them look right because they result from long co-operation between man and nature.

If the land has dictated the course of farming, farming has in its turn been the most powerful influence in shaping the countryside as we know it. Most things of interest in rural life are, at some point in the past, linked with the story of farming, and without some understanding of that story today's countryside does not always make sense.

Agriculture is not one industry, but a complex of industries, and its history is too big a subject for us to tackle comprehensively. The best we can manage is a quick look at some of the more dramatic changes in farming methods and their effects on the countryside.

The making of farms

The Roman 'villas' were large farmsteads, but few in number relative to the expanse of forest and wilderness which was Britain at the time of the Conquest. The Saxon tribes which followed the Romans were true settlers,

71

Driving cows in Wiltshire (*MERL*)

Oxen ploughing in the 1880s. They are harnessed with collars, probably because both horses and oxen were employed on the same farm, but there were then many ox teams still harnessed with traditional yokes (*MERL*)

clearing forests, establishing villages in the fertile clearings, and driving the 'Britons', the indigenous half-Romanised Celtic peoples, westward and into the uplands. Perhaps this began the division of farming into the easier life of the lowland arable farmer and the hard existence of the livestock farmer up in the hills.

Peasant farming

The Saxons organised their new settlements on communal lines in the interests of defence and survival. Norman feudalism settled the peasant village into a pattern which endured in some form for a thousand years, until the last eighteenth-century Enclosure Acts destroyed it completely.

The medieval peasant farmed in an open landscape of long, narrow, arable strips and large areas of common grazing land. This was the communal 'open field' system, regulated by a host of laws and customs, manorial rights and duties, of which fragmentary survivals may be seen in the rights of commoners and verderers in a few places.

The form of the strip fields was dictated by both technical and social considerations. Ploughing was mainly done by oxen and the heavy plough and its team were not easily manoeuvrable, so that a certain minimum distance between headlands was essential. No individual was allowed to have all his arable land in a single piece, lest some should be more favoured than others in respect of natural fertility, drainage or other factors. Hence the allotment to each individual of a number of strips in different positions.

Cattle on the common grazing land usually had to be continuously herded, since the arable areas were seldom fenced. The range of crops was by our standards very limited and the yields poor. Eggs, fresh milk and dairy products, with the exception of cheese, were mainly seasonal summer things. Winter meat supplies were salted, the limited stocks of fodder being devoted to keeping breeding stock and draught oxen alive until the grass came again in spring. Sugar was a rarity in Tudor times, honey was otherwise the only sweetener and even this could be obtained only by killing off the bees, retaining a few colonies to multiply by swarming the following year. Most of the work was done with hand tools, though ox-drawn carts, ploughs, rollers and harrows were common. Seeds were broadcast on the soil and harrowed in, often with thorn bushes. Throughout the Middle Ages agriculture remained primitive, yet it kept an increasing population fed and generated enough surplus wealth to leave lasting monuments.

The wool trade is the most obvious example of this truth, but it must be remembered that the majestic abbeys and wool churches are not the only

Overleaf: Nine-bay cart shed, still in use in the early twentieth century (*Lionel E. Day*)

reminders of the peasant communities. Somehow, they financed and maintained a multitude of parish churches during a great period of church-building; they slowly extended the areas of cultivation and, equally slowly, improved its methods.

The new farming

What we now think of as the traditional farming pattern became established in the late eighteenth century. Most of the remaining common land was then enclosed, some of it being farmed by the new owners, no longer peasants working for subsistence, but capitalist producers and employers of labour, and much went to large landowners who rented it out. The relative proportions of owner occupiers to tenant farmers varies in different parts of the country, but tenant farming, with the landlord bearing the cost of fixed capital equipment and the farmer using his resources as working capital, has proved a sound arrangement. In the period of agricultural prosperity during and after the Napoleonic Wars, new farmhouses and farm buildings sprang up; thousands of miles of hedges were planted, giving the countryside the irregular patchwork-field pattern; land drainage was undertaken on a massive scale; selective breeding of livestock expanded on the pioneer work of men like Coke and Bakewell and there was a willingness to experiment with machines despite a super-abundance of labour.

In the first years of the nineteenth century, home food production was a major priority. To the pressures of war were added the needs of a fast-growing urban population, the new phenomenon of millions of people clamouring for food which they could not produce themselves. The new farming fed them, made large profits and improved the land in doing so.

This so-called Golden Age, which ended in a sequence of disasters in the 1870s, was based mainly upon mixed farming. Soil fertility was maintained by the manure from stock, by the bare fallow which rested the land for a season and facilitated the destruction of weeds by summer cultivations—in the eastern counties it was a tradition that a fallow should be ploughed seven times between Whitsun and Michaelmas.

The principles of 'high farming' were fashionable by the time of the Great Exhibition. They involved heavy capital expenditure on plant and equipment and were vigorously preached by a new breed of farmers who had made fortunes in industry and wanted to apply their methods to agriculture—not, in those days, to show tax losses, but to demonstrate profitability.

In this they succeeded, for the period, looked back to as the Golden Age, was one of high prices and cheap labour. But we have reason to be grateful to the Victorian high farmers; their curious moral standards may have

Old farm buildings still in use in the 1940s (*MERL*)

permitted the exploitation of their workers, never the exploitation of the land.

It was thought better to feed crops to livestock rather than turn them directly into cash, for in this way much of their fertility returned to the farm. The sale of manure off the farm was unthinkable; its purchase from the towns with their teeming horse populations a prudent investment. Two chemists, Lawes and Liebig, were working out the mineral requirements of plants and inorganic fertilizers were a possibility, but the Golden Age was based on the use of vast quantities of organic manures. Britain became a great importer of fertility, especially in the form of guano, the putrified droppings of millions of seabirds. Most regrettably, even Egyptian mummies were put to the same use, whole shiploads of them being landed at Liverpool and ground down into a sort of bone meal.

The cleanness of most arable land was on a par with its fertility, overseas visitors often commenting that British farmers kept their fields as though they were gardens. Root crops were repeatedly hand-hoed and horse-hoed and corn was hand-weeded, long lines of men and women advancing slowly through it, pulling up every stray dock and thistle. One still hears the story of the farmer returning from his morning ride of inspection to announce that he has seen a tuft of couch grass in the Twelve Acres and forthwith despatching a man with a fork to eliminate it—a folk tale now, but quite relevant to a time when two months' wages would not have bought a can of modern herbicide.

In a single lifetime agriculture moved from the primitive to the sophisticated, from the sickle and the flail to the reaper and the threshing machine. More than that, the cult of high farming poured wealth into the land itself, manuring, liming, ditching, draining, tree planting. This was a reserve to be drawn upon in the hard times to come.

Depressions and revivals

The Golden Age came to an end in the 1870s. From 1872 to 1879 there were only two good harvests, and 1879 itself was a year of total disaster. The spring had been late and wet, the summer grew steadily wetter. Day after day a cold rain fell relentlessly. Where the hay could be mown it blackened in the swathe and rank new grass grew through it. Grain sprouted in the ear before it was cut and when it was stooked the sheaves merged into a tangled mass of green. The sheep population was decimated by liver fluke, an internal parasite whose intermediate host is the water snail. Myriads of snails infested the waterlogged pastures and not less than a million sheep died. (Probably it was nearer three million.) Their carcases lay rotting under the sunless skies as dispirited workers strove to keep pace with the task of burial.

High farming could have survived the climatic disasters of the 1870s had it not been weakened by the economic forces leading to the Great Depression. So writers of the time called it, and innumerable parliamentary commissions, and so Rider Haggard was still calling it when, at the turn of the century, he rode the length of the land recording the sad decline of British agriculture.

The immediate cause of trouble was a sort of delayed explosion. Thirty years earlier the Corn Laws had been repealed against furious opposition from farmers and landowners who foresaw the market being swamped by cheap imports of grain. Their fears were groundless; most of Europe had no exportable surplus, with the possible exception of Russia, and trade with her was interrupted for years by the Crimean War. The price of wheat, the indicator and pacesetter, remained high, the poor suffered, and farming prospered.

Across the Atlantic, the wagons rolled westward on the American plains and the cabins of the homesteaders followed them. Steel ploughs bit into the sod. 'Wrong way up', an old Red Indian is supposed to have commented as

The bean dibbler. At the turn of the century considerable acreages of beans were still planted by hand (*MERL*)

Nineteenth-century traction engine preceded by a man with red flag. Threshing and ploughing tackle could only move from farm to farm at walking pace (*MERL*)

he watched the furrow slice turning, and perhaps the dustbowls of the next century would have confirmed his doubts. But for the moment there was fertility here, riches, acre upon acre of waving gold.

American wheat appeared on the British market in 1875, in the middle of a run of bad home harvests. In a few years the trickle became a flood and prices slumped. Hitherto it had been taken for granted that poor yields were partly offset by higher prices, now this compensation no longer operated. Industrial Britain welcomed cheap grain, it meant less insistent demands for wage rises and more competitive exports. Cheap food came to be seen as an important element in the nation's industrial supremacy and for that reason, despite much debate, the Great Depression in agriculture settled into a chronic condition.

With falling grain prices the old adage of mixed farming, 'Down corn, up horn', was remembered. Arable land was grassed down and low-cost livestock farming began to replace the more intensive forms of production. But there was no escape from foreign competition; in 1883 a refrigerated ship docked at London with a cargo of Australian beef.

Much technical progress took place during the period from 1880 to 1914. The reaper-and-binder was introduced, the tractor became a practicable proposition, the milking machine was invented. Adoption of new methods in farming has often been held up, as was now the case, less by the farmer's innate conservatism than by sheer lack of resources. World War I not only compelled farmers to change many time-honoured ways but gave them the ability to finance the changes.

The possibilities of the submarine blockade were not immediately realised on the outbreak of war and the organisation of home food production got off to a slow start. Key men on farms joined up, the Army swallowed up horses, farriers and saddlers, and reduced the rate at which land could be brought under the plough. It was a near thing, and in 1917 reserves of essential foods dropped to a few weeks' rations, but somehow a record area of tillage was achieved and with the help of the Women's Land Army vital harvests were secured.

1920 saw farming prosperous again, more mechanised, accustomed to a smaller labour force. War had taken from the village tens of thousands of working men who returned no more and were not replaced. What was called 'the drift from the land' was at last beginning to affect the balance of rural society.

What happened next affected it more drastically. Brief prosperity was followed by a new slump, worse than the Great Depression because it was part of a universal phenomenon. The Corn Production Acts, which had underpinned prices, were repealed in the early 1920s, and a disastrous slide began. By 1932 wages in some counties had fallen to 31 shillings (£1.55) a week, but even this was more than many farmers could afford and workers drifted to the towns to search for employment or to lengthen the dole queues. Wheat prices reached the lowest of the century, eggs were less than one old penny (½p) each, milk was almost unsaleable to an urban population gripped by mass unemployment.

Fields were left to fall down to weedy grass or were poorly cultivated. Harvesters in Suffolk wore leather gloves to handle the thistle-infested sheaves. Outgoing payments were cut to a minimum and the farmer and his stock lived off the land. It is always possible to do this in evil times, avoiding starvation and bankruptcy by drawing on the accumulated assets of the past, a fact that, combined with the unwillingness of farmers to adopt any other way of life, seems to have ensured the viability of British farming through a chequered history. Nevertheless, some gave up the struggle, and in 1932 it was possible to buy a 100-acre Essex farm with house and buildings for £500. A freehold cottage in the village was available for £50 upwards. Many farmworkers' cottages stood empty, some falling into ruin but more increasingly under the ownership of townspeople.

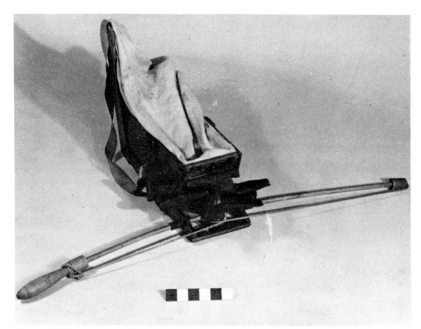

The seed fiddle, as preserved at the Museum of English Rural Life, Reading (*MERL*)

Some recovery from the slump came before 1939. Wheat prices were stabilised by a quota payment system, a new crop, sugar beet, gave guaranteed returns. The Milk Marketing Board, and other authorities, gave producers some control over distribution. But once again it was the dire imperatives of war that made farming profitable.

Today, after a generation of reasonable stability, the farms of Britain produce more than half the nation's food, a considerable achievement in a small crowded island. Growth of output per man and per acre has been remarkable, but we can do without statistics. The countryside has a well farmed look about it now that the see-saw of boom and slump has ceased its wilder swings. Maybe there are questionable practices in modern farming, but they *are* being questioned. The day of the mixed farm, of organic manures, respect for traditional methods and concern for the structure of the soil is not over.

'Hodge'

That was Richard Jefferies' name for the nineteenth-century farmworker, and it fitted perfectly the traditional conception of the straw-sucking

Broadcast sowing with the seed fiddle. The method was used until fairly recently to undersow corn crops with grass and clover (*MERL*)

unskilled labourer. Jefferies should have known better—he was often lacking in perception where human beings were concerned—for the regular farmworker still is just as he was in those simpler times, a skilled man.

'Only a man harrowing clods', wrote Hardy, seeing him as one of the simple and enduring things in a collapsing world. The Victorians who saw him from the comfort of their new railway coaches, scarcely moving across the landscape, thought him picturesque and sometimes called him a peasant. But Hodge was the most important of all manual workers in the first half of Victoria's reign. His labour alone fed the exploding towns. Bowed over the stilts of the plough like a stumbling Atlas, he was the ultimate prop of the Industrial Revolution.

Hodge's misfortune was that he was too numerous. Nineteenth-century villages, especially in the southern half of England where there was little recruitment into manufacturing industry, were usually far more populous than now. It was always a buyers' market in labour and to this were due the great advances of the Golden Age.

The size of the rural population was a legacy from the previous century. The English peasantry ceased to exist with the completion of the eighteenth-century enclosures and the improvers, as they thought of themselves, achieved a double objective. They brought the common land under private ownership and they left beyond their new fences a dispossessed race of landless labourers who must either work or starve. The once semi-independent peasant lost at one blow his common rights, his plot of land, his access to fuel, even the freehold of his cottage.

The enclosures did not in themselves stimulate the growth of population, but were followed by a piece of social legislation that went disastrously wrong. In 1795, faced with wartime famine and increasing burdens of relief for the poor, a group of Berkshire magistrates met at the village of Speenhamland and brought in regulations linking wages to the price of bread. It was further decided that farmers employing paupers would receive a subsidy towards the cost of their wages. A pauper was strictly defined as a person owning neither land nor property; moreover, to qualify for the subsidy he or she must have children. An unmarried man, or a childless married one became less attractive to the farmer, no matter how good a workman he might be, than one whose wages were largely the responsibility of the parish. The legitimacy of the children was irrelevant. A woman at Swaffham, in Norfolk, drew 18 shillings a week for her five illegitimate children, leaving her employer to add a purely nominal amount to her wages. An unmarried man, if he got a job at all, would be offered no more than 6 shillings a week, and on that he would starve. The system, as Lord Ernle has said, encouraged 'early and improvident marriages'. It also encouraged the production of a large family as the surest way of finding work.

The Speenhamland system spread far and rapidly. At first its effects were disguised by reasonably full employment, but soon it became clear that a premium had been placed on huge families of paupers, and that only by deliberate pauperisation could able men find employment. A Mr Hickson, giving evidence to the Poor Law Commission, described a carter with whom he had been 'forced to part'. This man owned a little property, and although locally recognised as a good and responsible workman he was classified as a non-pauper and his wages were unsubsidised. 'While I have these things,' he told Hickson, 'I shall get no work. No one will employ me . . . I must beggar myself.'

In 1834 the Speenhamland system was replaced by a new Poor Law, the harsh regime of the workhouse and the overseers of the poor. Its only virtue was that it stopped the deliberate pauperisation of the rural worker whose conditions, because of his overwhelming numbers and a deeply ingrained habit of subservience to his masters, were slow to improve.

We must skip this depressing chapter of social history, the story of men going to work on a breakfast of bread soaked in warm water; of a month's wages mortgaged to buy a sack of wheat; of squalor and hopelessness in the teeming villages. Outbursts of useless anger, of arson and machine-smashing, occurred throughout the century, but true militancy came only with the revival of hope and self-respect in the 1870s. The National Union of Agricultural Workers was founded by Joseph Arch and at least one of its measures struck at the root of the problem. It sponsored the emigration of its members, and during the last quarter of the century many thousands of men, women and children took ship for Australia and other parts of the Empire. It is some measure of their desperation that these people, many of whom had never before ventured more than a few miles from their villages, should have risked this leap into the unknown.

The farmworker improved his bargaining position during the Great Depression. His cash wages remained fairly static while food prices fell. On the economic see-saw he began for the first time to go up as his employer went down, and from then on the steady decline in his numbers continued, which has changed the village from an agricultural community to one in which only a small minority is directly involved in farming.

It is easy for us to appreciate the skills of the modern farmworker which are largely those of the technician. It is less easy to grasp those of his predecessor, Hodge, because they were traditional and conveyed by practice from one inarticulate man to another.

If you would see Hodge's monument, look around. Modern farming owes more to him than to all its other creators; his labour fashioned it out of the old peasant agriculture before most European countries had attempted the task. His skills went unrecognised in a society dazzled by industrial marvels and were taken for granted by his masters. Yet the evidence is that in the worst decades of the last century he retained a certain dogged pride in his work. Perhaps because it was all he had.

In the nineteenth century British agriculture was the indispensable foundation of the Industrial Revolution; in the twentieth it twice staved off defeat in war. That much is as clear as the fact that it has suffered long periods of neglect and, frequently, farmers and their workers have suffered the rawest of deals for most of the last fifty years.

The efficiency of farming today, the sheer speed of modernisation and its effects on the countryside and the people who live there, is not apparent until we take a closer look at some basic bits of farming. A very few of them, like shepherding, have not proved amenable to revolutionary change, but the old methods have vanished in a generation.

Tilling the land

The basis of agriculture is tillage—the cultivation of the soil so that seeds may be sown in it. This was the great invention that divided the settled farmer from the nomadic herdsman who had to follow his flocks wherever they chose to go in search of food. It was also the means by which food surpluses could be accumulated and cities created.

Ploughing

Primitive man did little more than scratch the surface of the soil and leave his crops to fight it out with the indigenous vegetation. Celtic and Roman Britain had ploughs which performed the essential function of turning the soil over to bury the weed growth and leave a clean surface, but they did it inefficiently and fields were usually cross-ploughed, first in one direction and then at right angles. Square fields were preferred, giving an equal length of run in both directions.

The mould-board plough, which cuts under the soil and turns the slice over in a continuous furrow, was introduced by the Saxons and has remained the basic design. Saxon ploughs were cumbersome affairs drawn by teams of eight oxen; they needed plenty of room to operate and no more turning on headlands than necessary. The square field gave place to the strip $\frac{1}{8}$ mile long. This was the 'furrow-long' or furlong and it remained the standard length of the peasants' arable fields for a thousand years.

Design and construction of ploughs improved as iron replaced wood and steel superseded iron, but up to the eighteenth century they still needed enormous tractive power. The great Kentish plough, for instance, required sixteen oxen to drag it through heavy land. Lighter ploughs permitted the

Horse ploughing was widely practised up to the 1940s and soaring fuel costs are now creating new interest in the working horse. The World Ploughing Championships still have a section for the horse plough (*MERL*)

change from oxen to horses in the nineteenth century and the attainment of high standards of work, later fostered by ploughing matches which still survive as a world-championship contest.

Single-furrow ploughs were the most common, though two-furrow types for teams of two or three horses were also employed. An acre a day was the traditional work target—equivalent to an hour or so's work today by a crawler tractor with a multi-furrow plough—but under bad conditions the acre was not always attained.

Much working time was taken up in the care of the horses. The ploughman, generally known as a horseman or carter, was among the more important of the regular farm staff. He had some security of employment, unlike the day-men who could be laid off without wages when weather held up their work. A large farm at the turn of the century might have twenty or thirty working horses and their efficiency depended on the men who, under the head carter, looked after them and worked them in the field.

When winter ploughing, the carter's day began before dawn. By the light of a lantern he would feed and groom his horses, a process which might take up to two hours. Men and horses would be in the field by first light and ploughing would continue until two o'clock. Then back to the stables for the carter to have his dinner, the horses to be fed and groomed again and harness to be cleaned and receive minor repairs.

The advantage of the tractor over the horse lies not only in speed of work but in the huge disparity of the time taken up in maintenance. The horse cannot be run into a shed, switched off and left until needed again. Working or idle it must be cared for. Its working day was strictly limited, unlike that of the tractor. The horse era was of necessity one of abundant human labour to service its motive power.

Four principal breeds of heavy horse shared the work until well into the present century: the Clydesdale, the Shire, the compact and powerful Suffolk Punch and the somewhat lighter but beautiful and active Cleveland Bay. All are probably descended from the medieval warhorse, and all are still being bred. To them was later added a horse from northern France, the Percheron.

Interest in working horses is on the increase and rising fuel costs may yet bring them back to the farm for certain limited functions. For this there would be an historical parallel; at the end of World War I farms had lost many of their horses and workers, and large numbers of tractors were in use. Then came the slump and the trend was abruptly reversed. Tractors were still unreliable, repair bills were crippling, fuel for them could not be produced on the farm, and the wretched machines couldn't reproduce themselves. With plenty of labour available again, many farmers returned thankfully to horses and continued to use them for all purposes, including ploughing, right through the 1930s. This, of course, will not happen again, barring a too-rapid exhaustion of the world's fossil fuels, but already the cost of those fuels means that the horse has some things going in its favour.

Attempts to apply mechanical power to ploughing and other arable operations were a frustrating business for the Victorians. The steam engine was soon at work driving threshing drums and barn machinery, but in the traction of land implements it was a failure. As in the attempts to produce a steam-powered aeroplane, the ratio of weight to power proved a fatal obstacle. The engine used for driving threshing tackle developed only about 7-brake horsepower and this was associated with a weight that under wet conditions did enormous damage to the soil structure. More powerful engines were of course heavier still and there was no way of reducing the havoc created by their wheels. After some attempts by the more lunatic inventors to produce a machine that travelled on a large number of legs it was generally agreed that steam engines should be kept off the land. The tractor had to await the internal combustion engine.

In spite of this, steam ploughing became a reality and was practised until the 1950s. The method adopted was to employ two engines on opposite headlands of the field, hauling a plough back and forth by a steel cable attached to winding gear. The plough was a multi-furrow reversible type which could travel up and down the same side of the work, ploughing a

Muck-spreading becomes a one-man job with the mechanical spreader. Formerly, manure was placed in small equidistant heaps and laboriously spread by hand (*Farmers Weekly*)

continuous area instead of the separate 'lands' of the ordinary one-way plough. The engines moved slowly forward as the work progressed, and the sound of their whistled signals to one another, and the sight of the plough, one beam pointing to the sky and a small hunched figure riding uncomfortably and monotonously adjusting and resetting the implement at the end of each trip, were for long part of the country scene. The steam tackle brought new power to the plough and permitted deeper work. On clay soils it was widely used for mole draining, in which a conical implement is pulled through the subsoil, leaving tunnels in the stiff clay which stay open for years.

The work of the steam ploughing tackle is now done by the crawler tractor, far more powerful than earlier generations of wheeled machines and exerting great tractive force with less concentrated pressure than that of the wheel. Even so, there is some fear that soil structure may be more seriously damaged by the continual use of heavy machines than by any other farming development.

Substitutes for the plough include various forms of rotary cultivator, larger versions of the garden machine, but they have proved of limited value. A 'no-ploughing' movement was started in America in the 1940s, sparked off by the horrors of erosion and the spectacle of millions of tons of topsoil literally going with the wind. A return to elementary rules of good husbandry and the resting of overcropped and exhausted land put matters right and the plough continued in use.

In the last few years, however, new no-ploughing techniques have been used with success. They depend on killing off old crop remains and weeds with a contact poison such as paraquat which destroys them in a few days but then breaks down and becomes harmless on contact with the soil. A new crop may be sown immediately, a special drill being used to plant the seed in the very firm undisturbed surface. The method has been found useful in sowing quick-growing fodder crops in stubble after harvest and has also been used for major crops including cereals. It is claimed that without disturbance the soil reaches a natural equilibrium, that the humus content is built up by decaying roots, and that the earthworm population, often regarded as an index of fertility, increases. Fertilisers are applied in liquid form, or drilled with the seed, and liquid organic manure in the form of drainage slurry may be injected below the surface.

Seed-sowing and weed control

A variety of cultivators and harrows are used to prepare a seedbed after ploughing, though on the heavy clays the most effective agent in producing a good tilth is frost. This shatters the clods from inside by turning their water content into ice and causing it to expand. The result is better than could be achieved by any amount of 'knocking about' and explains why a spell of hard winter weather is welcomed by arable farmers.

The actual sowing of the seed brings us to a long-running dispute comparable with the oxen versus horses controversy which smouldered for much of the last century. Traditionally, seed was sown broadcast on the surface, the sower carrying it in a basket slung from his shoulder and strewing it in rhythm with his stride. The land was then harrowed to cover it. Peas and beans were dibbled, the worker making small holes, slipping a seed in each and covering. (Incidentally, the dibbling of beans continued into the present century because the seed was too large for many types of corn drill then used—and a back-breaking job it must have been.)

The disadvantages of broadcast sowing were that the seed was covered to varying depths and so the crop was uneven from the start, that crop and weeds grew up together making hoeing impossible, and that amounts sown varied and were usually larger than necessary. The last defect was corrected to some extent by the seed fiddle, worked by a bowstring wrapped round a spindle, the fiddler scraping away regularly with each step. The fiddle was still used for sowing grass and clover seed until quite recently.

Attempts were made in the sixteenth century to devise mechanical ways of depositing seed and covering it to a uniform depth. Sir Hugh Platt employed a servant girl to plant carrot seed by dibbling, but she dibbled wheat instead. The resulting crop was so much better than average that Sir Hugh was led to make extravagant claims and everyone in the business started turning out useless machines for making rows of little holes in the ground. The peasants continued to broadcast their corn and cover it with bush harrows.

A new approach came in the eighteenth century from Jethro Tull, a law student who took to farming when his health broke down. He hit on the idea of cutting a miniature trench or drill with a coulter and feeding the seed down a tube immediately behind it. From this came a machine with a number of coulters to cut equally spaced drills and a feed system which ensured a regular flow of seed down each tube. This was essentially the modern drill and it ensured even planting depths, regular spacing and control of seeding rates.

The new methods soon proved their value to the landed gentry who had taken up farming during the craze for enclosure and improvement. Coke set 3,000 acres of corn using the drill on his great estate at Holkham. Lord Townsend gained the nickname of 'Turnip' from his enthusiasm for this root as winter feed for cattle. Robert Walpole was said to open letters from his farm bailiff before turning to government correspondence. Tull's contention that far better crops could be grown in rows with space between them for cultivation was amply confirmed in practice during the reign of 'Farmer' George, but it was so radical a conception that the farming rank and file clung to the old ways for another two generations. In the year of Queen Victoria's accession, a Suffolk farmer who had bought a drill was asked by derisive neighbours when he was going to start using his pepper caster. Fortunately for the growing and hungry population the ensuing years of high farming and high profits brought a rapid change of mind.

The seed drill has increased in size and consequently in speed of work over the years, but the only fundamental innovation has been the combine drill which sows granules of fertiliser along with the seed.

Having a crop in rows meant that weeds could be dealt with in a way impossible if it were broadcast. It was this development that made possible the high cultivation standards of the mid-nineteenth century. Even cereal crops were hoed between the rows while young, and root crops until the leaves met in the rows. Despite the wide use of first horse and then tractor hoes the amount of hand-hoeing that went on up to the outbreak of World War II was remarkable. Today, the familiar draw hoe has virtually disappeared from the field operation of thinning and 'singling' root crops, and soon this is likely to be taken over by machines equipped with electronic sensors.

The hand labour of weed control has been replaced by the herbicide spray, a change as revolutionary as any in modern farming. The first experiments in killing weeds amid growing crops used diluted acid solutions on cereals; the acid ran off the smooth narrow leaves of the corn but accumulated on broad-leaved weeds sufficiently to scorch and inhibit them. One of these weeds was charlock, a cruciferous plant with yellow flowers, and many readers will recall cornfields blazing yellow with its flowers in pre-herbicide days—a sight to depress the farmer and gladden the heart of the beekeeper, for this flower was a generous source of nectar. Now one rarely sees charlock in bloom and a yellow field betokens mustard or a new crop, oil-seed rape.

The harvest

The harvesting of cereal crops is the climax of the farming year. It is also the end of it, for Michaelmas (29 September) is traditionally the day on which farm tenancies begin and end. The crops have been gathered in and the autumn ploughing, which marks the beginning of a new season, is about to begin. This is the nearest to a 'natural break' that occurs in the cycle of arable farming.

The harvesting of bread grains has always been of tremendous economic importance and this is reflected in the symbolism and legend gathered around it. Bread is the 'staff of life' and in temperate climates a failure of the harvest once meant starvation or something very near it. The Old and New Testaments are full of cornfield story and imagery; the great American family festival is one of thanksgiving for the desperate colonists' first harvest; Harvest Thanksgiving alone in the Christian calendar fills our country churches, and Russian communism chose the sickle, the age-old reaping tool, to represent one half of the union of workers and peasants.

The harvest is of particular interest to us in the context of a changing countryside. The reduction in the farming labour force, which in a single lifetime has changed the character of the village and sometimes the whole appearance of the countryside, is more clearly seen in harvesting than in any other farming operation. From the time when the exiled Ruth 'stood in tears amid the alien corn' to the opening of the Stockton & Darlington Railway, nothing changed. By the end of the next 150 years nothing was the same.

Reaping

In assessing the transformation of the harvest field it will be as well to keep to the harvesting of bread grains. To us, this means wheat, to our ancestors and even today in some parts of the world it could mean barley or rye. The point is that grain, intended for direct human consumption, has always been treated with almost reverential care, and this set the corn harvest apart from the gathering of lesser crops. Not that any part of the cereal harvest, whether destined to feed humans or livestock, was treated lightly.

The sickle This tool dates back to the farmers of the New Stone Age, and the finest specimens made in Britain were produced after 1820. In that vast span of time, throughout which innumerable harvests were reaped by it, the basic design never changed. The improvements that came in the nineteenth century, when the manufacture of so many tools passed from the village smith to the new workshops of Sheffield and the West Midlands, were in the quality of steel and the forging of cutting edges. It is impossible to say when the manufacture of sickles ended, if indeed it has. Corn was being cut with them in the 1930s and maybe some are still in use by gardeners who prefer this tool to the conventional hook.

The sickle is a light, narrow, pointed, crescent-shaped blade with a serrated edge like a modern breadknife. The reaper stoops low, gathers a handful of the crop in the left hand and severs the straw with a gentle sawing stroke. Straw bands are laid ready on the ground and each handful is added to the bundle which, when tied, forms a sheaf.

There is no violent impact on the straw as it is cut, no swipe which in a very ripe crop would shake some of the grain from the ear and cause loss by 'shedding'. Up to the middle of the last century a great deal of reaping was done by women, and exhausting as the work must have been to the reapers, bowed all day under a fierce sun, the sickle is in some ways a feminine implement. Its effective use is a matter of skill and endurance rather than of brute strength. The quality of its work was higher than that of any other manual reaping method, though the worker could only cut about one quarter of an acre a day with it as compared with an acre when using the scythe.

In the north of England and in Scotland, reapers using the sickle were organised into a gang called a 'bandwin' consisting of seven persons, of whom only three or four would be actually reaping, the others making bands, binding the sheaves and setting them up in stocks. The whole bandwin, which might be of either sex or both, could not deal with more than one full acre in a long day.

Scythe and bagging hook These tools were increasingly used in harvesting after the middle of the eighteenth century when the new large-scale farming began to put more stress on output per man-hour than on the meticulous gathering of every grain of corn. A good man with the incentive of piece-work rates—and all reaping was paid for this way—could cut an acre a day with either tool.

For most of its long history the scythe's primary use was in grass-mowing, not only for hay, but in trimming the lawns of the gentry. Some of the best steel obtainable went into scythe blades, and with the practised honing of the skilled mower it was a wonderfully efficient tool. Not that proficiency is easily attained, for sharpening the scythe is as difficult to learn as using it, the beginner invariably applying the whetstone, or rub, at the wrong angle and creating a 'shoulder' on the blade instead of the smooth progression to a razor edge which is essential for clean mowing. The novice can make a fair showing with a scythe sharpened by an expert, the expert could do little with one sharpened by a novice. Much folklore attaches to the treatment of the scythe, and many an old scytheman would refuse to keep his tool under cover, saying that to leave it outdoors would 'rust the iron out of it'—if possible he would hang it in an apple tree, though unable to give a reason for this preference.

The scythe was in occasional use for cutting corn right up to the advent of the combine-harvester in the 1950s. It was the custom to 'mow round' the outside of a field of corn by hand before the entry of the binder and so give the latter a clear passage with no corn flattened and wasted. The combine, cutting the crop immediately before it, opens up its own path into the field and has finally ended this survival of hand-reaping.

The bagging hook is still widely known by that name and is used in various trimming jobs. Its use in reaping had a number of local names in addition to 'bagging'. It could have been 'fagging', 'chuffing', or 'slashing', though the tool itself was essentially the same smooth-edged, rather heavy hook. Like the scythe, it was used by men only, and an acre a day was an accepted target.

Both the scythe and the hook treated the grain more roughly than the sickle. The scythe was fitted with a 'bow', a bent rod of hazel, which gathered the corn into a thick swathe at each stroke and made it easier for the binders to collect it into sheaves; the hook was used in conjunction with a hooked stick held in the left hand to pull the straw together. The careful placement of each handful of corn by the user of the sickle did not fit in with the ideas of the new agriculture. By the early nineteenth century the farmer was looking for profit, not subsistence.

The reaping machines

By the late eighteenth century reaping machines began to obsess the inventively minded. Joseph Bryce took out a patent for one in 1799, but it never got beyond the experimental stage and was lost along with other mechanically nightmarish attempts to couple horse traction with systems of moving knives. The work was hampered by obstruction from farmworkers who feared the loss of employment, and farmers who regarded the whole idea as unnatural and even devilish. The pioneers were sometimes compelled to conduct their experiments by moonlight under conditions of great secrecy.

The Reverend Patrick Bell, a Scottish clergyman, developed a practicable machine in the 1820s, but only about a score were manufactured. Labour was still abundant and cheap and there was little incentive to eliminate the defects in Bell's invention. Three models were, however, exported to America, where labour was scarce and expensive, and this may have influenced future developments.

McCormick's reaper came from the United States in 1851 and was shown at the Great Exhibition. Whether Bell's machine was truly its ancestor cannot be said for certain, but it must have owed something to the Scots parson. It was already widely used in its native land, and with one or two similar makes soon gained acceptance in Britain. By 1871, 40,000 machines of the McCormick type were in operation and 25 per cent of the corn acreage was being harvested by them.

The change that this machine brought to this part of the harvest operation is shown in the testimonial written by one farmer to his supplier. His entire crop, he said, had been cut by two machines driven by two lads of fourteen and fifteen years. The two-horse reaper cut slightly more corn in an hour than could the strongest labourer in a day.

The reaping machines cut and delivered the crop in ways which made it increasingly easy to gather up and bind into sheaves, but this was still a manual operation, the sheaves being tied with the traditional straw band. Then, in 1878, the McCormick reaper-and-binder appeared, to be universally known as the 'binder' as the combine-harvester became the 'combine'.

The binder is a triumph of agricultural engineering. It cuts the corn and transports it on wide canvas belts to a platform where it is compressed into a sheaf, tied with twine and ejected. The ingenious heart of the machine is the knotter which ties the sheaf, but the whole is a complex of moving parts built around, and driven by, a single large driving wheel. The horsedrawn machine depended for its power on the satisfactory adhesion of this wheel to the ground; if it slipped on a wet surface the moving parts lost their power. This was a defect of all horsedrawn machinery and was only remedied when machines came to be hauled by a tractor which supplied an independent drive to the moving parts through a power take-off. It says much for the quality of their design that hundreds of thousands of horsedrawn machines, of varying degrees of complexity, served British

Overleaf: Gang stooking oats. A universal harvest scene until the combine made them redundant in the 1950s (*MERL*)

farming so well over more than a century of expansion and revolutionary change.

Stooking, stacking and threshing

The reaping machines drastically reduced the harvest labour force and the teams of reapers and binders, the bandwins and the gangs of itinerant Irish workers who followed the ripening corn northwards with scythe and hook, were all on their way to redundancy by 1880. The progressive farmer replaced them with a binder, one man and a team of two or three horses.

Reaping, however, is only the first part of the job. The crop must be dried so that it will store safely. The object of stooking, or standing the sheaves up in groups of ten or twelve, is to dry off weeds and green matter in the straw and to evaporate some of the moisture in the grain itself. Stooks are built in a tent shape with a clear passage for the circulation of air between them. If well built they will not collapse in strong winds and the shape ensures quick drying after rain. In very wet seasons, however, there may be serious damage to corn in stook, the ripe grain germinating and the heads of the sheaves growing together in a mass of shoots and roots. One speaks of stooking in the present tense because some farmers, especially those producing high quality straw for thatching, still harvest in the old way. Their total acreage is small in relation to that harvested by the combine, but ten years ago 60,000 binders could be found in working order on small farms.

Stooking requires a minimum of two workers and entails a lot of to-ing and fro-ing in collecting the sheaves and setting them up. On large acreages a much bigger gang is usually put on the work. For carting, at least seven are necessary for a continuous rhythm of work; two pitchers and a loader in the field, an unloader, a pitcher and a builder at the stack, and a driver to take in the full wagons and bring back the empties. None of the work comes easily to the inexperienced, as thousands of volunteers found to their cost in the two world wars. A tall load on wagon and trailer that will not suffer disaster in its passage over rough ground is an expert job, as is the building of the stack.

A corn stack is more than a neat round or oval heap of sheaves; it is made to eliminate the possibility of penetration by moisture through rain beating on its sides. It starts with a base of brushwood and straw, or with a permanent iron frame on rat-proof 'staddle stones'. The first sheaves are placed in a conical pile in the centre with the heads pointing inwards. More sheaves are laid round them in overlapping circles until the circumference is reached, and this process is repeated, layer upon layer. At the completion of each layer the centre is always the highest point and every sheaf in the outer layers slopes slightly upwards from its exposed butt end. This is known as

A Surrey harvest field in the 1940s. It was basically the same for centuries past; in a few years it was to be transformed (*Keystone*)

'keeping the middle filled' and it prevents water working its way inwards along the straw. It also means that the overlapping sheaves can only be removed in the correct order and the stack must be un-made in the proper sequence at threshing time. Attempts to lift the sheaves haphazardly are exhausting and well nigh impossible.

Threshing machines With the crop safely stacked and thatched against the weather, or stored in a barn, the most interesting part of the old-style harvest is now imminent. Until now the yield has been guessed at and argued over—with threshing comes the moment of truth.

Threshing before the late eighteenth century was an almost continuous winter job and also important because it provided work under cover. A clean, smooth area of the barn was the threshing floor and the whole operation absorbed a good deal of labour. Corn was laid on the floor and grain threshed out of the ears with a flail—the ancient hinged stick—usually by two men working in unison. Straw would be raked away

Threshing in January. The threshing tackle provided work for many odd characters who followed it from farm to farm throughout the winter (*H. D. Keilor*)

and the threshed grain and chaff piled into a heap. This was then winnowed by exposing it to a draught from a winnowing machine, a large hand-operated fan. The corn was then passed down a series of sloping riddles or screens, the weed seeds and smallest grains falling through the holes and a reasonably clean sample accumulating at the end. Finally, an expert worker would throw the grain from a shovel so that it fell in a long band with the heaviest corn carrying furthest from the thrower and the lightest dropping near him. Thus the 'head-corn', suitable for milling or grinding, was at one end of the strip, and the 'tail-corn', good only for poultry and the like, was at the other. This medieval classification remained in general use when machine threshing was adopted and is still applied to combined corn dressed on the farm.

By the eighteenth century, farmers were looking for speedier methods. They wanted more straw to provide litter for increasing numbers of

WE the undersigned Magistrates acting in and for the Hundred of Gallow, in the County of Norfolk, do promise to use our utmost Endeavours and Influence we may possess, to prevail upon the Occupiers of Land in the said Hundred,

To discontinue the use of Thrashing Machines, and to take them to pieces.

Dated this 29th. day of November, 1830.

CHAS. TOWNSHEND.
ROBERT NORRIS.
EDW. MARSHAM.

STEWARDSON AND SON, PRINTERS, FAKENHAM.

Magistrates' notice of 1830 (*MERL*)

livestock and did not like having workers spend the entire winter dealing with the corn crop in penny packets. The first attempts at mechanisation were made in the seventeenth century with a contraption of flails on the rim of a wheel, but the real advance came 150 years later with the invention of the rotating drum within a concave surface.

With the drum-and-concave threshing became the first farm operation to be completely mechanised. In the early 1800s machines worked by four men could turn out over a ton of threshed corn a day and, although this compares badly with the 10 tons of the later steam tackle and six or eight men, it was a vast improvement on the flail. Large farms began to install machines driven by horses or waterwheels, and by the 1840s the first steam-driven installations were at work.

In southern England, where villages were over-populated and, owing to the pernicious Poor Laws, single men and those with no families were desperately short of work because they brought no subsidy to their employers, the threshing machine was seen as a menace. In 1816 and again in 1830, there were savage outbreaks of machine-wrecking and arson. In some areas the magistrates tried to ease matters by persuading farmers to dismantle their machines. Where the employment situation was better the machine was welcomed as a relief from the backbreaking labour of the flail.

Incidentally, the flail was still being used by a stalwart rearguard in 1900, and possibly still in parts of Scotland in the 1930s. Certainly many farmworkers kept the old tool at home before 1914 to 'knock out' the grain gleaned by their womenfolk, though the most popular method was to lean a ladder against the cottage wall, hold the gleanings in a small sheaf and dash the heads against successive rungs with a downward movement. A sheet placed under the ladder caught the grain, and if a breezy day were chosen most of the chaff would be blown away. In those days, of course, gleanings were still potential flour or meal and not unimportant to the household economy.

The first steam-powered threshing machines were usually worked by a stationary engine driving other barn machinery, such as chaff-cutters and mangold-slicers. However, these expensive installations were beyond the average mid-nineteenth-century farmer. He compromised by having his own machine erected in the barn and hiring an engine when necessary. The early engines were not self-propelled and were taken from farm to farm by horses. Then the threshing drum was mounted on wheels, the engine provided the traction, and farmers found it economical to hire the entire outfit from contractors. This was the pattern from about 1860 to 1950, the only changes being in technical improvements to the tackle. The threshing drum has about it an aura of noisy excitement absent from the combine, and many countrymen past middle age remember threshing days with nostalgia.

Using the flail in East Anglia. It was the loss of this arduous work to the threshing machine that led to outbreaks of violence and the magistrates' notice in the preceding illustration (*MERL*)

Steam-powered threshing machine c 1860. The number of workers required for the job hardly varied over the next 100 years (*MERL*)

The tackle arrives late on a winter's day and is set against a stack ready for an early start. The farmer's own staff is joined by the little group of casuals who follow the machine—'sheenin', they call it. The engine driver, captain of the team, surveys the heap of steam coal and the arrangements for supplying water with a critical eye—these are the farmer's responsibility.

At first light steam is raised, the main driving belt is eased on to the flywheel and the driving-pulley of the drum, with another belt to the straw baler. The machine is in fact a mass of exposed belts.

The thatch is stripped from the stack, the 'feeder' takes his place, sharp knife in hand, to receive each sheaf, cut the string that binds it and deliver it into the ravenous mouth of the drum. Hour after hour he gathers each sheaf as the pitcher places it near his hand, perched in his little recess with the machine shaking under him and a form of ordered Bedlam all around.

The din is unrelenting. The engine's rhythmic beat is lost in the clack of belts, the rattle of the shaking screens as they clean the grain, the heavy thud of the baler, the incessant *whoosh* of the drum with every sheaf it gulps down. Clouds of dust begin to blow from the machine's innards, black smoke beats down from the newly fired engine, men scurry from one job to another, bending double under the flapping belt. At the corn take-off, where empty sacks are hooked up and the full ones carted away, there is relative peace, merely a shouted argument about quality and yield in which every passing worker joins from time to time. And at last the engine driver looks at his watch and the engine hisses and dies. Dinner-time or knocking-off time, and the next step will be to move the drum to another stack and start all over again.

This was the typical last act of the harvest up to a few years ago. the only thing wrong with it by today's standards is that it had too large a cast.

The combine The combine-harvester was a logical method of eliminating entirely a major part of the harvesting process. It cut out binding into sheaves, stooking, carting, stacking and, later, passing the stacked corn through a stationary threshing drum. The idea was to marry a reaper with a mobile threshing machine and pass the crop straight into the latter as it was cut, carting away the threshed corn and, if desired, the straw.

The technical obstacles to the idea were enormous, but by 1890 many combines were at work in the new American and Canadian prairie wheatfields. The machines were huge and heavy, drawn by teams of a dozen horses or mules. They would have been unusable in the small fields of Britain, and it was in fact another fifty years before a new generation of smaller, motor-powered combines gained a foothold in British cornfields. They were slow to be adopted, and less than a hundred were at work by 1939. The reasons were economic: farming was emerging from a major depression and capital was short; the climate made it essential to dry the grain artificially if the natural drying period in stooks was eliminated, and labour was still cheap enough to justify the old routine of the binder, the stack and the threshing drum. The smallest area of corn to justify the capital outlay was 200 to 300 acres and there was no incentive to change the old ways.

With the outbreak of war, labour became scarce, wages higher, and corn-growing more profitable. Eventually the combine and its ancillary grain-drier and storage silos became worthwhile for the grower of quite modest acreages of corn. By 1950 some 20,000 of the monsters were crawling round the harvest fields, and soon their dominance was unchallenged.

The combine became steadily more labour-saving. At first, it was often drawn by a tractor and decanted the grain into sacks like the stationary drum. It needed a driver and two or three more men to attend to the sacks. Then it became self-propelled, and the grain was stored in a tank from which it could be discharged into a waiting truck for transport to the drier. In theory, one man could conduct the entire harvest; combining until the tank was full, taking a truckload to the drier, and returning to resume combining. Finally, he could switch to the pick-up baler and deal with the straw.

That may be a fantasy, but the telescoping of all the skills and labours of harvest into the brief passage of an immensely sophisticated machine epitomises the completeness of the farming revolution.

The harvest today

The combine is saying two things as it marks the landscape with its patterns of straw. It is telling a remarkable story of increased production. In 1850 Britain harvested nearly 6 million tons of cereals from 9 million acres; just over a century later 11 million tons were gathered from 8 million acres. Now the yield from a slightly larger acreage is more than 14 million tons. The plant breeders may take much of the credit for doubled and trebled yields and the engineers for the virtual disappearance of the harvesters.

For this is the combine's second message. A generation ago the field would have been lively with stooking or the loading of wagons or trailers. Fathers of the older workers would have told tales of the reaping gangs when this was indeed a 'field full of folk'. Now the combine drones on in its little individual dust-cloud, a solitary figure controlling it like a captain on the bridge.

Return to the village and speculate on the new cottagers. Most of them are erstwhile townsfolk, but it is not they who have changed the character of the place. It was the combine.

Harvesting today. In 1650 nearly six million tons of grain were gathered; in 1950 eleven million tons were harvested with one-tenth of the labour force (*Fox*)

Baling straw near Wantage. The cartage and storing of the bales will be the last act of the mechnical harvest (*MERL*)

Making hay on tripods. When ready, hay and tripod are carted to the barn. The system was used in high-rainfall districts but is now replaced by methods of indoor drying (*MERL*)

Snatching hay while the sun shines. Modern methods have speeded up the process and ensured better hay crops in bad seasons but a less perfect product in good ones (*Farmers Weekly*)

Haymaking

Like harvesting, haymaking is one of those events in the farming calendar which attract the attention of non-farming people. Coming in high summer, it has traditionally associated a certain carnival spirit with the hot and heavy work of its serious business. Today most of the hard work has gone, the fun has gone with it, but the hay crop remains vitally important.

The historical pattern of haytime matches that of the corn harvest—unchanged methods based on limitless hand labour from time immemorial; the introduction of machines in the nineteenth century, and a period when man and machine seemed to have reached a state of balance; then a sudden transformation during and after World War II.

Haymaking is all about the evaporation of water. The crop of grasses, or leguminous plants such as clover or lucerne, is cut when its protein and carbohydrate content is high and its indigestible fibre low. This stage is reached in early summer when the plants are coming into flower and are also full of sap. The problem is to get rid of the surplus water and preserve the dry matter with the smallest possible damage to the delicate leaves which contain many of the nutrients. It is not a minor problem. Since about 10 gallons of water evaporate from every bale of hay, drying has to be completed as quickly as possible and with a minimum of handling, hence the crucial importance of the weather. The artificial drying of hay—'barn drying'—has never caught on, and is not likely to do so in view of the high energy consumption entailed. Making hay while the sun shines is still an economically sound objective, and when it fails to shine at the right time the dairy and beef industries feel the effects for many months to come.

The day of the haystack

The rectangular thatched haystack in the yard or a corner of the field finally vanished from the landscape some time in the 1950s. The casual observer may have been vaguely aware of its passing, may even have realised that it was sometimes replaced by a shapeless pile of bales covered with plastic sheeting, but he probably failed to notice that the old-fashioned hayfield had gone with it.

The haystack had its place in the country scene, in proverb and in rustic stories. Most aspects of haymaking seemed immutable until a few years ago. If John Constable had returned in 1940 to paint a revised version of *The Hay Wain* he might have regretted the tractor and trailer, but the general scene would have been familiar to him. Yet the seeds of change were sown soon after his death.

Prior to the introduction of machinery, hay was mown with the scythe and, as at harvest time, groups of professional mowers moved from county to county during the season, supplementing the regular workforce. Gangs

The hay sweep, the first attempt to mechanise cartage from field to stack (*MERL*)

of Irish workers returned to the same farms annually and continued to do so up to 1914, long after the scythe had become obsolete. The fact that they found employment on the heavily staffed farms of the late nineteenth and early twentieth centuries shows how much hand labour haymaking continued to demand.

In 'making', the cut grass is allowed to lie in the original swathe for a day or so. In sunny weather a thin crop dries rapidly, but eventually the swathe is turned to dry the underside. There follows more turning and 'tedding' or shaking up the material to increase the rate of drying. The thicker the original swathe, the more humid the atmosphere, and the more rain that intervenes the longer it takes to complete the drying and the more handling the hay needs. Until about 1840 all this was done by hand with wooden rakes and two-tined forks. Then came the horsedrawn tedder, the swathe-turner, the horse-rake, the side-delivery rake and the mower with the reciprocating cutter-bar. With these machines the hay could be mown, turned, tedded, and raked into windrows ready for carting. In modified forms the machines are still in use, though they may not have entirely supplanted hand labour even now.

In the 1930s a lot of the work was still done by hand, and it was usual to see new stocks of gleaming white wooden rakes and shining pitchforks in country ironmongers' shops and agricultural merchants' stores by early May. To the layman all hayforks are pitchforks, but in fact only the fork with a long handle and large tines is properly so called, the smaller versions

Overleaf: Hay being raked into windrows ready for carting (*MERL*)

being simply 'two-tined forks'. This is used for dealing with crops at ground level, the larger tool for pitching hay to the top of a high load if necessary.

Carting and stacking

These parts of the operation remained labour-intensive despite the use of machines. A team in the field consisted of two pitchers and a loader, the wagon or tractor trailer passing between windrows and the hay being pitched from both sides. A leader for the horse (traditionally known as a 'whoa-gee boy') or a tractor driver was necessary, and another and more experienced driver to take the loads to the stack. Nothing was more calculated to raise temperatures all round than the news that a load had 'slipped' on its way to the stackyard.

The crop might sometimes be left in cocks instead of the continuous windrows. Cocking is an emergency measure applied when the hay is ready but cannot be carted before rain arrives or when it is being severely burnt by the sun. The hay is run up into small conical heaps and can stand appreciable amounts of rain without serious damage. Cocking is now out of fashion since it is by nature a rush job and needs more hands than the modern farm can usually muster in a hurry. Making hay on wooden tripods, a method still used in a few areas of high rainfall, such as western Scotland, is quite different to cocking. The crop may be quite green when hung on the tripods and continues to make as the air circulates freely under the pile.

In the 1920s the hay-sweep was introduced to speed up the work of carting. This implement had long wooden tines, steel-tipped and lying almost flat on the ground. Like an immense hand with outstretched fingers it slid under the hay, which was pushed back and piled higher and higher against a metal frame at the back. When it could hold no more the tines were raised enough to keep the tips of the fingers clear of the ground and the load taken with all speed to the stack. There the sweep reversed and slid from under the load, leaving it in a compact heap close to the elevator. The first sweeps were drawn by pairs of horses, one walking on either side of the tines, but later models were fitted to the front of the tractor or old car, traction being of little importance.

Use of the sweep virtually banished the haystack from the stackyard. It could not negotiate rough tracks and farm gateways and to be effective had to operate in the same field as the stack, shuttling swiftly to and fro with its relatively small loads. But it did enable the actual carting to be done by one man.

The central piece of machinery in stacking was the elevator. This contraption—there are still a few about—consists of a long wooden trough

Carting hay (*MERL*)

Stacking hay. The pony-driven elevator gear was replaced by the petrol engine in the 1930s.
A generation later the haystack had disappeared and hay was baled and stored in barns
(*MERL*)

which can be raised as the stack grows. A continuous chain carrying sets of metal spikes runs from top to bottom, picking up the hay as it is thrown into a large hopper and dropping it on the stack as the spikes swing over the top and begin their downward course on the underside of the trough.

The elevator's motive power was a pony, usually a semi-retired one who always seemed to remember the job from year to year. He was hitched to a pole and walked round in a small circle, turning a large gear wheel. This was sited some distance from the elevator and the drive was transmitted through a jointed rod running in bearings pegged to the ground. The pony would step delicately over the rod in each of his unending circles which, by the time the stack was built, would have marked out a ring of bare earth. In the 1930s the elevator pony was replaced by a small petrol motor, much more convenient when the elevator was shifted to a new site, but lacking the ability to stop and start on a shouted command.

A gang of at least four was needed at the stack and, with a good team or an able sweep driver in the field, there was little time for a breather. Hay has the peculiar property of growing heavier as the hot hours pass, and the work might well continue until dusk in an attempt to 'top up' the stack rather than sheet it over for the night against possible rain.

The stack-builder usually worked close to the edge of the stack, taking care over the placement of every forkful to maintain the proper shape. A well-built stack was narrower under the eaves than at the base, the eaves drawing out a little so that any drips from the thatch should fall well clear. The top was steeply pitched for effective thatching and there must be no sign of the stack listing to one side. This last was not always avoided since the whole mass would sink to about half its original height under its own weight and the internal heat that produces good hay. These factors might start the stack leaning and then heavy poles, known in many parts of the country as 'lawyers', were wedged as buttresses along the overhanging side. The name appears to indicate a slightly contemptuous view of the legal profession as being useful in propping up what would otherwise fall down—for the unfortunate stack-builder the report that he had 'called in the lawyers' meant a serious loss of face.

The internal heating of a stack sometimes led to spontaneous combustion, and the appearance of wisps of steam and an increasingly strong smell would signal the need to make tests with a rick-iron. This was a long metal probe with a barbed point, thrust deep into the stack it was left for a few minutes and then withdrawn with a tuft of hay from the interior caught in the barbs. Temperature was assessed on the feel of the iron and the condition of the hay, and on rare occasions the stack might be partially unmade to allow it to cool. This was a measure of last resort, since the admission of more oxygen might start an uncontrollable blaze. Stacking the hay while too green was the cause of overheating, but some degree of heat was necessary if the hay was to attain the rich treacly aroma that signified quality and made it a pleasure to handle and, visibly, a pleasure to eat through the long, hungry days of winter.

Haymaking now

The pick-up baler now takes the hay from the windrows and compresses it into neat oblong blocks, or wraps it into short Swiss rolls, in both cases tying it neatly with string. Bales may be left in lines for collection or accumulated on a sled towed behind the baler and left in piles to make the eventual carting quicker. Or they may be the new large bales, monstrous things that even a hydraulic fork-lift can only raise one at a time. Two or three men can now package and store the hay crop without lifting a fork.

Along with the haystack the countryside lost a skilled ancillary worker whose trade, pursued in solitary independence, is seldom mentioned. The hay-trusser worked summer and winter when the weather permitted, usually single-handed and calling no man master. He was paid on piecework, his earnings depended on his skill, and that was how he liked it.

The job began with the purchase of a stack by a merchant who had to remove it. The trusser was engaged and his equipment, press, weighing machine, knife and tarpaulin, dumped on the site. He would arrive daily on his cycle until the stack had been converted into lorry loads of trusses.

The hay-knife is a formidable tool, a stout blade with a convex cutting edge and a horizontal handle slightly offset from the line of the blade so that it may be grasped with both hands and the knife moved up and down with the full strength of the body. The hay was cut with a vertical sawing motion, the trusser standing on a small rectangular area, about 2 by 3ft and cutting downwards around its edges. His little platform became a detached slab of hay, prevented from slipping by a long spike pushed through into the uncut portion below. Once severed from the stack, the block of hay was carried to the weighing machine, adjusted by addition or subtraction to a weight of 56lb and squeezed tight in the long-handled press before being tied. The weight of each truss was precise, their size and shape as uniform as packets on a production line. The cut face of the stack would be as smooth as if a giant had sliced it with a single sword-stroke. Very skilful was the solitary hay-trusser, and often one would find him on a winter's morning, when the hoar frost lay thick upon the tarpaulin that covered his pile of trusses, shirtsleeved and bowed in concentrated energy over his knife.

Growing the hay crop

Technical changes here have been less obvious than those which have swept the fields bare of haymakers, and few people are aware of them.

The plant breeders have been busy on grasses, evolving more productive strains. Grasses and clovers may be sown as temporary leys to be ploughed up again as part of an arable rotation, or they may constitute a permanent crop, staying down indefinitely. Temporary leys are 'undersown', the seed being drilled in spring corn when a few inches high. After harvest the clovers and grasses develop rapidly in the stubble and provide a heavy crop of hay the following year.

Good permanent grass has always been regarded as very valuable—almost irreplaceable. 'Break a pasture, make a man; make a pasture, break a man', says an old proverb. It means that to plough up old grassland and cash its fertility brings quick profits, while the process of re-establishing a good sward is ruinously expensive. Now, however, new techniques of grassland improvement are in use. Old pastures may be re-seeded without breaking up the soil structure; the existing grass with its weeds is killed by spraying with a contact herbicide which does not affect the soil, and the seed of improved varieties drilled direct into the bare ground. Another method is to 'inject' the grassland with new varieties while leaving most of it intact. A specialised type of drill is used, spraying narrow strips of herbicide and simultaneously burying a line of seed down the centre of each strip. The result is innumerable bands of bare soil, about 2in wide, in which the seedling grasses establish themselves and from which they spread to permeate the old sward.

As grazing, silage or hay, grass is a main source of meat and dairy produce. We are every bit as dependent on it as we are on those greater members of the grass family, the cereals.

Dairying

The production and distribution of milk have changed drastically since the turn of the century. The dairy cow gives a lot more milk now than in 1900; she has become more important and her lifestyle has varied with farming fashions and economics. Although temperamental at times she is an adaptable animal. She does not give of her best unless reasonably happy and contented, and this has protected her from extreme forms of exploitation. The dairy herd is probably better cared for today than ever before.

The liquid milk market

Some of the milk produced goes to make butter, cheese, cream, powdered milk and other products, but providing the daily 'pinta' is the main task of the dairy industry. Average consumption is about 30 gallons per person per year and more than three million cows are needed to ensure this supply and provide a surplus for manufacturing.

The provision of a clean, safe and regular supply of milk is a fairly recent

Shorthorn cow, c 1830. Although a supposedly dual-purpose (milk and beef) breed, she would probably have had a milk yield of only 300–400 gallons per lactation (*MERL*)

development and one which would have seemed fanciful even a century ago. The problems lay in the cycle of production and the peculiar nature of the product.

In the first place, a cow may be expected to milk for nine months after the birth of her calf. She is then dry for three months until the next calf is born—that, at least, is the ideal sequence, not always achieved. In the past cows most often calved in the spring and produced their greatest quantity of milk from summer grass. This was the case in the South West and parts of the Midlands, where most of the milk went into producing cream, butter and a whole range of famous local cheeses; it is still the case in many parts of Europe today. But if the priority is a continuous output of milk for the liquid market, it is no use concentrating production in the spring and summer, and dairying spread from the traditional grazing areas to other parts of the country where the production of winter milk became an important element in mixed farming. Increasing numbers of cows were allowed to calve in the autumn and by the 1930s the newly created Milk

A modern champion dairy cow. Herd averages of more than 1,000 gallons per lactation are now regularly attained (*Farmers Weekly*)

Marketing Board, which had taken over the distribution of all liquid milk, had established seasonal price differentials which made winter production profitable.

The other difficulties in the way of a universal supply of fresh milk lay in the nature of the product. Milk is highly perishable and a perfect home for micro-organisms. The most familiar of these now are the ones which turn it sour, but it was once a frequent carrier of tuberculosis, typhoid and other infectious diseases. Pasteurisation, a form of limited sterilisation by heat, was a partial solution, but the real revolution in dairying has been in producing clean milk and getting it to the customer in a fresh condition. Until the railway formed a fast link between town and country, urban populations got their milk from urban cows. Well into the nineteenth century cows were kept in London, sometimes in conditions of considerable squalor. It was considered a good selling point to advertise milk 'warm from the cow', and only when it began to be transported long distances by rail was it realised how vital to the keeping quality was the swift cooling of milk to prevent the multiplication of bacteria.

The 'milk train' ran from almost every country station and older readers will remember the cohorts of churns cluttering local platforms and those of the London termini.

By the 1920s the distribution of milk was well organised, though old methods still lingered. The milkman's barrow still carried a large brass churn and a range of measures for the benefit of customers who liked to see the commodity ladled straight into their own jugs, but bottling at the dairy was becoming standard practice and producer-retailers were bottling on the farm.

Change on the dairy farm

As the milk industry grew, standards of hygiene became stricter. Milk was continually tested for cleanliness and quality. It had once been the easiest foodstuff to adulterate, since all one had to do was to add water, but testing for fatty and non-fatty solids (the nutritive elements from which butter and cheese are made) put a stop to this ancient practice.

Milking out of doors was prohibited to reduce contamination by dust;

Hand milking. Four expert milkers were required for a herd now milked by one man with modern equipment (*MERL*)

Modern tandem milking parlour. The cows are in it for only a few minutes and the milk passes by pipeline to be cool-stored for collection (*Farmers Weekly*)

hand milkers were required to wear clean overalls and use buckets partially covered by a dome top; coolers were introduced, the most popular being the type in which milk passes in a thin film over the outside of a corrugated casing while cold water flows through the interior.

The most important step in the provision of safe milk came in 1922, when the eradication of bovine tuberculosis began. Herds were subjected to the tuberculin test and when free of reactors a premium was paid on their milk. In the 1960s this task was completed and the national herd was declared 'TT'. The dairy farmer's work in complying with a host of regulations and keeping the milk flowing summer and winter increased rapidly in the years of modernisation from 1920 to 1970, yet in that time the labour force declined even faster, so that eventually the work of eight men in 1920 was being done by one in 1976.

The old-fashioned way was to keep the cows tied up in stalls during the winter—October to April in most parts of the country. Keeping the building clean and the cows fed was an almost continuous operation, occupying the staff between the morning and evening milkings. Water was supplied to each standing in an automatic drinking bowl, but everything else, including milking, was a matter of hard slog and long hours.

The introduction of machine milking was a major step forward. The machine was in use before World War I, but early models were not entirely reliable, though they established the pattern of a suction pump which created a vacuum in closed buckets and drew off the milk by a rhythmic sucking and squeezing from the cups fitted over the cow's teats. Improved design made it possible for one man to milk four cows simultaneously, and the fact that the milk was not exposed to the air but remained enclosed in its passage from the cow to the cooler was a further advance in hygiene.

A complete change of system came with the advent of the milking parlour. Instead of the long cowshed with each animal in her own standing, milking is done in a small building designed for a limited number of cows. In quick succession they enter, eat their ration of concentrated foods while being milked, and are replaced by others. In winter the herd lives in a covered yard, no longer tied, and the work of dung clearance, the provision of clean litter, and the supply of bulk foods like hay and silage is largely mechanised.

The milking equipment no longer requires the carrying and emptying of heavy buckets, the milk passing straight through a pipe-line to a cooled storage vat. The churn has been replaced by the refrigerated tanker, and this change has eliminated more backbreaking labour.

Cows and cowmen

The average milk yield thirty years ago was between 700 and 800 gallons

Milk churn awaiting collection at the end of the farm road (*Leslie F. Thompson*)

per cow in each lactation. Now it is about 1,000 gallons. The first breed to be systematically selected for milk production was the Dairy Shorthorn, a dual-purpose animal which provided useful calves for the beef herd. Today, as is obvious when travelling through dairying country, the chief milk producer is the large black-and-white Friesian. Two Channel Island breeds, the Jersey and the Guernsey, are of commercial importance, the high butterfat content of their milk earning it a special price. The small, gentle, attractive Jersey cow is the better known of the two; the Jersey bull, with elements of the Spanish fighting bull somewhere in its ancestry, has a somewhat evil reputation.

The cow is a creature of habit. If thirty cows are let into a shed with thirty standings each will go unerringly to her familiar place. The routine of the milking parlour is soon accepted, cows entering and leaving quickly and without fuss. The herd instinct ensures that large numbers live fairly peaceably together in the confined space of the covered yard through the

A two-thousand gallon tanker collects milk at a dairy farm. The change from churns to tankers has been completed in ten years (*Milk Marketing Board*)

winter months. A 'pecking order'—in this case a pushing order—is established and a cow rarely challenges her superiors or tolerates any nonsense from the lower orders.

The modern herdsman, despite the mechanisation of his craft, still has to be a stockman first and a technician second. Stockmanship is an indefinable quality, a mixture of knowledge and observation, an awareness of possible trouble that comes from an understanding of every individual animal. He must be aware of a failure in appetite, an unexplained drop in milk yield, a hint of possible difficulty in calving. The head herdsman is the highest paid of farmworkers, reflecting the exacting nature of the job. Many small and medium-sized herds are run by the farmer himself with family assistance.

Butter and cheesemaking

At one time the manufacture of butter and cheese was a farmhouse activity of great importance. On many West Country farms all milk was processed and, with the major markets for liquid milk too far away, the sale of these products plus clotted cream provided the only cash return from keeping cows. There was usually an additional bonus in using the by-products, skimmed milk, buttermilk and whey, in the feeding of pigs.

Buttermaking remained exclusively the province of the farm dairy until about 1870, when small dairy factories started up. However, farmhouse butter held a large share of the market up to 1914 and many a farmer's wife and dairymaid staked her reputation on the unvarying quality of her output.

The techniques employed during most of the nineteenth century had scarcely changed since the days when Jael offered the stuff in a lordly dish to Sisera before she murdered him. Milk stood in large shallow pans, and when the cream had risen to the top it was skimmed off and churned. It was not cooled at any stage and even though the dairy was a cool, damp, stone-flagged place, there was endless trouble from souring in hot weather. It was a popular allegation against supposed witches that they caused the souring of cream, but the millions of airborne micro-organisms that settled on the milk needed no help from witchcraft. The churn in general use was of the plunger type, tall and narrow and activated by a long handle moved up and down. It was tiring to work and difficult to clean.

Butter, once it has emerged as a solid mass, has to be 'worked' to eliminate the droplets of liquid it contains. This involved a lot of pummelling and kneading and there was sharp disagreement among Victorian advisers over the relative merits for the purpose of bare hands or wooden 'spades' or 'pats'. One writer admitted that traditional methods were not perfect: 'A woman having hot, heavy, clammy hands should never be a dairymaid, for butter is very susceptible of taint and its freshness will doubtless be spoilt by the heavy smell of sweaty hands.' Washing the hands with cold water and oatmeal is recommended—soap would presumably result in more 'taint'—but it is interesting to note that worries about contamination were confined to its effects on flavour.

Methods improved after the invention of the centrifugal separator in 1890. This ingenious machine divides the whole milk into its heavier and lighter parts, collecting the cream more efficiently than by skimming and reducing contamination from the atmosphere. Rotary and box churns replaced the ancient plunger type and easily sterilisable metal superseded wood in dairy utensils. But the dairymaid slowly disappeared from the scene and buttermaking became fully mechanised in the creameries.

Cheesemaking is another extremely ancient way of preserving the nutrients of milk in solid form. The Prophet Job asks, 'Hast thou poured me out as milk and curdled me like cheese?', and no doubt cheese made from the milk of goats and ewes was a familiar enough food in his time.

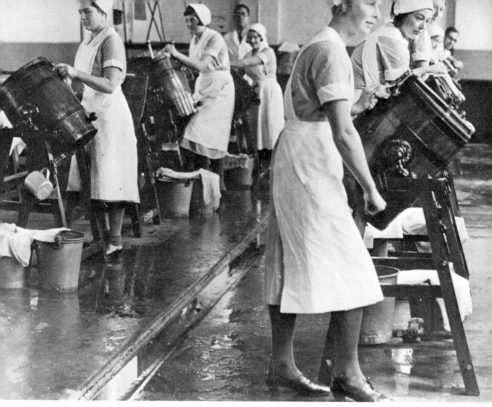

Butter-making class at Reading University in the period between the wars (*MERL*)

Wensleydale cheeses drying. Although most English cheeses are made in large creameries there is great demand for farmhouse cheeses made in traditional ways (*MERL*)

The Romans knew all about cheeses and probably introduced their manufacture to Britain, but although their own methods were fairly advanced those of the islanders remained primitive until the eighth century when the use of rennet as a curdling agent became general.

Cheese is simply milk which has gone sour and has separated into two obviously different constituents—a solid mass, the curd, and a thin liquid, the whey. It was discovered that, with suitable treatment, the curd could be preserved and kept for long periods, and that a great variety of textures and flavours could be obtained by varying the process.

At first the milk was allowed to sour in its own time, either whole or after the removal of the cream. Natural souring is an erratic business, taking different times according to temperature and other factors and leaving the eventual flavour of the cheese to be decided by the particular strain of micro-organisms involved. Controlled manufacture became possible only when it was found that milk could be curdled in an hour or so by the addition of small quantities of certain substances generically described as 'rennet'. The most widely used is that prepared from the stomach lining of calves, but various vegetable substances have been used at different times. The familiar weed, lady's bedstraw, was once known as the cheese rennet plant because its juice was used for curdling milk.

The usual farmhouse procedure was to use the morning milk warm from the cow, mixed with that of the previous evening raised to the same temperature. If skim milk was used the cream had to be taken off as soon as possible and all the milk warmed to blood-heat. The harder cheeses were produced from skim, the softer, high quality ones like Cheshire and Double Gloucester from whole milk.

The curd, which formed very soon after a small quantity of rennet was added to the milk, was strained and kneaded to get rid of some of the whey. It was chopped up to release the imprisoned droplets, squeezed more vigorously, and packed into cheese presses. Here it was put under gradually increasing pressure for days or weeks. What at last emerges from a press is recognisably a cheese, though unripe and immature. Thereafter, it will stand on a shelf in the storeroom, being turned daily and perhaps rubbed with salt, anointed with butter, or receiving other individual treatment.

The arts of cheesemaking, evolved by trial and error in remote farmhouses in Somerset and Cheshire, in Gloucestershire and the Midlands grazing lands, have not been entirely lost, though machines have taken over most of the work. It is no small thing for Cheddar and Stilton that they should be known worldwide because of their cheeses.

Sheep

No animal holds quite the same place in our history as the sheep. It has made a major contribution to feeding and clothing us for most of history. It established Britain as an exporting nation in the Middle Ages and founded the first great personal fortunes derived from trade. It paid for schools, bridges and some of the finest ecclesiastical architecture in Europe. It is a vital element in the history and symbolism of both Judaism and Christianity—the bishop's pastoral staff, the crozier, is not a cross but a stylised shepherd's crook. The Lord Chancellor presides over the High Court of Parliament seated on a woolsack.

Breeds of sheep

The sheep population of Britain is larger than that of any other country except New Zealand. The number of distinct British breeds is believed to be about forty, and this is probably unique for such a small area.

The continuity of so many breeds, the fact that they have maintained separate identities up to the present day, reflects the adaptation of the sheep to a particular environment and also the isolation so characteristic of rural life in the past. Both by force of circumstance, as in the island and mountain breeds, and through local pride and prejudice among the lowland flockmasters, the breeds have survived unchanged over long periods, though of course there has been much crossing in the interests of better economic performance. One does not have to search for the ancestors of the modern sheep, it has, so to speak, brought its ancestors with it. They may be seen in the fields, on the hills and islands, and at agricultural shows, and a quirky, fascinating lot they are.

It is said that sheep are not native to Britain, but whence and when they came is anybody's guess. Domesticated forms were known before the Roman conquest and there were, no doubt, many introductions in later times. The St Kilda sheep were said to have been established on their remote island by the Vikings, and the black-spotted Jacob sheep, which became popular as ornamental lawnmowers in eighteenth-century parks, were brought from the Mediterranean. Whether they are indeed the 'spotted and speckled' breed which Jacob is credited with producing by a form of magical suggestion, will never be known. What is certainly untrue is the legend that they got here by swimming ashore from the shattered galleons of the Armada.

Breeds fall into three large and very varied groups. The longwools are represented by the Romney Marsh and Border Leicester. Their wool goes to make the finer worsteds. Then there are the shortwools, the other lowland group, typified by the Suffolks and the Downs. They have dark faces, their wool is used in a variety of fabrics, and their meat is of fairly high quality. Hill breeds are the most numerous and economically the most important since they utilise land which might otherwise be completely

unproductive. The varieties are sometimes very localised, but among those of wide distribution are the Cheviot, the Welsh and the Blackface. Hill-sheep fleeces go into a variety of manufactures, ranging from the finest tweeds to carpets.

The insulation provided by the fleece is demonstrated by the capacity of hill sheep to withstand very severe cold. Sheep in hot desert regions—and these may be the animal's original habitat—are equally well protected from the intense heat. Tests have shown that the temperature at the skin surface may be as much as 40°F (4°C) lower than in the outer layers of the fleece when the sheep is in intense sunlight. A newly shorn sheep under these conditions suffers badly if unable to find shade, it has no interior heat-losing mechanism to compensate for the loss of its insulation, and pants rapidly like a dog. However, the sheep's fleece, like its adaptability in matters of diet, has helped it to feel at home in many lands from Australia to Iceland and has provided mankind with clothing suitable for a similar range of climates. The wool clip from a single sheep may weigh anything from 4–20lb according to breed. A South Devon ram holds the record with a fleece of 45lb, and that by anyone's reckoning is a pretty formidable overcoat.

The carcase weight of the fat lamb depends, of course, on the age at which it is slaughtered and on the adult size of the breed. The smallest is probably the Shetland, with other island breeds, the Orkney and the Soay, not much larger. These types can pick up a living under the hardest conditions, the Soay especially, eating seaweed when other grazing fails.

Shepherding

The sheep does not lend itself to intensive or factory farming. It is very much an outdoor beast and the shepherd's life and work are equally so. In essentials the work has changed less than that of any other branch of livestock husbandry, and if the shepherd's life is today often far from idyllic it was little different in the past. He has long been an idealised figure in the rural scene, and even when most farm animals were tended in the open air for much of the year, the pastoral poets ignored their attendants. It was never a case of 'Nymphs and swineherds, come away'.

Undoubtedly a good shepherd has a special dedication to the job and a very close association with his flock. The routine of work may appear leisurely compared with the continuous slog of dairying, but the shepherd must be ever on the watch. The ewes must be in good condition when mated in the autumn and their nutrition before and after the rams are introduced into the flock directly affects the coming lamb crop. They must be counted, given supplementary feeding, perhaps rescued from snowdrifts

Shepherd and his dog at the turn of the century (*MERL*)

Jacob sheep. This ancient Mediterranean breed, once popular for keeping down the grass in gentlemen's parks, was almost extinct in the 1930s. Its numbers are now increasing because the odd-looking creatures may have characteristics worth preserving (*Fox*)

during the winter. Lambing is a time of sleepless tension with the lives of hundreds of ewes and lambs literally in the shepherd's hands, and weather conditions frequently appalling. Ewes may bear one lamb, twins, or occasionally triplets, and the shepherd's final achievement is measured by the ratio of surviving lambs to the number of ewes in the flock. In lowland flocks the higher it gets above one-to-one and the nearer to two-to-one the greater the shepherd's achievement.

Shearing comes with the warmer weather, the sheep are dipped as a protection against skin disease and insect attack, old ewes are culled from the flock and replacements selected from among ewe lambs. Then the seasonal cycle starts again.

On mixed farms where sheep form a major enterprise the shepherd usually has a reputation for intransigence, of placing the interests of the sheep first and those of everybody and everything else nowhere. In the

Dorset Down ewes with their lambs (*Farmers Weekly*)

131

Sheep shearing in the 1890s (*MERL*)

Sheep dipping in Wiltshire. Note the footgear before the age of the rubber boot (*MERL*)

recent past it was the custom to fold flocks on arable crops such as roots, using gate hurdles to make the enclosures and moving them as the sheep cleared the crop. It was a valuable system in maintaining soil fertility, but in its traditional form used a lot of labour in moving and setting up scores, perhaps hundreds, of hurdles at frequent intervals. It was 'shep's' prerogative to ask for the required number of men, horses and carts when needed, and he expected absolute priority over other operations.

On hill farms where sheep are the mainstay of production the shepherd is of even greater importance. Human help is limited and he may rely heavily on his dogs, with co-operative efforts between neighbouring holdings for major events such as shearing and dipping. It is in the lonely hill districts that shepherding has evolved many strange words and kept them alive along with the local breeds.

The most remarkable example of this specialised vocabulary is the system of numerals used in counting sheep in the west and north and still known to older shepherds in Cumbria, Northumbria and Scotland. Hill flocks must be counted accurately at every opportunity, especially when the sheep are mustered for shearing or dipping—though why a specialised counting method should have appeared and survived remains a mystery.

The numbers run from one to twenty, at which point the shepherd presumably made a mark or dropped a pebble and returned to one again. The count from one to ten is *yan, tan, tethera, pethera, pimp, sethera, lethera, hovera, covera, dik.* From eleven to twenty the sequence is *yan-a-dik, tan-a-dik, tethera-dik,* and so on with a divergence at fifteen, which is *bumfit,* and terminating at *gigottt* or *figgott* for twenty. The last appears to be a local variation. The idea of counting in small equal batches and marking off each batch on completion is a sound one, lessening the chance of confusion when the numbers reach the hundreds and the counter's attention begins to wander. The change in word structure at every fifth numeral is another aid to keeping the counter fully awake. But the origins of the words have never been explained, guesses ranging from Gaelic to pre-Roman Celtic with a dash of Latin. Certainly *yan* and *dik* for one and ten suggest Latin roots, but equally they suggest French and possible Norman influence.

The general terminology of sheep husbandry has more local variants than most branches of farming. A sheep which has got on its back and cannot right itself is generally described as being 'cast', but in some places it is 'wigwelted'. A ram lamb may be a 'diamond tup' or a 'dinmont' and a ewe lamb a 'chilver'. A barren ewe is sometimes sardonically described as a 'guest' in recognition of the fact that she is not pulling her weight in the production line. A hand-reared lamb is a 'cade' or a 'tidden', and an inferior specimen, equivalent to the runt in a litter of pigs, is a 'pallie'.

In some respects, such as the control of disease, sheepfarming has become

Prize-winning pig of 1872 (*MERL*)

steadily more efficient, but without basic changes of method. It is still possible, and will long remain so, to see a sight which has gladdened many a heart for centuries past: a great flock grazing in peace upon the hillside.

The changing shape of the pig

Odd as it may seem to us, the fat pig was once fat. Today, a fat fat pig is worth a lot less than a lean fat pig because changes in dietary habits have made so much of him unsaleable.

The difference between description and reality is not peculiar to the pig. Cattle ready for slaughter are officially 'fat cattle' and the pre-Christmas shows are 'fatstock' shows. Until recently the term was accurate. Animals were grown to large sizes and a great part of their total weight was fat.

The way in which nineteenth-century prints and paintings emphasised the fatness and bulkiness of champion pigs and bullocks shows how desirable these characteristics were thought to be. They were exaggerated by the artist to please the owner, just as he might portray a thoroughbred horse with an impossibly long neck and small head.

Shepherd near Blandford with twin Dorset Down lambs. His work has not changed basically over the centuries and still requires a high degree of skill and dedication (*MERL*)

Artistic exaggeration apart, meat animals in the past were bred and fed to satisfy very different standards to those of our own time. The modern pig, of which the Scandinavian Landrace is a perfect example, is long and lean, with its heaviest development at the rear end. The breeder has before him a vision of the ideal pig consisting almost entirely of lean back rashers and lean hams. The Victorian pigbreeder looked for an animal that would gain overall weight as economically as possible no matter whether he put it on equally fore and aft or whether it was as much fat as lean.

As with pork and bacon, so with beef. The nineteenth-century beef animal had an almost rectangular outline, carrying as much weight in the forequarters, where the cheaper joints come from, as in the back and hindquarters which are the source of the more expensive cuts. A progressive change of shape in the beef breeds has taken place over the last century and with it has come quicker growth and more attention to food conversion rates—the ratio of live weight gain to the animal's food consumption. Our native breeds such as the Aberdeen Angus and the Hereford are famous the world over, but many European breeds are now being imported for experimental cross-breeding to improve still further the proportion of lean meat. Many Continental breeds of cattle are lean and muscular, having been bred for hundreds of years as draught animals.

Dying breeds and the gene bank

The survival of a breed is a matter of economic performance, though personal preference and sentimental attachment may outweigh the harsher criteria with individual farmers. Some old breeds remain unaltered and still profitable, in others important characteristics are modified to suit the changing times. But many once-popular breeds are superseded by new ones and drop out of commercial farming. This happened with poultry between 1940 and 1965, the familiar laying breeds, the Wyandotte, White Leghorn, Light Sussex and Rhode Island Red, being almost universally replaced by more productive layers, hybrids known only by numbers. Which brings us back to the story of the pig.

There were once nearly a dozen breeds of pig, the Large White, the Essex and Wessex Saddlebacks, the Tamworth, the Gloucester Old Spot, the Berkshire and others. Their names indicate local origin but in fact they were widely distributed. The pig industry is now largely based on the newcomer, the Landrace, and the Large White. Other breeds are on the way to extinction.

It may be thought that there can be no objection to the disappearance of a breed of livestock which is no longer commercially viable. However admirable the instinctive skill of old-time breeders, who created it by painstaking selection and no theoretical knowledge of genetics, it has served

Fat Berkshire pigs of the 1890s (*MERL*)

The modern pig has changed its shape: this one was sold for 500 guineas in 1967 (*Farmers Weekly*)

its turn. But it is not as simple as that, and today a move is afoot to preserve the old breeds of farm livestock.

It is now realised that future breeds can only be derived from existing genetic material and that a breed which is *in toto* unsuited to modern requirements may have valuable characteristics. The Berkshire pig, for instance, may be quite the wrong shape but have the ability to produce and rear larger than average litters. It may have genetic factors of fecundity which will fit into a new bundle of characteristics being assembled. The hereditary make-up of a breed is an asset in what has come to be known as the 'gene bank' and when a breed is lost the asset has been dispersed.

The lead in preserving old farm livestock has been taken by a voluntary organisation, the Rare Breeds Survival Trust, and their farm at Guiting Power, in some of the loveliest of Cotswold country, is open to the public. It is a good place in which to get acquainted with a varied and colourful aspect of farming history.

Boundaries and barriers

Good fences, they say, make good neighbours, and to livestock the other man's grass is always greener. Two methods of fencing are of particular interest in that they involve specialised skills. One is hedge-laying, and this is of comparatively recent origin. It dates from the eighteenth century and is fast becoming a lost art now that the mechanical hedge-trimmer has taken over.

Dry-stone walling, on the other hand, is very old indeed and its practitioners are much in demand. There are no substitutes for walls in hill-sheep country and no machine has yet been invented which can rebuild a damaged wall.

Hedge-laying

When looking at landscapes we saw that the hedge took its present form as a result of the enclosures and the abandonment of the open-field system. Estate boundaries had to be drawn and field divided from field in the patterns of the new farming. This, once established, was a self-perpetuating fence, but it was soon found to function better and look better when strictly controlled. Economics would have generated the art and craft of hedging if the requirements of foxhunting had not done so first.

At one time every farm of any size had a reasonably proficient hedge-layer, and hedge-laying competitions were almost as common as ploughing matches. This was especially so in the major hunting counties where the hunts provided the prizes, where well kept hedges were synonymous with good farming and where to reinforce a hedge with barbed wire was an offence only slightly less horrible than shooting a fox.

A Kentish hedger at work. The saplings are cut lightly without being completely
severed (*John Topham*)

The purpose of laying a hedge is to keep it to a uniform height and width
and to ensure that it is strong and stock-proof at all points. Left to itself it
grows upwards, and as the individual hawthorn and other plants become
more tree-like, gaps appear between them. Spreading growth is transferred
to a higher level and the base of the hedge ultimately consists of a number
of thick stems too widely separated. Such a hedge is said to be 'thin at the
bottom' and is a standing invitation to any enterprising animal to put its
head through and push. The simplest way of controlling the hedge is, of
course, to trim it. By continually cutting the top and sides a dense interior
growth is promoted and the hedge at least looks impenetrable.

Laying a hedge is simply a method of forcing it to grow in a different
direction, training the upright growths to become more nearly horizontal
and so permanently fill the thinning and gappy part. It has the merit of
retaining the strong growths already there and persuading them to carry on
growing in a more effective position.

Hedge-laying is a winter job, undertaken when the sap is down and the

The boom of this modern Hedgeater swings to cut on both sides (*Farmers Weekly*)

leaves gone. The hedger can then see what he is doing; which useless growths to cut away and which of the stronger ones to retain as the hedge's framework. He works from left to right, first clearing away the scrub and rubbish from the hedge-bottom. Then he begins bending down the tall stems so that they all lie obliquely, pointing from right to left, and with their tops at the same level. The angle of slant will vary with the length of the growth. If the hedger has determined on a height of, say, 4ft for the finished work, an 8ft stem will form a much more acute angle with the ground than a 5ft one. The skilled worker does, however, like to see the entire hedge laid at approximately the same angle, and will select and trim the growth to that end.

A deep cut is made on the right-hand side of the stem when it is bent over so that it stays in position and is easier to bend. With very strong growths this may have to be done with an axe, but as a rule the hedger can make the cut with a bill as he pushes the growth over with his glove-protected left hand. In this operation lies the real art of hedge-laying; the cut must be deep

The hedge being laid into position (*John Topham*)

enough to permit bending without breaking and yet it must leave enough wood and bark intact to support life and growth. The wound heals, and the hawthorn plant grows more slowly in its new circumstances, throwing out masses of prickly shoots along its entire length and soon producing a close-growing hedge right down to the ground. The framework of the hedge no longer consists of vertical elements with increasing spaces between them, but of semi-horizontal, overlapping growths as difficult to break through as the rails of a fence. Not only is the hedge now an effective barrier, it is a far more effective windbreak, giving protection at ground level with its dense growth.

As the hedger proceeds he drives in stakes of hazel or hawthorn every few feet, interlacing them through the stems, and strengthening the hedge until natural growth has bound it together. The top is finished off level, with the thinner ends twisted or plaited together, and at one time it was usual to save long brambles during the initial trimming, strip them of their thorns and weave them along the top, binding in the stakes. The toughness and flexibility of brambles was also recognised in their use as cord for tying the first layers of thatch to roof timbers (see Thatching, p233).

A properly laid hedge could be kept in order by regular trimming with a slasher for many years without developing weak spots or needing to be patched with wire. The powered hedge-trimmer now does the work of a man with a slasher in a fraction of the time, and although we may regret the roughness of its work it has meant that many thousands of miles of hedges have been saved from grubbing. However, a neglected, runaway hedge can still only be restored by hand, with skill and patience.

Dry-stone walling

Over the dales and fells and moorlands the stone walls run for mile upon mile, marking boundaries and providing the only windbreak for sheep on many a bleak upland.

The dry-stone wall is a perfect example of the economy of true craftsmanship. With no materials other than those lying at his feet the wallbuilder erects a fence capable of withstanding the most atrocious weather conditions and of containing the born escaper, the Blackface sheep. It is an ancient craft, many of today's walls having been in existence for centuries with only a minimum of repair. The wall, or 'dyke' as it is known in many parts of the country, probably began as simple boundary marks and developed into something more valuable when hitherto unused uplands became the home of profitable flocks.

The craft had geographical limitations; it was never a universal farm craft as was thatching, for example, and the number of skilled 'dykers' in any district was always limited. It is now a fairly highly paid activity for the

Building a dry-stone wall in the Cotswolds. Rubble is packed in the centre cavity (*Fox*)

Repairing a dry-stone wall. The craft is still much in demand for the wall is the only practical sheep-fencing in upland areas (*MERL*)

proficient, but proficiency in dyking is not easily acquired. The fact remains that modern technology has not come up with any form of fencing to compete economically with dry-stone walling in its own particular terrain.

The dry-stone wall is constructed of irregular pieces of rock held together by their own weight without mortar. It usually consists of two separate walls of flattish stones piled up so that they lean slightly inwards towards each other. The space between them, known to the dyker as the 'heart', is filled with carefully packed smaller fragments of rock. The top is finished off with large stones laid crosswise to act as a coping and bind the whole together. The final product is a stout wall whose sides have a slight inward 'batter' and the stones of which are so firmly held by the adhesion of weight that even if one projects far enough to be grasped in both hands a strong man is unable to pull it out.

The use of large stones for the coping completes a process followed throughout the building. The smaller stones are used at the base of the wall and they get progressively heavier as it grows. At first glance this seems slightly crazy, one would expect a solid foundation of heavy stones to support a superstructure of lighter ones. But if it is remembered that the wall is held together by weight it becomes obvious that the weight must bear on all its components. If heavy stones are piled up to a height of, say, 2ft and lighter ones piled on top, the upper courses of the wall are easily dislodged. However, if the reverse procedure is followed, the upper stones will be too heavy to budge under the impact of a scrambling sheep and the whole mass of the wall will be compacted by the weight at the top.

The durability of dry-stone walling is partly accounted for by its resistance to erosion. A more sophisticated wall of dressed stone bonded with mortar would soon begin to suffer from the effects of rain and frost. Drops of water find a lodgement, expand on freezing and loosen a crumb of cement here and a flake of stone there, leaving larger cavities for more water to repeat the process. Such a wall, dependent on the mortar for its strength, would need constant repointing. But the rock fragments in the dry-stone wall do not fit together exactly, the whole thing is honeycombed with small spaces and channels through which water gaining an entrance immediately drains away. The stonework dries out and the hardest frost leaves it untouched. The secret of the dry-stone wall is quite simply the dryness of its stones.

Regional differences

Seen from a distance the walls look much alike, switchbacking over landscapes in which they alone are sometimes the only evidence of man's existence. But they differ somewhat with the terrain and the temperament of the sheep they have to restrain. Two main types have evolved.

A Cornish version of the dry-stone wall (*Field*)

Northern or Pennine walls They are found from the Peak District northward, on both sides of the Pennine ridge and in Scotland from the Clyde–Forth valley to the Roman Wall. Many are built on steep slopes at altitudes where gusts of wind have the impact of a bulldozer. In spite of this these walls may have endured from the early eighteenth century with only minimal repairs. They are wide-based double walls in which both faces and the 'heart' are so carefully laid that wind pressure on the sides merely consolidates the whole.

A sheep-proof wall is not easy to maintain where hill sheep are concerned. Their instinct is to go through or over wherever the chance offers, and they are ever watchful for a weak spot. They have, however, a peculiar inhibition, no doubt born of generations of unfortunate experiences among the rocks; they will not attempt to scramble over or through a wall which looks as though it might be in danger of collapse.

From their knowledge of sheep psychology the Scottish dykers evolved the so-called Galloway wall. It is very solidly built up to a height of about 3ft, but the top part, a further 2ft, is narrower and so laid that light can be seen between the stones. The layout seems to create an impression in the sheep mind that the whole thing is unsafe and the risks involved in getting over it unacceptable.

The Cotswold wall The Cotswold country is kinder than the Pennine slopes; the walls are lower and the Down or crossbred sheep accustomed to a softer

Old millstones have been incorporated in this wall at Lower Slaughter, Gloucester
(*Leslie F. Thompson*)

and less active life. This is a land of stone and stonemasons, of stone cottages and incredible churches born of the wealth of wool and the skills which it fostered. The stone and the sheep symbolise the history of the Cotswolds over the last 700 years, and the beautifully regular walls, dividing the rolling landscape as they have done for much of that time, are a constant reminder of both.

The great limestone hump of the Cotswold Hills extends from a point near Bath to the steep escarpment that falls into the Midlands plain. Nowhere does it rise much more than 1,000ft above sea level and as hill country it is undramatic. Nevertheless, the underlying rock, the stone which J. B. Priestley saw glimmering with the sunlight of lost centuries, has stamped its character on the area.

The soil is poor and shallow, the rock often a few inches below the surface, and the maintenance of any fertility in this stony ground has traditionally depended on the sheep. The stone is easily quarried without blasting and near the surface the action of frost has often left it fissured horizontally so that quite thin slabs may be prised up and used for roofing 'slats' with very little trimming. Similar horizontal cleavage occurs at greater depths and much larger blocks are also quarried with relative ease.

The waller thus has an almost limitless source of raw material at hand, even if he has to do a little digging for it. It comes in flattish pieces which tend to fit rather closely together and would impede free drainage if laid perfectly flat. So the Cotswold waller gives his stones a slight slope from the centre to the face of the wall, leading the water out by the shortest route. The topping stones of Cotswold walls are sometimes bound with mortar, a unique deviation from the pure doctrine of dry-stone walling. On the other hand, the massive pillars which are a feature of the angles and gateways of the Cotswold wall will often consist of squared blocks closely fitted and standing apparently immovable, without mortar.

West Country walls have in many cases been neglected because of changes in farming practice and have often collapsed and been swamped in vegetation. The dykers here were no less skilful than those in other parts of the country, and Cornish craftsmen especially made very effective use of fragmented granite in the building of early stone cottages as well as walls.

4 The Country Church

The best way to understand what the Church has meant to countrymen is to look at the churches. They are an accumulated history, pages of timber and stone whose intrinsic beauty, like the monastic chronicler's illuminations, so enthrals us that we make little effort to decipher the writing.

The Church of England, whose material inheritance is so much older than its name, is, of course, country-based and rooted in a time when city folk were a tiny minority. So it is that a village with no church seems incomplete, and the word 'parish' has more meaning in the country than the town. It retains something of the combined religious and civil significance that it once possessed universally. Time was when the government of the self-sufficient, self-contained parish loomed much larger than the distant shadows of government and the king's officers. At the centre of the parish, physically and in the affairs of life, was the church. In religion and politics, loyalty and subversion, peace and war, and through all upheavals, it was a continuity which has held to our own time. How could it not have stories to tell?

The feeling that the church is almost a symbol of the true village comes out in a vivid little passage in Jacquetta Hawkes' *A Land*:

> When returning from hill or moor one looks down on a village, one's destination, swaddled in trees, and with only the church tower breaking the thin blue layer of evening smoke, the emotion it provokes is as precious as it may be commonplace. Time has caressed this place, until it lies as comfortably as a favourite cat in an armchair, caresses also even the least imaginative of beholders.

Here the church tower, visible through the gathering haze, signifies the very existence of the village. One feels too that it symbolises the sense of comfort and continuity that always comes from the sight of clustered dwellings grouped, as it were, around the church for protection.

The image of comfort and protection may be illusory. The village may have been rent by sectarian strife, utterly neglected by pluralist parsons, or embittered by disputes over tithes many times in its existence. But the continuity is undeniable, the church may well be the oldest building

Wiltshire vicarage and church (*Leslie F. Thompson*)

in the village, and in a way the oldest record of the lives of its people.

To write only about the buildings of the established Church is of course to ignore a great part of the Christian tradition in Britain. This book is an affair of arbitrary choices, and things gleaned at random, and no value judgements are intended.

The parish church

If you visited a fresh parish church every single day of the year it would take you some thirty years to see them all. Taken collectively they form the greatest accumulation of artistic treasures and historical relics in the land—greater by far than all the museums put together.

It is difficult to imagine the village or country town without the dominating presence of its church. Even where new roads and the modern dwellings of new populations have engulfed the old community, the spire

Overleaf: Milking in the shadow of the cathedral of Ely (*H. D. Keilor*)

or tower of the parish church still looks over the scene to the fields beyond as it has done for perhaps 700 years.

The church will have seen and suffered the effects of many changes. It may have lost some of its valuables during the Dissolution of the Monasteries and seen its wall paintings obliterated and replaced by the royal arms. During the Civil War and the Commonwealth the priceless work of sculptor, woodcarver and stained-glass artist may have been destroyed as idolatrous. In Victorian times the restorers may have wrought almost equal havoc from the best of motives. Yet the proportion of the national wealth and technical ability that went into churchbuilding over the centuries was vast enough to ensure us an incomparable heritage—'incomparable' in the literal sense that no other area of equal size anywhere in the world can muster such a collection.

Its role in history

The first people to build churches in any number were the Saxons. Their building period is generally given as AD 600 up to the Norman Conquest of 1066, and like all epochs of architectural styles in ecclesiastical building, this one is only very approximate. The Saxons were around long before 600, conversion to Christianity by the Celts had been in progress, and the Celts themselves were building churches in the west. The Saxon Christians in England began by erecting stone crosses as emblems of their faith and congregating for open-air worship around them. But it was during the Saxon period that the idea of the parish church took shape.

The Saxon lords took to erecting churches on their manors, the church and its priests specifically associated with that particular feudal community. The local church turned out to be more lasting than feudalism, the village changed and grew around it, but for a very long time it was a focal point of the village life.

Not merely was it often the largest, most splendid structure in the village, visible to the traveller above the treetops long before any other sign of human presence, it was in rural areas the centre of communal life. Baptism, marriage and burial repeated the tale of the generations. It was the only welfare centre for the destitute once the monasteries had been ravaged by Henry VIII. The 'parish chest' within its walls contained more than ecclesiastical records; it was often the safe deposit in which parishioners kept their wills and title deeds. From 1597 the compulsory parish registers of births, marriages and deaths provided the first population records. The nave of the church, uncluttered by pews, was a place for parish meetings, church-ales and general revelry on saints' days and holidays. It was the village hall, the place of entertainment, as well as the place of worship. The church-ale was an approved form of revelry, and many churches had their own cauldrons for brewing the essential refreshment. (A few still have them.) The church of St John the Baptist at Cirencester in Gloucestershire, one of the great 'wool' churches, and said to be the finest example of the Perpendicular style in the country, has thirty-eight carvings showing a church-ale on its unusual parapet. Some of the figures are hotting up the proceedings with pipe and tabor, and one carries the injunction 'be merry'. The varied functions which the church came to assume and their importance to people who seldom left the confines of their village explain why some 15,000 parish churches are in existence now.

The number and magnificence of our churches also tell us something of mercantile history in the countryside. Here the size of a church bears no true relation to the size of the parish, either now or in the past. One often hears it said that an enormous church in a tiny village must indicate a much larger population in past times, but the chances are that even when church-going was universal the congregation could never have filled it. The grandeur of the church is more often a reflection of the wealth and religious devotion of its patron. This might be individual or collective, a rich merchant or a powerful guild. The motives were no doubt mixed; it has been said that many of our churches are monuments to the glory of God and the conceit of man. The element of prestige was a frequent ingredient; the merchant wanted a church worthy of perpetuating his name, wherein he might eventually lie in his canopied tomb; the guild wanted one consonant with the dignity of its craft and perhaps dedicated to its patron saint; the community as a whole might strive for generations to raise an edifice outshining those of its neighbours.

The influence of the guilds is seen mostly in churches built from the fifteenth century onwards, when they would sometimes contribute their own chapel to the parish church, and occasionally play a major part in the initial construction. It must be remembered that churches as we know them are seldom the product of an exact plan, executed swiftly and in detail according to contract. They were altered and added to as new religious concepts evolved or new resources became available. The Witney church of St Mary in Oxfordshire occupies four times as much land as it did in the twelfth century. The writer's own parish church, begun in the fourteenth century, consisted of nothing but a chancel for fifty years.

Repeated reference to the 'wool' churches is inevitable. They are scattered all over the Cotswolds, East Anglia and eastern England. The profits of the wool trade and cloth manufacture in these areas paid for their wonderful and enduring craftsmanship. But other trades, not always associated with quiet rural districts, have also contributed. The small Essex town of Thaxted, for instance, was once a centre for cutlery manufacture—a southern Sheffield. To the west lies the hamlet of Cutler's

The parish church, Long Melford, Suffolk. A magnificent 'wool' church, it recalls the days when the wool merchants poured their surplus wealth into monuments to their piety (*Suzanne Beedell*)

Green, and the ancient guidhall is a relic of the trade. But the supreme monument to the cutlers is the parish church which they helped to build. Seemingly lifted above the roofs of the town, its spire visible over miles of rolling cornland, the great church of St John, St Mary and St Laurence is overwhelmingly impressive.

Thaxted church prompts a small digression to a subject which was bound to crop up sooner or later. The interior has been kept almost in its medieval state, with the nave and aisles bare of fixed pews and only as many chairs in place as are needed. It is bare and light and vastly spacious, so that one's eye is drawn upwards to the splendid timbering of the roof far above, or forward to the chancel and the altar; one feels that the men who raised these soaring columns and worked intricate carvings on scarcely visible beams were trying to express something of eternal value in the language of their craft.

Having seen this, leave Thaxted and drive the few miles to the market town of Saffron Walden, which became wealthier by growing the autumn-flowered saffron crocus for dyes and flavourings than ever Thaxted did by cutlery. Here too the town is crowned by an enormous church, possibly the largest in the county of Essex. In its building it had architectural links with King's College, Cambridge, and its stonework betokens craftsmanship of

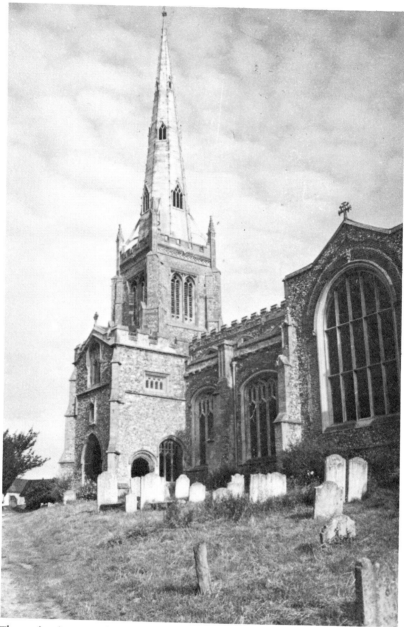

The wool trade was not the only commercial interest in the Middle Ages to go in for church-building. The great parish church of Thaxted, Essex, is associated with the Cutler's Guild (*Suzanne Beedell*)

the highest order. The interior, however, was extensively 'restored' in the nineteenth century, overcrowded with pews and over-embellished in other ways. The impact of size and design is dispersed and lost in too much detail.

Restoration is an essential and continuous process, it has gone on through the centuries and without it we should have no churches at all. But the restorer should have the humility to ask himself what the original builders intended and to respect that intention in his work. The Victorians, replete with new ideas and materials (including cheap, highly polishable, imported pitch pine), were fatally apt to assume that they knew better than their predecessors. Comparison of these two grand churches illustrates the point.

Architectural styles

The dating of a church by its manner of construction is a complex subject. The layman who just happens to like old churches will do well to avoid the more expert writer on the theme lest he becomes hopelessly bogged in technical argument. It helps to carry a simple guide to styles in one's pocket, to make as good a guess as possible at the age of a church, and then to check this from a local source. In this way it is possible to absorb the general 'feel' of buildings of different periods and eventually to place them within a century or two and to spot later restorations.

It is often the small, unnoticed features that tell us more of the past than the actual fabric of the church; some of them will be mentioned here after a very brief chronological sketch of the way church architecture developed.

The Saxons (600–1066) During this period the basic plan of the modern church evolved, the Celtic single-celled building giving way to the chancel at the eastern end containing the altar and separated by an arched opening from the nave or main body of the structure.

Only the later Saxon churches have survived, the earlier ones were really glorified log huts later rebuilt in stone or brick. An example of Saxon timberwork is still preserved in the church of St Andrew at Greensted-juxta-Ongar, Essex, where reconstruction has preserved a wall of massive split oak logs.

Stone and brick Saxon churches were mostly built of materials salvaged from Roman ruins. Although accustomed to the use of timber—they were great shipbuilders—the Saxons had no experience of stone-dressing and their masonry is rough and ready. Sometimes they worked stone and brick in herringbone patterns; frequently they plastered the exterior, hiding its defects. Traces of this rendering may still be seen on some Saxon churches. Lacking a theoretical knowledge of the principles involved, the Saxons were guided by simple rule-of-thumb ideas of compactness and solidity. Their windows are narrow, either rounded or triangular at the top. Wider

St Andrew's, Greensted, Essex, dates from AD 845 and is the world's oldest wooden church. The original Saxon timbers can be seen along the nave wall (*St Andrew's Church*)

windows are divided into lights and the vertical divisions, or mullions, are often gently bulged like balusters. These balustered windows are very typical of Saxon work.

Doorways are also narrow and fairly high. This distinguishes them from the Norman doorway, though both are topped with the rounded arch. Saxon towers are a rarity, though over fifty still exist. All are from the end of the period and most have been extensively altered. Usually they have been raised by the addition of extra storeys with a battlement finish. Two Saxon churches are worth visiting for their towers alone.

One is at Earls Barton, Northamptonshire, where the tower has been somewhat altered but remains completely Saxon in its lumpish solidity and obvious suitability as a military strongpoint when necessary. Like another

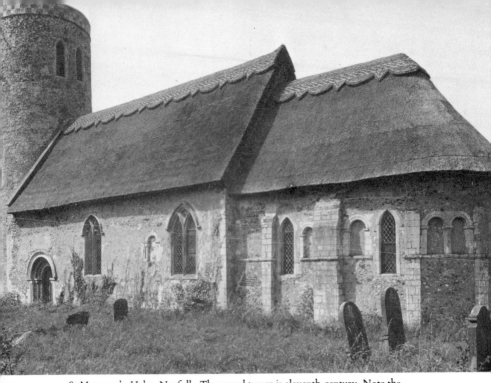

St Margaret's, Hales, Norfolk. The round tower is eleventh-century. Note the traditional Norman door on the south wall

Saxon church in the same county, that at Brixworth, there is a room in the tower with a window into the nave, intended, like the royal box at a theatre, for the use of VIPs. The second remarkable tower is at Sompting, Sussex, and this is the only one of its kind in England. It is topped with a 'Rhenish helm' spire, a four-sided gabled roof, purely Saxon and still familiar in the Rhineland.

The Normans (1066–1200) The latter date is purely arbitrary but by then the typically Norman was giving place to the Early Medieval English or Transitional style. Norman building had at first a touch of megalomania about it. They concentrated for half a century on abbeys and cathedrals before turning their immense energies to building or rebuilding parish churches. The number of basically Norman churches to be found in England and parts of Wales testifies to how well they built.

Continental craftsmen crossed the Channel to work on major projects and their skills gradually spread. Norman carvings in Durham Cathedral are reproduced in the parish church of Kirkby Lonsdale in Westmorland. The view from the churchyard here is said to be the finest in a county of magnificent views; Ruskin rhapsodised over it and Turner painted it.

Churches became more spacious in Norman times. Aisles running parallel with the central nave were introduced, so that the church kept its traditional form of a main axis running west to east with the chancel and altar at the east end, but widened this axis and introduced the transept. As the whole building was widened so the problems of roof construction and increased thrust on the walls had to be tackled. Stone vaulted roofs began to replace timber ones, and an early example of vaulting may be seen in one of the most famous Norman churches, at Elkstone, Gloucestershire. This church has a splendid late medieval tower, the Norman one having collapsed. In general, of course, Norman work did not collapse, it endured, whether in church or castle, and they coped successfully with their technical difficulties. The outward thrust on walls, for instance, brought about their use of the buttress, thereafter universally employed in many forms.

Norman doorways are round-arched, but far more decorative than those of the Saxons. The wide Norman doorways with sculptured surrounds depicting everything from floral designs to the harrowing of Hell is a typically Norman feature. At the south door of the fine late Norman church at Kilpeck, Herefordshire, are carvings of Welsh men-at-arms in peaked caps, a local reminder of the bloody clash of cultures in which Saxon, Norman and Celt had been so long involved.

Gothic styles (1200–1660) This, the greatest period of church building in Britain, is divided into three sections, Early English, Decorated and Perpendicular. The non-expert finds this pretty confusing, wondering why the same church should sometimes be simply described as 'Gothic' and sometimes by one of the other titles. In fact, all the developments of more than 400 years are the evolution of the one style.

The hallmark of Gothic is the pointed arch. Around it grew the conception of space and light, of thinner walls and flying buttresses to sustain them, of ceilings that culminated in wonderful fan vaulting, of windows ranging from narrow 'lancets' to great expanses of stone tracery and stained glass, of slender columns with richly sculpted capitals, of elaborate porches with niches for holy water stoups and the figures of saints.

The strength of the Gothic style, however, lay not in the scope it gave for decorative craftsmanship but in the soaring strength and lightness of its great structures. Even in the starkness of ruin the beauty survives and it was in the abbeys and cathedrals that it first developed. From them it percolated down to the humble parish church, which became steadily less humble and more magnificent.

The thirteenth century saw many parish churches in the Early English style built in England. In Scotland there was greater concentration on monastic building and many fine abbey churches were erected. For the first half of the fourteenth century the Decorated style evolved and building continued apace. Then it virtually ceased, and you will find few churches ascribed to the period 1350–1400. The reason was bubonic plague, known in this manifestation as the Black Death. Spreading from China across Europe it entered England at Weymouth in 1348. By the autumn of 1349 it had killed between a third and a half of the population; whole villages were destroyed, the manorial system broke down and there was not enough labour for essential production, let alone non-essential building.

The most important Gothic phase, the Perpendicular, came with the fifteenth century. It was dominant for 300 years, and more British churches bear this label than any other. The style takes its curious name from the outlines of arches and windows; in the earlier Gothic these are more curved, in the Perpendicular the verticals go straight up and only begin to curve inwards near the top of the arch. This small difference provides the distinguishing names of the later Gothic, but the changes that followed the dismal standstill of the Black Death went far beyond it. The new capitalists and the new craftsmen lavished money and talent on churches across the land. From the West Country and the Cotswolds to East Anglia and northwards, the fifteenth- and sixteenth-century churches are not merely magnificent but full of inventive artistry. Where the plentiful stone of Somerset and Gloucestershire was not available, as in East Anglia, the outpouring craftsmanship was diverted into woodcarving.

Perpendicular is the most truly British style in church architecture. It is the ultimate achievement of the Gothic builders and throughout the countryside their noble towers and soaring spires, often rooted in some quite small community, have proclaimed the measure of that achievement down the centuries. Other styles were to come, notably the Classicism of the late seventeenth and eighteenth centuries. The pillared, porticoed and steepled churches which were part of Wren's rebuilding of London developed more as an urban style in England, though in Scotland the Classical period coincided with a major churchbuilding era and many fine Classical churches are found in rural areas there. Classicism in England found full expression in domestic architecture, with every landowner wanting a Palladian mansion, and such Georgian churches as showed the same influence were often the work of architects whose reputations—and fortunes—had come from satisfying them. The fine church of St Peter and St Paul at Blandford, Dorset, was the work of John Bastard, one of a family of architect builders famous for their country houses. This church, incidentally, was the subject of some really brilliant alterations by the Victorians, who in 1893 moved the sanctuary, on rollers, to new foundations and inserted a chancel. At Hardenhuish, Wiltshire, the little church of St Nicholas is also the work of a man bred in the Classical style, John Wood of Bath, who, in that city, built the then unique Royal Crescent and the Assembly Rooms. The Hardenhuish church is a rarity, with a domed tower and Venetian windows of clear glass, all beautifully proportioned.

The nineteenth century saw the Gothic Revival, which produced so many great buildings, sacred and secular, under the influence of a visionary genius like Augustus Pugin and so much rubbish from lesser architects. It was a tremendous century for building churches, but one feels that the builders who looked steadfastly back to the best of the Middle Ages were the ones who really justified all that outpouring of energy and stone.

Building materials

The design of churches, like that of cottages and castles, was always affected by the availability of materials. Before the canals and the turnpikes the builders had little hope of getting heavy freight from a distance—like the farmer, trader, craftsman and housewife they had to make do with local products. The exceptions were a river or sea route, or work of special importance justifying a special effort. The latter might apply to a cathedral or an abbey but not to a village church. There was no question there of ordering stone from a distant quarry or sawn timber from a far off mill.

Stone was the most important material, and the most useful and easily worked variety was limestone. It occurs in a great belt from Yorkshire down through the east Midlands and the Cotswolds into Wiltshire and Somerset; all these have magnificent churches with a lavish use of stone in every way. Some of this limestone was transported by river to Cambridgeshire and Huntingdonshire, but most of East Anglia was chronically short of stone in the Middle Ages. One form of limestone known as Kentish Rag was shipped across the Thames into Essex as well as being extensively used in Kent, Surrey and Sussex, but it is very hard and was used more for facing stone than for detailed sculpture.

West of the limestone belt you will find many churches of warm-tinted sandstone in the counties of Cheshire, Shropshire, Herefordshire, Warwickshire and Worcestershire. Sandstone is very easily worked and there is a temptation to execute very intricate carvings. Unfortunately it weathers badly, and sandstone churches sometimes look older than they really are.

East Anglian churches reflect the variety of local materials used as substitutes for worked stone. Some are brick-built, and this continues a Saxon tradition, though the Saxons collected bricks from Roman ruins instead of making their own. Timber is widely used in East Anglian churches, which often have timber porches of great age. The standard of medieval woodcarving is high and its sheer quantity and variety is remarkable. Roofs were often thatched, as befitted corngrowing country where not more than a handful of dwellings in a village were roofed in any other way.

Perhaps the most widely used material was flint, found wherever there was chalk. In Norfolk the flint mines known as Grimes Graves supplied the Neolithic tribes with axeheads and were still furnishing materials for the flint-knappers who, up to 1914, were kept in business by the flintlock muskets used in Africa. Building true walls and towers of knobbly, multi-shaped flints is a considerable art, and in what is known as 'flushwork' it reached extraordinary perfection. Flushwork uses 'knapped' flints—cracked open down the middle to expose smooth, black surfaces—in conjunction with a certain amount of dressed stone. The latter forms the outline of patterns and designs which are filled in with the flints, the whole producing a level finish in varying shades and often elaborate patterns and tracery. Perhaps nothing to be found in the parish church speaks so clearly of the patience and dedication of the true craftsman.

Churchyards

Country churchyards are almost as worthy of study as the churches themselves, but the casual visitor usually scampers through the churchyards in his haste to look round the church and so misses a lot of accumulated history.

The churchyard we see today, if it is an old one, will have changed its appearance completely since the days when the church was built. Sometimes the churchyard is older than the church and has been a pagan burial ground. In the Middle Ages it was often a place of assembly, like the village green; fairs and markets were held in it and the popular game of 'fives', a form of handball later confined to public schools, would be played against the church walls.

The ground level reflects the age of the burial ground. The base of the church walls and the path encircling them may be lower than the burial area and the north side of the churchyard lower than the south. Occasionally the south side is raised quite a lot above an adjoining road, giving the impression of a deliberate embankment, but in reality this is due to centuries of burials one above another. Kenneth Lindley, author of *Of Graves and Epitaphs,* has pointed out that with only six burials a year a twelfth-century churchyard would by now have received some 4,800 interments, enough to produce a very substantial rise in the ground level. The south side will contain more graves, and the oldest ones—people objected to being buried on the north side where the shadow of the church fell across their graves, for the Devil lurked in shadows and approached from the north. So only when the southern parts of the churchyard were unbearably crowded was the remainder brought into use.

It must be remembered that conditions of burial in the past were very different to those of today. Until the seventeenth century there were no headstones to obstruct the digging of fresh graves. Clerics might be buried inside the church under a memorial slab, and by the thirteenth century important laymen were accorded the same privilege and began the fashion of canopied tombs and recumbent effigies, but the common people rested without memorial. Nor were they buried in coffins, but merely wrapped in a sheet or shroud. This became a matter of economic importance in 1678 when an attempt was made to revive the declining wool trade by passing an act compelling everyone to be buried wrapped in woollen cloth under a penalty of a £5 fine. This remained the law until 1814. As to the funeral arrangements of these humbler members of the community, the body would be carried to the churchyard in the parish coffin, from which it would be removed at the last moment.

Apart from the general layout of the older country churchyard there are a number of items of special interest that one should keep a lookout for.

Crosses An obviously ancient cross with no memorial inscription may be as old as, or even older than, the church. Crosses were erected by the earliest missionaries to these islands to serve as reminders and rallying points for their converts and they continued to be used to mark a gathering place for the community. An example of this is the number of market crosses to be found in old towns, the cross being a location for holding meetings, reading proclamations and transacting business. The village without a market place would have its cross in the churchyard or possibly on a burial ground before the church was built.

The oldest crosses are Anglo Saxon, with broad, elaborately carved shafts, though very few of these are left. Some medieval crosses have deep niches in their shafts, as in one at Great Malvern, Worcestershire. There is no good explanation of the purpose of this feature. The Celtic cross, with the arms enclosed in a circle, is usually early, and so is the curious lantern cross.

Yew trees The yew is more commonly seen in the churchyard than any other tree, it is a longlived species and some of the gnarled and twisted specimens to be seen are obviously old. Various explanations for the number of churchyard yews have been advanced; it is said to be a funereal tree like the cypress, or a symbol of immortality because of its longevity. It was useful, in that branches of yew were often carried in Palm Sunday processions when green boughs were hard to come by. Edward I is supposed to have ordered its planting around churches to reduce structural damage from wind, though in view of its low maximum height, its windbreak value for a large building would be very limited.

The famous yews in Painswick (Gloucestershire) churchyard. Many churchyard yews are probably remnants of the medieval armaments industry, planted to ensure timber for the deadly longbow (*MERL*)

Lych gate of Flowton church, Suffolk (*Rev. R. W. Francis*)

Almost certainly its planting in the thirteenth and fourteenth centuries was encouraged by government, not for the structural protection of churches but as an essential part of the armaments industry. The decisive weapon in the French wars was the English longbow, which was made of yew. This wood was also imported from Spain in some quantity but homegrown supplies were a vital insurance, as great a cause for concern then as the supply of oak for the navy was to become later. The training of archers devolved upon the local authorities and so no doubt did the planting of yews. The churchyard would be a suitable site for a tree which is poisonous and not to be dotted around where the wandering cattle of the commons might nibble it. Many of the churchyard yews seen today may well have been planted at this time and are by now only middle-aged. The lifespan of the species is 1,000–2,000 years.

Lych gates This type of covered churchyard gateway is fairly common, but few lych gates older than the seventeenth century now exist, and most of the older ones have been extensively restored. the open timberwork of the sides, exposed to wind and rain, is unlikely to last for many centuries.

The purpose of the lych gate was to enable a coffin to be set down on a stone or wooden table while part of the burial service was read. It provided shelter for bearers and mourners who might well have walked a long way in bad weather.

The word *lych* is Old English for a dead body, and this is its only surviving use. The wake—the watching over the dead—was once known as a 'lych-wake' and the route along which the dead were taken for burial as a 'lych-path'. These footpaths were closely followed and the funeral procession did not stray because wherever a corpse was carried a new public right of way would be created.

Watch boxes A construction resembling a sentry box may be found in some churchyards, recalling a very odd black market that flourished in the late eighteenth and nineteenth centuries. The development of systematic medicine, and the fact that dissection of human bodies was illegal, led to a brisk trade in subjects obtained by grave-robbing. The 'resurrection men' did so well out of their nocturnal activities that many burial grounds were guarded from dusk to dawn by armed volunteers to stop the desecration of fresh graves. Not all watch boxes conformed to the simple open-fronted, sentry-box pattern, some were more like miniature forts or blockhouses with windows commanding a view of the graveyard. Body-snatching gradually became more hazardous, even in lonely and isolated churchyards. In Edinburgh Messrs Burke and Hare found it easier to kill than to dig, but after selling at least fifteen victims in 1827–8, Hare turned king's evidence

The sexton at Fairford church in 1916 (*MERL*)

and Burke was hanged. Doctors and hospitals thereafter became very wary over their purchases and the resurrection business faded away.

Gravestones Headstones earlier than the seventeenth century are very rare. The oldest ones are short and solid, with inscriptions usually on the east-facing side only. By the eighteenth century the headstone had become more elaborate, with many variations in outline, longer and better executed inscriptions and decorative scrollwork. On late eighteenth-century stones the influence of Thomas Chippendale and the Adam brothers is often visible. Monumental masonry was becoming a craft in its own right and the masons were adopting ideas from great designers in other fields.

Flat slabs known as ledger stones were among the earliest outdoor memorials, but were apt to sink and become overgrown with turf. There was a renewed interest in large and heavy ledger stones, however, during the body-snatching epidemic when some of them were covered with a heavy iron grill.

Table tombs or altar tombs were first used in the church, but later outside. The name describes their appearance, though this has changed with time. Many early ones consisted of a stone slab supported on four, squat, stone legs, later the sides were filled in to give plenty of scope for decoration and inscriptions. Table tombs are to be found everywhere, but they did seem to become locally fashionable in some areas. There is a surprising concentration of them at Painswick, Gloucestershire, famous for its church clipping ceremony. A variant of the table tomb is to be found in the Cotswolds, especially around Burford. This has a curved corrugated top and at first sight makes one think of a Nissen hut. It is known as a 'bale tomb' and the top is said to represent a tightly bound bale of wool. This is likely enough and one more instance of the impossibility of forgetting the sheep when looking at Cotswold and East Anglian churches.

The use of the cross as a headstone was not widespread until the later nineteenth century. It is a simple and therefore cheap design and it helped to maintain the dignity of Victorian churchyards. The force of tradition in rural parishes also tended to keep things simple and to save the country churchyard from gesticulating angels and other excesses in Italian marble which were being mass produced to symbolise the status of the dead.

Old gravestones are usually made of some local material. Until a real transport system began to develop with the canals, the transport of stone was impracticable, though a little came south from Yorkshire by sea. Oxfordshire and Gloucestershire had their own soft Cotswold stone; North Wales and parts of the Midlands have many fine and almost inde-structible headstones in slate; the churchyard at High Easter in Essex has the remains of a memorial in oak. These wooden memorial boards were frequent in the seventeenth century in ares with no available stone.

Another alternative to stone was cast iron, and the presence of iron memorials in places now remote from industrial centres is of interest to the industrial archaeologist. They exist in Kent, Surrey and Sussex, cast in local foundries in the days when iron smelting in these counties was fuelled with wood from the forests of the Weald. Iron grave slabs may be seen inside the parish church of Wadhurst, Sussex, dating from as early as 1614, with others at Rotherfield and East Grinstead. A very intricate piece of casting imitating a carved headstone is at Brightling, also in Sussex. But the greatest concentration of iron monuments is centred on Coalbrookdale in Shropshire, where the ironmasters brought about the birth of the modern smelting industry. Castings from this district were quite widely distributed and there are excellent iron monuments, including cast table tombs, in the churchyard at Madeley, not far from Hereford.

Epitaphs

Memorial inscriptions are frequently the most interesting things in the churchyard, telling us as they do of the manners and mores of the past, but always in the context of a human story. Even the deliberately humorous epitaph has its inevitable aura of sadness.

Many good collections of epitaphs are in print, but they account for only a fraction of the inscriptions to be found in our thousands of churchyards. The choice of themes is wide, references to trade and crafts being one of them. Farmers are badly represented in this, their profession seldom getting a mention, but shepherds are often remembered. An epitaph to Samuel Horrell at Miserden, Gloucestershire, is typical of the pious hopes that the shepherd's calling seemed always to evoke.

> From youth through life the sheep was all his care,
> And harmless as the flock his manners were,
> On earth he held the faith to Christians giv'n,
> In hopes to join the fold of Christ in Heav'n.

Blacksmiths—or their next-of-kin—have everywhere appropriated some verse by the poet Hayley (1742–1820), a friend and biographer of Cowper and author of an amusing autobiography. The lines which have become a sort of blacksmith's requiem begin:

> My sledge and hammer lie reclined,
> My bellows too have lost their wind;
> My fire's extinct, my forge decayed,
> And in the dust my vice is laid . . .

Bellringers and town crier in the nineteenth century. The rosettes suggest they have won the contest (*MERL*)

With local variations the poem may be seen on blacksmiths' gravestones in many parts of the country.

There is nothing borrowed about the acid humour of one 'Robert Commonly Called Bone Phillip', buried at Kingsbridge, Devon:

> Here lie I at the Chancel door
> Here lie I because I'm poor
> The farther in the more you'll pay
> Here lie I as warm as they.

Many memorial inscriptions record awful and violent deaths, and if a moral could be drawn the mason was able to charge for a great deal of lettering. A very long and extraordinary example occurs not on a churchyard memorial but on the market cross at Devizes, Wiltshire.

On Thursday the 25th January 1753, Ruth Pierce of Potterne in this county, agreed with three other women to buy a sack of wheat in the market, each paying her due proportion towards the same. One of these women, in collecting the several quarters of money discovered a deficiency, and demanded of Ruth Pierce the sum which was wanting to make good the amount. Ruth Pierce protested that she had paid her share, and said that she wished she might drop dead if she had not. She rashly repeated this awful wish, when, to the consternation of the surrounding multitude, she instantly fell down and expired, having the money concealed in her hand.

On a different level to this cautionary tale, and giving sound technical advice, is an epitaph on three well-diggers at Marton, Yorkshire, who died after

> Venturing into a Well at Marton when it was filled by Carbonic Acid gas, or fixed air. From this unhappy accident let others take warning, not to Venture in Wells Without first trying whether a candle will burn in them. If the candle burns to the bottom they may be entered with safety; if it goes out human life cannot be sustained.

This warning was given in 1812 and was much needed. Well digging was a vital occupation in rural areas where piped water supplies were virtually unknown until the present century. In the deeper wells many fell victim to carbon dioxide through lack of even such rudimentary precautions as the coalminers employed against methane.

Contrasting with the very explicit epitaph is the briefly uninformative as at Old Dalby, Leicestershire:

> 1835 Henry Wells who was killed

And the slightly ambiguous, like this Edinburgh inscription:

> Erected to the Memory of
> _____
>
> John McFarlane
> Drown'd in the Waters of Leith
> _____
>
> By a few affectionate friends

The exploring visitor will find in many a churchyard inscriptions that tell much of the place and its people. But one thing must be said. Do remember that the burial ground of the parish church, however great its historical interest, is to be treated with no less reverence than the church itself. In some country churchyards well off the beaten track, it is not impossible to share the feelings of Francis Kilvert when he came out of church on Easter Sunday into the sunlit peace of the Wye valley.

> When all the people had left the Church and no-one remained but the Clerk putting away the sacred vessels I walked alone round the silent sunny peaceful Churchyard and visited the graves of my sleeping friends . . . There they lay, the squire and the peasant, the landlord and the labourer,. . . the infant of days beside the patriarch of nearly five score years, sister, brother by the same mother, all in her breasts their heads did lay and crumble into their common clay. And over all she lovingly threw her soft mantle of green and gold, the greensward and buttercups, daises and primroses. There they lay sleeping well and peacefully after life's fitful fevers and waiting for the great Spring morning and the General Resurrection of the dead.

To us it has a morbid inflection, but Kilvert's village parishioners in the 1870s would have understood well his simple faith and his awareness of God in nature. To him the green and gold mantle of spring vegetation over the graves had as clear a message as the vestments he had just left in the church. And, as one is in such places, he was conscious of the uncounted generations beneath his feet, having no memorial but laid to rest century after century in that same faith that here was holy ground and that in the end all would be well.

Tithes and tithe barns

A tithe was a form of local taxation for the upkeep of the Church and the financing of its services to the community. King Offa made its payment compulsory in Mercia in 794 and by the end of the tenth century it was compulsory everywhere. It was in theory paid to the rector of a parish, but he might be an individual priest or a monastic foundation. With the destruction of the monasteries it was likely to go to whomsoever the king had granted their lands. In the Middle Ages it was the recognised source of relief for the poor, but later the proportion of it allocated to this purpose varied with the circumstances and consciences of the clergy.

Payment was made in kind, one tenth of the annual produce of the land and one tenth of the annual increase in livestock. No-one with land was exempt; even if a farmer deliberately let land lie fallow he was still liable for a payment based on what it might reasonably be expected to produce. Collection was enforced under a range of penalties extending even to excommunication.

Overleaf: Tithe barn, Lenham, Kent (*Lionel E. Day*)

The assessment of the amount due from every crop, flock and herd was a time-consuming process at best, at worst it caused endless friction and ill-feeling. Where payment was made to an incumbent who lived among his parishioners and valued good relations with them, disagreements could be settled amicably, but if the tithe-holder were a distant abbot or bishop, or a pluralist parson who claimed the revenues from several parishes and doled out miserable pittances to curates who did the work, the results of the system could be deplorable.

The inherent physical difficulties from the Church's point of view are obvious. The size of the surviving tithe barns, which we now admire, indicates the storage space that had to be provided. Add to this the wagons, horses and stabling, threshing floors for the grain and facilities for dealing with all the odd lots of cattle, sheep, pigs and poultry, and one can see that the clergy did not get their tenth without a good deal of toil and trouble. Then there were the unusual and perishable items and the problems of their disposal or immediate use. In many fishing villages, for instance, the incumbent was entitled to a tenth of every catch—and how many clergymen today could cope with *that* situation?

It is natural to assume that the whole archaic system ended with the Middle Ages, but the astonishing thing is that it remained the law of the land until 1936, when the Tithe Commutation Act finally legalised payment in cash. Long before then the various parties had sought ways of simplifying it; there might, for instance, be an agreement to convert the many bits and pieces into a single commodity, as in a case at Drayton Basset in Staffordshire where one tithe-payer discharged his entire debt in cartloads of wood. By the late eighteenth century the common lands were being enclosed, the seed drill and the horse-hoe were in use and modern farming was on its way. Men who had fought Enclosure Acts through Parliament and backed their ideas on agricultural improvement with huge capital investment were not going to waste time and labour on setting aside every tenth load of turnips and every tenth piglet in the litter for the parson. In many cases they made a once-for-all settlement by giving land to the parish church and in effect telling the parson to grow his own crops.

Church land, known as 'glebe-land', already existed in many parishes, and in Scotland the manse was occasionally known as the glebe-house. Many of the clergy farmed their land efficiently and the work gave them a link with the community, a common interest in weather and prospects, a mutual understanding which quarrels over tithes had at times eroded. It must be remembered that, up to the Reformation, the tithe was widely regarded as 'God's portion', that part of the fruits of the earth set aside for the Church to administer in the relief of poverty and suffering. As such it was widely accepted, however bitter the individual disputes. It became the

Tithe distraint protest in 1935 (*MERL*)

cause of estrangement between the farmer and parson only when it was seen to be devoted solely to the latter's stipend. Especially in periods of agricultural depression.

Although quite a few incumbents farmed their own acre of glebe and so shared, with spiritual profit, the trials of many of their parishioners, the farming parson's lot was not always an easy one. Some might think he had unfair advantages, like the West Country farmer who complained to the Bishop that 'parson always claps on the prayers for rain the minute he's got his hay in' to the detriment of those still in the middle of haymaking. More seriously, the nineteenth-century Church increasingly disapproved of farmer-parsons, preferring them to be socially set apart from all but a minority of their flocks. As the Bishop of St Asaph put it in 1803: 'The clergy should be kept apart from those occupations which would degrade them from the rank they ought to hold in Society, and mix them in familiar habits with the inferior orders. . .'. He spoke with horror of the country curate who 'will wield the scythe and the sickle, he will fodder the kine and help to throw out the dung upon the land'.

The widening separation of the country clergy from any close involvement in the very basis of country life did nothing to help in the continued wrangling over tithes. The Act of 1836 abolished the now unworkable collection of tenths and substituted cash payments based on the land's estimated potential production of corn. Farming was then moving into a period of great prosperity and farmers paid up, albeit grumblingly.

With the onset of depression at the end of the century, resistance to the tithe became widespread and bitter, but the profitable war and postwar years that followed 1914 temporarily smothered it.

In the deeper depression of the 1930s the old resentments boiled over. Many farmers were unable to pay the levy, others said they were Nonconformists or had no religious beliefs and why should they support the Church of England when they were faced with ruin? Distraint orders on stock and equipment were followed by forced sales to pay the debts. The auctions became the scenes of demonstrations, packed with farmers who made only derisory offers for the goods, knowing that outsiders would not bid against them. At the end they would hand everything back to the original owner and the authorities might be left with barely enough to cover the expenses of the sale.

The long history of tithe now entered upon its last phase. In 1936 the Government abolished the tithe-owners' rights and gave them in compensation a Tithe Redemption Stock paying a 3 per cent interest. The tithe-payers contribute to the redemption annuities of the stock through a tax collected by the Inland Revenue. They pay less and the owners get less, but the latter's income is guaranteed. In 1996, the redemption date, all these payments will cease and, almost exactly 1200 years after King Offa first made it compulsory, tithe will be among the things of yesterday.

Before long only the remaining tithe barns will remind us of the days when Holy Church operated one of the most complex taxation systems ever devised. As so often happens, the craftsmen have left us a window on the past and through it we may glimpse the priest gathering God's Portion from the peasant's strip-fields, and all the subsequent troubles that ended the barn's original function.

5 Communications

The ways along which people and goods have moved from place to place have done much to change the look of the countryside. Some are new features in the landscape, some are very, very old, and all of them, roads, railways and canals, have in their time affected the lives of country people, whether by physical impact on their surroundings, or by the slow breaking down of village isolation and the destruction of village crafts and trades by the freer distribution of factory products.

For the greater part of our history communications improved very little; often they worsened for long periods. With OS maps and a little imagination we can recreate most phases of the story. We can walk for miles along the tracks used by men of the Bronze Age and follow the roads that sustained the military dominance of Rome; we can admire medieval bridges and trace the packhorse trails along which the 'golden fleece' of the flockmasters was borne to the ports; we can find the last tollhouses of the turnpike roads still in existence, and stay the night at inns which were bustling centres of activity when the stagecoach gave people their first taste of speedy overland travel; we can enjoy the peace of a newly cleared canal, and wonder at what manner of men scooped out thousands of miles of these great ditches by sheer muscle power; or we can note the magnitude of some railway cutting or embankment and imagine with what bewilderment the folk of a century ago must have watched the immemorial face of the land being reshaped before their eyes.

Roads

Before the Romans came, according to G. K. Chesterton, a rolling English drunkard made the rolling English road. It seems a fair assumption to anyone who has sought an unfamiliar village in an inadequately signposted part of East Anglia or the West Country, but the pre-Roman settlers are not to blame. The meandering minor roads are much more recent in origin; like all roads they have a story to tell but it is often as difficult to follow as the directions of the local populace when the land was denuded of signposts during the last war.

The smaller country roads do not wriggle over the map out of a perverse desire to cram in as many miles as possible between A and B. They behave like this because of their history and if you take the trouble to investigate their errant ways you will discover that the apparently pointless twists and turns are clues to changes in the landscape. That mile-long loop that goes nowhere once skirted a piece of woodland long since felled. The sudden change of direction when all the land ahead is flat and open was to avoid a peat bog now drained and cultivated. And the road that runs aimlessly beside the river until it finds the bridge is making for the ford that was once the only crossing—the bridge was built there later because the road was there already.

Prehistoric roads

The first roads were tracks linking late Stone Age and Bronze Age settlements. As more settlements sprang up the mileage of linking tracks naturally increased, but one must think of these ancient ways as fanning out in all directions. The settlements were on the uplands, on the Downs and the high moorlands, and the trackways followed the highest ridges of these uplands, keeping to the watersheds which drained naturally in wet weather, and avoiding the forested, trackless valleys. There is a temptation to speculate on why these scattered primitive communities should have trodden out great trunk highways like the Jurassic Way, which crosses the land from the Humber to the Severn, or the Icknield Way, which links the West Country with the shores of the Wash. But of course they were not planned as long-distance routes, they grew by extension as the farms and fortified villages spread over more and more of the uplands where there was land clear of trees to be cultivated.

Occasionally the trackways left the highest ridges and ran along the lower escarpments of the chalk hills, though always keeping above the forests that covered most of the land. One such follows the southern escarpment of the North Downs and is popular with modern walkers who know it as the Pilgrims' Way and perhaps meditate on the pious folk who made it a route to Canterbury. However, it was trodden by other pilgrims also, three thousand years before Becket was canonised in 1172. These pilgrims were not bound for Canterbury but for Salisbury Plain and Stonehenge. If the Neolithic people had a cultural and religious centre it was based on those great stones and many of the ancient trackways of southern England seem to converge on the plain.

A few instances of prehistoric roadworks have survived; causeways of brushwood and split logs have been dug up in Somerset peat areas where they originally crossed marshland and connected two lengths of upland track. The wooden trackway crossed the swamps forming a barrier between the Mendips and the Polden Hills and it is thought that many of the Somerset 'green lanes' started as timber-surfaced tracks about 3ft wide.

A short stretch of metalled prehistoric road was uncovered at the entrance to an Iron Age fortified settlement at Oldbury, Kent. It was made up of broken stone, laid at the point where traffic in and out of the camp apparently reached its maximum and the track was likely to become impassable. This short stretch of Iron Age road is in line with an existing farm track, which itself marks the ancient parish boundary. Since boundaries were often marked by roads it seems that this prehistoric highway may have remained in use until a few centuries ago.

Roman roads

In Britain, the Romans not only made the first true roads, they planned their trunk routes for definite purposes—usually military—and they built different types of road to serve different needs. Having established a main network radiating from London they added many paved secondary roads in the more populous areas of Kent, Sussex and East Anglia.

The completed road consisted of a central metalled part and on either side wide verges bounded by ditches—a basic pattern for all time. The attention paid to drainage shows that the Romans had no illusions about the British climate and its inhibiting effects on movement. The garrisons at Colchester, Chester, the Wall, along the Welsh Marches and in scores of other fortresses were never left without reinforcements because relieving cohorts were stuck in the mud. And where troops could go dry-shod, so could civilians—far more easily in the third century than in the seventeenth when even main highways were no more than rutted patchworks of local effort.

Later roads

After the Romans there was no more thought of a national integrated road system until the motorway era. Or, rather, there was sometimes thought of it but never effective action.

Country life became localised and fell into the pattern of self-sufficient communities, which explains so much of our rural past right up to the present century. Villages needed interior roads or tracks between farm or house and field, and to the church and the mill and other key points. The road to the next village was less important and that to the nearest large town less important still.

The drove-roads were as indispensable in the supply of meat as the saltyways were in its preservation. They were the roads along which cattle were taken from breeding areas such as Wales and Scotland to the rich pastures of the Midlands, or as fat cattle to the towns for slaughter. From the sixteenth century onwards, especially with the growth of urban populations and the demand for fresh meat, the traffic increased. The cattle moved at their own pace, grazing as they went. Journeys were a leisurely matter of days or weeks and the condition of the stock on delivery was more important than the time factor. The drove-roads were much wider than any other type of track, as they provided grazing for hundreds of cattle during the droving season.

Drove road in Monmouthshire (*MERL*)

The turnpikes

By the time of Elizabeth I the amount of passenger traffic on the roads was increasing with the urge towards physical and spiritual travel that came with the Renaissance and the greatest problem was the maintenance of such roads as existed, a problem which no-one since the Romans had seriously attempted to tackle. An Act of 1555 put the onus of road repair on the parish, and every ablebodied man, under the direction of the Surveyor of Highways, had to contribute a week's unpaid work annually to the task. The law was unenforceable and the roads stayed as they were. A new Act substituted paid labour for compulsory service, with the parish doing the paying. Reaction to this was equally hostile. If the road was kept in repair a lot of strangers would use it and why should local people pay for that?

The Turnpike Trusts were formed to get round this difficulty of finance. They were essentially local bodies, and had power to levy tolls on users of the highways under their control, applying the money raised to maintenance and improvement of the roads. A 'turnpike' was in fact a fortified gateway and the roads were named after the gates, with their tollhouses and keepers, where payment had to be made for every vehicle and animal entering the next stretch of road. The tariff was usually nicely

A typical Roman road (*Cambridge University Collection*)

181

graded, from a coach-and-six down to a single sheep. Tollhouses were usually round or octagonal so that the keeper had windows facing up and down the road as well as towards his gate. Quite a few of these little houses remain, the only remains of the turnpike system surviving except for the tolls still charged at a few tunnels and bridges. It had a fairly long innings, the first Turnpike Act being passed in 1663 and the last road tolls being abolished in 1895. They were no more popular than any other form of payment for public services and in the early nineteenth century tollgate keepers in some country districts had a rough time at the hands of 'Rebecca's Daughters'. These protesters attacked tollhouses by night, usually dressed in female attire and seeking to fulfil the Biblical prophecy that the daughters of Rebecca should possess the gates of their enemies.

The turnpikes did nothing to change the landscape as motorways have and, indeed, few of them were entirely new roads. There was some re-routing in the eighteenth century but it resulted largely from the enclosures, the little local roads by which the peasants reached their strip fields being swallowed up by the new estates along with the fields themselves and a new highway being built beyond the enclosure boundaries. A wide detour with no town or village to justify it is a characteristic feature of an enclosure road.

The birth of modern roads

The turnpikes guaranteed some financial resources for making and mending roads but the technical means to use them effectively was lacking throughout the eighteenth century. Long-distance travel increased without becoming much faster or less hazardous.

The real improvement came early in the nineteenth century, when Telford and McAdam achieved general acceptance of the roadmaking methods they had been preaching for years. Their ideas were far from original, they simply reverted to Roman ideas and improved on them, insisting that roads have a foundation of large stones and a metalled surface of small ones, sufficient camber to shed the rain and adequate drainage to carry away the run-off. All very obvious, but forgotten or ignored for fifteen hundred years.

Road improvement brought exciting changes to country districts on trunk routes. Postboys on ponies gave place to Royal Mail coaches which, with the sound of the posthorn warning of their approach and passengers and sometimes an armed guard aboard, would clatter through the village at previously unheard-of speeds. The mail coaches ran on schedules sometimes worked out to half a minute, but the guard's watch would be the final arbiter of a coach's punctuality, since nobody could guarantee the accuracy of the clocks at the stopping points. It is hard for us to appreciate how much local time must often have diverged from Greenwich Mean Time in the days before the electric telegraph made instantaneous communication possible.

Average speeds for coaches increased from five miles an hour to seven and even ten on flat routes like the London to Norwich. Time lost on a hilly stretch could be made up on a recognised 'galloping stage' when the coachman would 'let 'em out'. A vital factor in maintaining average speeds was the time taken in changing teams, and this was reduced to two minutes for a four-horse team. The fresh team would be ready in its harness—black with polished brass fittings and brown leather reins—the famous 'ribbons' which all young gentlemen itched to handle.

Inns in country towns and sometimes in villages were obvious choices for development as staging posts in the great expansion of coach travel that took place in the first quarter of the nineteenth century. Easily identifiable coaching inns are to be found in all parts of the country, often with stabling and outhouses still grouped around a cobbled courtyard. Sometimes the yard is entered under an arch or through a passageway, and occasionally it will be found that this entrance has been enlarged or heightened at some time in the inn's history to take larger coaches and those with outside passengers on top. Those intending to alight expected to do so within the precincts of the inn, not in the road outside, a sensible arrangement in view of the pickpockets and footpads who increasingly swarmed round coaching inns as the number of well-heeled travellers multiplied.

Really efficient long-distance travel by horsedrawn vehicles had a gloriously spectacular life but died young. It was indeed very nearly stillborn, for the canals were firmly established at its beginning and the railways had virtually replaced it by 1840. It ushered in a long period in which the horse became the short-haul extension of the railway, with private equipage almost a middle-class necessity and the cab-rank waiting at every fair-sized station. Coachbuilders had overcome many of the problems encountered in combining lightness with strength and their vehicles, from the two-horse, two-seater curricle for the madcap young, to the sedate and shining carriage of the dowager, ranked with farm wagons and farm machinery as the finest in the world. All the modern forms of powered transport were either introduced or perfected in the nineteenth century, yet to the countryman and to some townsfolk the horse was supremely important.

Despite their new solidity, country roads remained puddly in wet weather and appallingly dusty in summer. The general use of bitumen and asphalt surfaces—dubbed tarmacadam in memory of the great roadmaker—is quite recent. Sixty years ago most secondary roads would have looked quite normal to the Romans and repair was very much a matter of filling in holes with broken stone and gravel. Early motorists swaddled

The age of this post bridge on Dartmoor is not known (*Fox*)

Bridge over the River Tamar (*Western Morning News*)

themselves in veils and long coats against the dust-clouds, and even in the 1920s it was possible to stand on high ground and track the progress of a car along a distant road without being able to see the vehicle itself.

Of the motorways themselves one may say that they are not roads in the traditional sense. They pass through the countryside but are nowhere a part of it. They connect no small towns and villages, rather they avoid them. Access to them is limited, as is the type of traffic using them; they are no more roads than the railroad is a road, being virtually enclosed tracks for high-speed motor traffic between major built-up areas.

Bridges and other things

Bridges are not only essential to communications, they are often of historical interest and sometimes intrinsically beautiful, which is more than can be said of most roads. Unfortunately, just as the best thing to do with an ugly house is said to be to live in it, so the surest way not to see a bridge is to drive or even walk over it. To appreciate a bridge you must leave the road and look at it from the bank of the waterway which it spans.

The earliest type of bridge was probably a tree which could be felled so that it fell across the stream. This developed into the simple single-span foot-bridge and the origin of such bridges is still preserved in placenames. Trowbridge, in Wiltshire, could be named after a *treow* bridge, or tree-bridge, and in the same county there is the oddly named Pantry Bridge—almost certainly Pine-tree Bridge. In several parts of the country you will find towns and villages called Stockbridge, 'stock' meaning, among a host of other things, a treetrunk.

Stone packhorse bridges of a narrow and primitive kind are often found alongside the site of an ancient ford. The ford would provide the easier passage when the river was low and the bridge would keep the trail open when it was in flood. On Dartmoor, Exmoor and in parts of Cornwall, where some of these ancient, dateless bridges survive, they are known as 'clapper' bridges, from the medieval Latin *claperius*, a heap of stones. Some are indeed not much more than that and their survival for centuries is perhaps due to the fact that they are so easy to repair.

Signposts and milestones

Guideposts of one sort or another have existed for a long time, though the early ones were designed less to tell the traveller where he was going than to assure him that he was actually on a road. In the thirteenth century, for instance, granite crosses were put up to mark one of the safe tracks across Dartmoor. In the late seventeenth century local justices were ordered to set up signposts, but the order was usually ignored. Private individuals sometimes took over this civic responsibility and Nathan Izod's signpost has

Milestone on the Penzance–Zennor road (*John Topham*)

(*P. Racher*)

stood on Broadway Hill in the Cotswolds since 1669. At Bicton, in Devon, a square brick pillar dating from 1743 encourages the traveller with directions and biblical texts. In 1773 the Turnpike Trusts were finally ordered to equip their roads with both signposts and milestones. The tall fingerpost is an example of the persistence of traditional design and is still widespread on secondary roads. The benighted motorist climbing the post and striking matches to read the directions has been a familiar comic figure for more than a lifetime, but of course the signs were meant for stagecoach drivers and travellers on horseback. Within the last forty years it has dawned on the authorities that directional signs should be within range of the motorist's vision and the beam of his headlights. The result, like most things to do with modern roads, is aesthetically horrible.

The Romans set up milestones on a few major routes, and one may be seen in situ at Stanegate, in Northumberland. Several museums have quite good examples, including the British Museum.

Canals

Compared with roads these artificial waterways have but a brief history. It was one of sudden and explosive growth, less than a century of unchallenged importance, decline and demise.

The great age of 'inland navigation', as they called it, began when the third Duke of Bridgewater wanted to bring coal from his Lancashire pits at Worsley to Manchester. The Mancunians of 1760 were partially surrounded by coal which reached them only in expensive driblets on horseback, and the Duke proposed to revive an old idea of his father's and dig a canal from Worsley to connect with the river Irwell at Barton. From there the coal barges could sail to Manchester by the navigable Irwell–Mersey route.

At this point Bridgewater met James Brindley and the scene was set for the greatest outburst of canal-digging in history. Brindley, a crofter's son, was a millwright by trade; he was a mechanical engineer and he understood the management of water. He was actually surveying the line of a projected canal joining the Trent and the Mersey when the Duke engaged him to dig his own more modest 'cut'. Brindley, typically of the great engineers of his own and succeeding generations, was a man of powerful assurance and originality. He knew what should be done and whatever the apparent difficulties usually succeeded in doing it. His originality extended to his spelling, for he had little formal education. He reported to the Duke that he had carried out an 'ochilor survey or ricconitoring', and as a result of this the original plans were radically altered.

The canal for which Parliamentary approval had already been obtained would have needed a series of locks where it joined the Irwell at Barton, owing to its much higher level. Also, the barges would have had to pay the

The canal village at Stoke Bruerne, Northamptonshire. The pub was used by the 'boaters' when canal traffic was in its hey-day (*Roy J. Westlake*)

A stretch of the Macclesfield canal (*Leslie Bryce*)

Hazlehurst aqueduct on the Caldon canal after its restoration (*Leslie Bryce*)

Irwell and Mersey Company a navigation toll on every ton of coal carried. Brindley advised that the rivers should be bypassed, the canal itself being extended to Manchester and constructed all on one level, crossing the Irwell at Barton by an aqueduct.

The concept of a canal crossing a river on a bridge was received with some scepticism, and the great John Smeaton, then rebuilding the Eddystone Lighthouse, made snide remarks about 'castles in the clouds'. But Brindley completed his project, aqueduct and all, and the land was thereafter greatly changed.

The countryside was not ruined by the canal-builders. Far from it, for though in the pullulating industrial towns the waterways eventually became grimed and filthy, they remained clear and sweet in rural areas, great trade routes where traffic moved continuously at the gait of a horse, and waterfowl and fish made the highway their home.

The bright-painted narrow boats and plodding horses on the towpath, the lockkeepers' cottages, the navigation inns with their barge-horse stables, these things fitted into field and village once the upheaval of construction was past. The countryman benefited from cheaper transport of goods, manure from the towns was carried free of toll, and by 1782 the once barren fields along the banks of Brindley's Trent–Mersey canal (the Grand

The Grand Union canal at Blisworth (*Derek Pratt*)

Junction) were ecstatically described by a contemporary writer as being in consequence 'clothed with a beautiful verdure'.

Between 1760 and 1840 some 3,000 miles of canals were dug, as compared with the 1,500 miles of navigable rivers. This colossal feat of civil engineering was carried out with a minimum of damage to the environment, as modern canal cruisers and those working on their restoration can appreciate. Many of the constructions blend with the landscape or have their own superlative quality of design. Telford's great aqueduct at Pontcysyllte, bestriding the Dee valley on its nineteen slender legs and carrying the Llangollen canal in a cast-iron trough 1,000ft long, has been called the greatest monument in stone to the canal age, but several of Telford's works, as well as those of Brindley, Rennie and others, run it close in daring, technical skill and the ability to build on a large scale without blotting the landscape.

The boatmen
Waterborne traffic grew with industry and population and then slowly

declined in competition with the railways. As late as 1900 it was still quite important, the narrow boats plying on short hauls where their slowness was no great disadvantage. Now the canals have an increasing role in the enjoyment of leisure, providing quiet travel and time to savour fresh views of an everchanging landscape. Their commercial life appears to be over, but even this is not certain in times of permanent fuel shortage. It still requires less energy to move a load on water than on land.

Throughout their active life the canals had a permanent population of their own, bound to them in a quite peculiar way. No-one ever expected a railwayman to live on wheels, but the canal boat crews were born, lived, married and died on the waters of their trade. The traditional narrow boat is 70ft long by 7ft wide, and that combined cargo space with living quarters for a family. The static villagers of the nineteenth century came to accept these curious folk in much the same way as they did the gypsies, familiar yet a race apart, perpetually moving on to strange places.

The canal-boat people have passed into history and their successors who are bringing new life to the abandoned waterways have different usages and a different language. The old terms describing the working of locks and other technical matters are still in use, but most of the language is forgotten. In the Fenland a lockgate or paddle may still be called a 'door', but is a very narrow cut in the Trent area still called a 'nip' as it once was? In the West Country does anyone remember that boats were once towed by pairs of 'animals', the canal-name for donkeys? Or in Yorkshire that the hirers-out of towing-horses were the 'horse marines', or in the Lake District that 'gonzooglers' were idle shiftless landlubbers who stood around watching the boats go by?

Present and future

Some 500 miles of canal are still registered as commercial waterways and many thousands of tons of cargo are carried annually on this relatively small length, though the traffic is limited to the larger craft and broader cuts. If the canals ever again become economically viable freight carriers, it will have to be by the use of large barges and modern techniques such as pusher tugs.

For the moment, derelict canals represent an integral part of the countryside that was shamefully abandoned, a wasted asset. If the voluntary work done in clearing these silted, rubbish-filled, weed-choked, scrub-grown channels is inspired mainly by a desire to provide holidaymakers with clean, attractive waterpaths along which to travel, then the leisure business is doing a worthy job.

Restoration is now officially in the hands of the Regional Water Authorities and the Water Space Amenity Commission, but all official

A holiday boat on the Caldon canal at Hazlehurst after its restoration (*Leslie Bryce*)

bodies respond to pressure from voluntary organisations. In this connection the enthusiasm of the Inland Waterways Association is as vital as ever.

The scope and variety of inland cruising increases all the time. The traveller may choose between a peaceful 20 miles a day on Telford's Shropshire Union with its varied country and deep cuttings and, if at heart a saltwater man, the very different passage of the Caledonian canal.

Railways

The Railway Age brought rapid changes in the appearance of parts of the countryside and in the lives of some country people. The canals had initiated the type of change that comes with great engineering works and the improved transport of people and goods, but their effect was more limited and the tempo of the changes they brought slower than that of the railways. The canal network was wide-meshed and many places were never reached by it; the railways penetrated far afield and within forty years of the opening of the Stockton & Darlington line there were 13,000 miles of them.

Without the railways the Industrial Revolution, which necessitated the movement of vast quantities of raw materials, could never have taken off, and compared with the monstrous spawning of the new industrial areas the

The 'juggernaut progress' of railway building. Despite the anguish of Victorian environmentalists, the countryside has assimilated the railway and made it part of the rural scene

Country station at the turn of the century (*Locomotive and General Railway Photographs*)

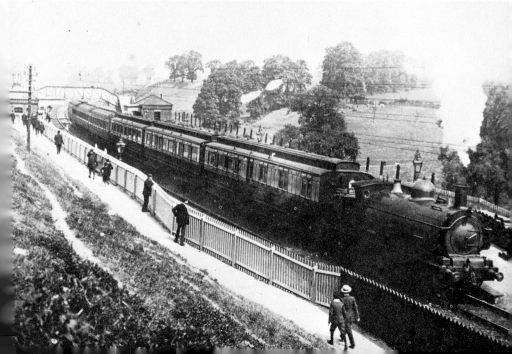

An express train passing a country station. Note the mixed gauge track (*Locomotive and General Railway Photographs*)

Electric train by the Grand Union canal. The two forms of transport that left the countryside relatively unscathed (*P. A. Dobson*)

changes that the railways brought to the countryside might seem trivial indeed. Remote towns and villages finding themselves suddenly on the line and the seat of a station no doubt found the social and economic effects dramatic enough, and the influence of these new centres of communication would spread slowly through the surrounding countryside: the faster movement of perishable produce, the delivery of new machines and tools from distant factories (to the detriment of the village smith), new consumer goods for the minority able to afford them. To the farm labourer, unable to afford even the cheap excursion that introduced industrial workers to the joys of travel, the railways made little difference during the nineteenth century. Later, they were to provide valuable alternative employment and in the depressions of the 1900s and the 1930s, many farmhands became railwaymen.

Apart from the economic consequences already referred to, the railway affected country life in two other ways worth mentioning. It changed the social character of many country districts, beginning the 'suburban sprawl' outward from the central city which has continued ever since, and in some instances it had dramatic effects on the landscape.

To the country-dwellers of the time this juggernaut-progress would have seemed either terrifying or inspiring, according to their temperaments. George Eliot, writing of railways in the Midlands, seemed to experience both emotions.

> There comes a crowd of burly navvies, with pickaxes and barrows, and while hardly a wrinkle is made in the fading mother's face, or a new curve of health in the blooming girls's, the hills are cut through, or the breaches between them spanned, we choose our level, and the white steam-pennon flies along.

We have to remember how things looked to the rural population of the time in evaluating the opposition to railways, for today, noting how inconspicuous they are, we may wonder what all the fuss was about.

6 Six Basic Crafts

There are certain skills without which the village, the rural community, simply could not have carried on. Those selected here may seem an arbitrary choice from among them, but they were essential to the supply of food, motive power and shelter.

Milling was a village industry until well into the last century and the processing of staple foods for man and livestock depended on the miller's expert manipulation of wind or water. This was surely more of a craft than a trade—the highly specialised business of millwrighting most certainly was, and many millers were also millwrights.

Without the blacksmith, the wheelwright and the harnessmaker, farming as we know it would have been impossible and road transport non-existent in the pre-motor era. And without the thatcher a large proportion of the humbler country homes would have been roofless, and harvested crops unprotected from the weather.

The universality of these crafts is evident in the countryside today and three of them, farriery, saddlery and thatching, are very much alive.

Windmills, millers and millwrights

A windmill is a very obvious feature in a landscape. It has a functional elegance that suggests a lighthouse and a sailing ship, and it always seems to be sited to produce the maximum visual effect.

The last idea is far from the truth. It was sited where it could be sure of catching some wind, therefore on reasonably high ground. Thus it was a sign from far off, and a community large enough to keep it at work would be grouped around it. The watermill, on the other hand, is usually invisible from a distance, tucked away in a valley near the lower reaches of a water-course. And just as windmills were ultimately more important in the dry, flat, or rolling lands of the south and east, so watermills became a more frequent source of power in the north and west. There were, and still are, more windmills in grain-growing areas because their use was mainly limited to the grinding of corn, though the Fens, under Dutch tutelage, set them to working pumps. But whereas the waterwheel could be used to drive all those types of machinery later powered by steam, the windmill was less structurally adaptable and dependent on an unreliable and intermittent motive power.

The vagaries of the wind could be neutralised by having some sort of auxiliary engine and no doubt this helped many mills to keep going well into the present century. The writer lives within shouting distance of a pair

Tower mill on the river Thurne, Norfolk. A small pumping mill (*Suzanne Beedell*)

of fine brick-built tower-mills, now without sails, standing a hundred yards apart on a ridge of high ground. Some way up the side of one of them a belt pulley projects, and to this, in periods of calm, the steam engine of a threshing tackle could be connected. Emergency milling of this sort was sometimes done at night, the threshing engine returning to its current job, perhaps on a farm miles away, at dawn.

It is not known when windmills were first erected in this country. The Domesday Book lists a great many mills, usually without specifying type. It nowhere mentions a windmill, but it does not follow from this that watermills were universal. Many mills at that time were worked by horses or oxen, others by men operating a sort of treadmill, while corn was still ground by the simple hand quern or mortar. Bread was the staff of life and corn must be ground; the windmill was a step in the mechanisation of that process, an industrial unit just big enough to cope with the produce, and supply the needs, of its own small area. The concentration of milling into fewer and larger set-ups began with better transport and was accelerated by the flood of imported grain into our ports in the 1870s. But windmills survived and carried on into the twentieth century and, indeed, were still being built in the nineteenth. When Stanley Freese wrote his classic *Windmills and Millwrighting* in 1957, he dedicated it to 'the last thirty

A Kent post-mill at Chillenden, the last to be built in the country. The sails have only skeleton shutters as the mill is not in use although all the machinery is there (*Suzanne Beedell*)

windmillers and millwrights who kept the sails turning'. Today one is hard put to it to find sails turning to any purpose, but thanks to the work of devoted enthusiasts enough fine specimens of the millwrights' craft have been preserved to make easy an understanding of their mechanism and of the millers' problems.

Post-mills These are the oldest type, the whole structure built around a central wooden pillar, usually of oak, having its base secured to a massive timber frame of horizontal 'cross trees' and 'trestle bars' or struts. The cross trees rest upon short piers of brick or stone, and this lowest part of the mill may have brick walls and be used for storage. The important part, however, is the boarded superstructure of two storeys carrying the sails and all the 'works', so made that it can be turned completely round about the central wooden 'post'.

The post-mill was an early attempt to answer two basic problems; how to make the structure stable enough to withstand wind pressures—which in a full gale might reach 50lb per square foot—and yet be capable of a swivelling motion so that the sails could always be kept facing into the wind. In the post-mill this requirement is met by the 'tail pole', a beam bolted to the floor of the revolving superstructure and projecting on the side opposite to the sails. It is a lever by which the mill is turned, sometimes by the miller himself, with his shoulders fitted into a sort of yoke (the traditional miller is a very strong man), sometimes by a horse or donkey, and sometimes by a winch and chain attached successively to a circle of chain posts placed around the mill.

Smock- and tower-mills Post-mills were largely superseded by smock-mills and tower-mills. The first is built of wood, the second usually of brick or stone. Tower-mills are circular in plan and smock-mills get as near to this as a wooden structure can by being octagonal or even twelve-sided. Both types have a pronounced 'batter', the sides sloping inwards towards the top, and only the topmost part, the 'cap', is moveable. The cap carries the sails; it usually has a domed or conical roof in the tower-mill, and it rotates like the whole body of the post-mill. In this design the mill can be made solid and stable, wind-resistance, especially in the tower-mill, is reduced to a minimum, and it can be built tall enough to have more than the two storeys of the post-mill and to house more elaborate machinery.

Another major improvement in design was an automatic device for luffing the sails—keeping them into the wind—and so easing the miller's work. This is the fantail, which you will notice projecting from the back of most smock- and tower-mills and some post-mills. It is a set of small sails at right angles to the main sails and driving a turning gear in the cap of the smock-mill or the body of the post-mill. The fantail is unaffected by the wind as long as the mill is facing directly into it, but as the wind shifts and acts less efficiently on the sails, so it begins to blow on the fantail. Working through a reduction gear of 2,000 to 1, it slowly turns the mill or, more likely, the cap, back to its proper position.

When the mill is in operation, the need to have the sails always facing into the wind can become more than a matter of mere efficiency. In sudden storms or squalls the wind may change direction by 180° and strike the backs of the sails if they cannot be turned quickly enough to face it. Then the mill is 'tail-winded' and may suffer a disaster similar to that of the sailing ship which is taken aback. Instead of the sails being pushed towards the mill by the wind and, as it were, held in place by it, they are forced outwards. The great windshaft that carries them may be torn from its bearings and perhaps tilted upwards through the roof as the lowest sails are driven down against the sides of the mill or even into the ground. The entire cap may be wrenched loose from the lower storeys, and mills have sometimes been abandoned as total wrecks after being tail-winded.

Millstones in position but not in use. The stone dresser's tools lie on the stone (*Suzanne Beedell*)

The miller

His reputation in the rural community has not always been good, partly as a result of his monopoly position in medieval times when the lord of the manor was apt to sanction only one mill in the district. Then the old-fashioned system of payment by 'toll', with the miller taking a fixed proportion of the flour and meal he ground, led to endless disagreement. Even when it was replaced by cash payment, millers were always suspected of helping themselves to a few bowlfuls from every sack. So the miller was crafty and dusty and powerful, and his thumb was flattened from incessantly feeling the quality of his output. (Hence the name 'miller's thumb' for the little minnow-like fish with the flat head.) And he was much too successful with women, even—or especially—married ones.

In reality, the miller had to be a fairly dedicated tradesman, holding down a responsible job sometimes single-handed. In a long period of flat calm after harvest the villagers might be without flour. Perhaps they could manage on a reserve of barley meal or perhaps even that was gone and the squealing of hungry pigs would float up through the still air and emphasise the dependence of farm and village on the mill. It would be little use seeking help from neighbouring mills for all would be at a standstill.

200

The day of the village miller is over, but on many a farm you will now find a modern hammer-mill grinding the farmer's own cereals to mix with proteins and vitamin additives for livestock feeding. Thus, after long reliance on distant manufacturers, grain is once more being ground and consumed where it is grown.

Watermills

The watermill is a venerable piece of mechanisation which developed from the idea of grinding corn between a stationary wheel and a rotating one. This was first done by the women of the household in a hand-operated quern, then on a larger scale by animals and slaves. Watermills in this country almost certainly pre-dated windmills and were eventually put to many other uses than flourmilling.

About 6,000 watermills were recorded in the Domesday Book, including many in drier areas where the windmill eventually predominated. Lincolnshire, for instance, which became famous for its windmills, had at that time one watermill to every three villages. None of these mills would have produced more power than a small car engine, but in the aggregate they provided perhaps 40,000hp of mechanical energy in eleventh-century Britain and this total increased considerably with the development of the windmill.

We can still find some well preserved mills, and even a few in working order. Millhouses, and other reminders of the watermill's former importance, crop up everywhere. For instance, in the days when the iron industry in Sussex was burning up the last of the great forests of the Weald, many of the forges had water-powered trip hammers, and Abinger Hammer is but one Sussex placename among many to recall the Tudor ironworks that reddened the south-country sky.

As new industrial centres and industries came to the Midlands and the North, water power grew in importance, driving textile machinery, in woodworking shops, paper and copper mills, and for pumping. While the windmills kept to their traditional grinding, majestically obvious against the sky, watermills performed a hundred different jobs throughout the land, their great wheels creaking away in the valleys of innumerable streams. From the cloth-stamping mills of Devon and Cornwall, to the gunpowder mill in Kent and the metal-working machinery of Sheffield, it was water that gave strength to the infant Industrial Revolution.

Smaller mills on fast-flowing mountain streams, known in Scotland as 'tirls' and in Cumbria as 'clicks', performed humbler duties such as working the blacksmith's bellows and turning large butter churns. A tirl at Shawbost, Isle of Lewis, may be seen working today, having been restored by schoolchildren in 1970.

Steam, of course, ousted the waterwheel, but the struggle was a long one. The largest wheel ever built in Britain, 'The Lady Isabella' (72ft in diameter) at Laxey in the Isle of Man, dates from 1854. It was erected to pump water from a depth of 600ft in a leadmine, but is now an awe-inspiring tourist attraction. To realise that Lady Isabella first began turning when steam was already well established is like finding an ancient mill building beside quiet waters in a village and discovering that a mill on this same spot was recorded in the Domesday Book. Such things bring home the length of time that water-powered machinery has existed in Britain and remind one that the roots of modern industry are to be found in the countryside.

For the greater part of its history the waterwheel was built of wood. The wooden axletree was about 18in square, and the problem of transmitting the thrust from the rim, where the pressure of water was applied, to the axle and the heavy machinery which it drove, was solved by the use of 'clasp arm' spokes. Had the spokes been simply mortised into the axletree as the spokes of a wagon wheel are mortised to the hub, the strain on these joints would have been very great. So, just two pairs of spokes were employed on each side of the broad wheel, each pair clasping two sides of the axletree and the pairs set at right angles to one another. Thus all four sides of the axletree were enclosed by the spokes. The construction may look clumsy, but it eliminated any possible weakness at the point of greatest strain. There were no joints at the centre, the spokes were strong continuous timbers spanning the diameter of the wheel.

One of the most interesting subjects of study at any watermill, or even at the site of one long vanished, is the way in which the designers chose their ground and laid out the watercourse to ensure the essential 'fall' of the water which represented its kinetic energy. Drought, especially in the eastern counties, was a perpetual menace, and the millpond—that symbol of placidity—was used to dam and store available water and release it in sufficient quantity to turn the wheel. Water had a clear advantage over wind in this business of storage—the windmill had to await an adequate breeze, it could not accumulate desultory puffs for future work as the watermill's pond stored the daily trickle. In wet and hilly country with unfailing streams the millpond was naturally less common.

The waterwheels still to be seen are of two main types. In one the water passes below the axle, acting on the paddles nearest to the sluice. This is the 'undershot' wheel, the easiest to construct and probably the oldest. In the 'overshot' type the sluice carries the water over the top of the wheel and projects it on to the paddles on the far side. The overshot is mechanically

Alfreton watermill and its miller, 1939. A few watermills are still in use (*MERL*)

the more efficient but requires a greater 'head' of water, whether from a fast-flowing stream or from damming. It will be noted that the undershot and overshot wheels have to turn in opposite directions.

We have been thinking of the watermill in the past tense and, in its traditional form, it is now little more than a very important part of our economic history. In its newer guises it is still important; the Scottish hydro-electric schemes have brought many changes to the Highlands, and the projected Severn Barrage, should it ever take shape, will be only a gigantic tide mill.

The village smithy

It still exists, for the craft of the smith has survived even though he is no longer the important rural personage he was up to a couple of generations ago. Nowadays he is part of a leisure industry, shoeing horses for riding and the developing hobby of driving. He has to spread his activities far beyond a single village and frequently operates a mobile workshop. Other smiths carry on traditional wrought-iron work such as the production of garden gates, and craftsmen as good as any in the past are to be found among them.

Reference to these two aspects of the blacksmith's craft reminds us of a distinction usually forgotten. A 'blacksmith' is really a worker in blackmetal, in other words iron, so called to distinguish it from the precious metals and the bronze which it began to replace 2,500 years ago. The smith who specialises in shoeing horses is properly called a 'farrier', though this word, too, probably derives from *ferrum*, the Latin for iron. A farrier was expected to be a horse expert and horse doctor as well as a shoeing smith, and cavalry regiments in the British Army recognised that he was in charge of the horses, coupling his trade with his rank, so that one could be a Farrier Sergeant. A blacksmith, on the other hand, might in theory not know one end of a horse from the other.

In practice, of course, the village smith usually had to exercise his craft in all possible ways and this made him a key figure in rural life. By the end of the last century he was essential in maintaining farm machinery and road transport, in mending and even making tools of all kinds and in providing vital ironwork for other crafts. He would be expected to hammer out ornamental curlicues for the squire's gates, forge a new link for a broken well-chain, or duplicate a fourteenth-century hinge on the church door. He must know how to handle an unmanageable horse and advise on the treatment of a sick one. By 1900 he was becoming a motor mechanic, not

Overleaf: A rare sight in 1955: horses waiting to be shod outside the blacksmith's forge at Crossthwaite, Westmorland (*Fox*)

Metal-working in a forge in Berkshire last century (*MERL*)

because he had any great affection for the newfangled horseless carriage but because he was the only man in the village who could be expected to understand machinery. In remoter places and extreme emergencies he functioned as dentist, employing his handier-sized pincers for extractions. (One smith is indeed reputed to have become so proud of his skill in dentistry that he displayed the notice 'Teeth extracted' in letters formed of the collected results of past extractions.) He might also be the parish barber, a subsidiary occupation which sometimes went to the cobbler or the harnessmaker. A smith named Alexander Fletcher, who worked at the Royal Smithy at Balmoral, was called in when one of Queen Victoria's guests, the Emperor Frederick of Germany, needed a haircut and no professional hairdresser could be found. The Emperor was probably lucky not to have needed a dentist.

Up to 1914, while the village retained much of its economic self-sufficiency, the smith, more than most local craftsmen, had to be a Jack-of-all-trades and master of several. The forge tended also to be a meeting place and central village news agency, always having its quota of legitimate customers and hangers-on. A sweaty, uncomfortable workshop in summer, where the reek of burning hoofs and coke fumes seemed to intensify the intermittent roar of the fire and the piercing clang of the hammer. But on a

An eighty-year-old blacksmith at work in Stone Allerton, Somerset, in 1950 (*Topical Press*)

winter's day, when thin wisps of snow spiralled in a freezing wind, it had its attractions. And if you had no horse to be shod you went to ask the smith's advice.

The blacksmith's role as an adviser and oracle—extending even to the conducting of a form of marriage over his anvil—derived from the mystique of smelting and working iron. The practical respect which a country community was bound to have for the blacksmith was reinforced by a certain subconscious awe of his craft, still to be seen in the accretion of legends and superstitions around the forge.

The modern craft

There are still horses to be shod, and indeed their number is growing. Wrought-iron gates and plant stands from craftsmen's workshops have a ready market.

The modern farrier chiefly uses mild steel bought in convenient bars. He may sometimes buy ready-made horseshoes in a variety of sizes, reshaping them to fit the individual hoof instead of forging each one separately from the bar in the traditional way. The term 'wrought iron' is often thought to describe finished forms of decorative ironwork, but may in fact apply to the raw material which is preferred to mild steel for this type of work as opposed to farriery. Wrought iron improves in texture with heating and hammering. Wonderfully delicate and complex shapes can be forged by the skilled smith, and all methods except forging are prohibited in true wrought ironwork. The metal may not be electrically welded, sawn, or bent when cold. Some of the basic designs in ironwork are very ancient. The earliest smiths discovered, for instance, that the beautiful spirals or 'volutes' like barley-sugar sticks, could be made by fastening one end of a flat bar of hot iron and twisting the other end.

Three basic items of equipment are common to the smiths of all ages: means of heating the iron enough to soften it, a solid surface on which to rest it when heated, and a hammer with which to shape it. The design of these things and of the many subsidiary tools has developed with accumulated experience and new resources.

The forge This is fundamental enough to be used as a synonym for the actual workshop or smithy. Scores of 'Old Forges' may be found in country towns, probably trading in teas, antiques, or even books.

The forge is an open hearth, raised to a convenient working level, surmounted by a canopy to carry off the worst of the fumes and sparks, and having a forced draught to raise the temperature level of the fire above that of ordinary combustion. The traditional bellows of our own smiths is worked by a lever; in some parts of the country it might have been worked by a waterwheel, but this gave less perfect control of the fire than hand operation.

The anvil The form known as the London anvil is the sophisticated end of a long evolution. Beginning merely as a solid base on which the iron could be hammered, the oddly-shaped anvil we know today was in general use by the nineteenth century. An anvil weighs from 1–3cwt and all its parts have a specific function. The flat upper surface on which most of the work is done is called the face; it is of hardened steel because the harder it is, the more vigorous the recoil of the hammer and the less the energy needed to lift it after each blow. Next to the face is the table, a narrow strip of softer iron or mild steel. On this is placed metal to be cut with a cold chisel, to ensure that the edge of the chisel will not be turned if it goes through the work and strikes the surface below. Beyond the table is the curious conical projection called the beak, or 'bick', designed for the shaping of curved objects, such as horseshoes, of varying sizes. At the opposite end to the beak is a small hole known as the punch-hole over which hot metal is placed when punching a hole in it, as in making the nail-holes in horseshoes. The punch goes through cleanly into the space beneath.

Tools The hand-tools of the smithy are numerous and of great interest to those fascinated by manual skills. Like the forge and the anvil they have developed from empirical observation and design. A smith would see what sort of tool was needed for a specific process and make it. Another smith would refine and improve it, or perhaps adapt a tool used in another craft. We cannot go into the uses of various tongs, pincers, buffers, flatters, hardies, rasps and hammers, for even the last simple object takes on many forms in the smithy. The farrier has a catshead (so called from its shape) for making shoes, and a shoeing hammer, which has a claw for withdrawing nails from the old shoe. For general ironwork there is the two-pound ball peen hammer, which has a head slightly rounded on one side, and a heavy sledge weighing up to 20lb. The smith may use the sledge himself or he may direct its use by his assistant. The forging is taken from the fire at the proper temperature as judged by its colour, manipulated on to the anvil with the tongs, and hammered into shape with all possible speed. The 'striker' wielding the sledge must do as much work as possible before the iron cools, the noise is considerable and verbal instructions from the smith may be replaced by a tap with his ball peen at the point where the next blow from the sledge is to fall. As a signal to the striker to stop his rhythmic swing he will tap the anvil himself and the clangour will cease.

Other fixed equipment in the smithy will be a mixture of ancient and modern. There will be a strong leg vice, bolted to the bench with its stem embedded in the floor; possibly a drill looking like a museum piece and another more modern electric job, and welding apparatus. Much depends on the needs of local customers; not many farmers are likely to be among them since modern farm machines are so complex that the local supplier or the manufacturer's field service will be summoned in case of a breakdown. But in a really dire emergency the smith who lives by children's ponies and garden gates can still do unbelievable things in the way of temporary repairs.

The horseshoe

The horse's hoof was not designed for the hard surfaces of metalled roads, for bearing greater weights than that of the animal itself, or for the strains imposed by traction. This gigantic toenail would soon be worn down to the sensitive quick without some sort of protection. The shoeing of horses and working oxen by nailing protective iron soles to the hoof was practised in Britain by the tenth century, and the village blacksmith, with farriery as one of his main activities, was an important craftsman in the medieval manor by the thirteenth.

The basic shape of the horseshoe has remained the same, though in detail it has varied from age to age and country to country. The Victorian era saw a spate of 'patent' shoes—spring-heeled shoes; unilateral shoes nailed on one side only to save time in shoeing; special shoes made to collect dirt and grit on the underside so that they should not slip on the new woodblock road surfaces. Mercifully for both horses and smiths they were soon abandoned.

In shoeing, the smith begins with one of the horse's forefeet. To start with a hind foot makes even the most placid horse suspicious, and the smith's conduct, touch and voice are aimed at reassurance. The old shoe is removed by drawing the nails and the hoof is trimmed with a special knife. This paring down is rendered necessary by the continued growth of the hoof when protected by the shoe from the natural abrasion of the ground.

The shoe is first fitted cold, then modified where necessary and fitted again 'black hot' (not quite glowing). This produces clouds of acrid smoke but evokes no reaction from a horse familiar with the process. The shoe now fits snugly and is cooled in the water trough which stands near the forge. The shoe for a hunter weighs less than 1lb, that for a heavy horse up to 4lb. It will be secured by seven or eight nails, according to the type, countersunk on the underside and clenched where they protrude from the upper surface of the hoof. It needs little imagination to see that a careless or incompetent smith means a lame horse and a rough or brutal one could mean a permanently nervous horse. But most farrier-smiths acquire a 'feeling' for horses as deep and instinctive as their feeling for iron.

The wheelwright's shop (*MERL*)

The wheel of the wagon

The sound of horsedrawn carts and wagons was once an insistent accompaniment to life in the countryside; the thud of hooves on turf or stubble, or the ring of iron shoes on the road. And always the rhythmic jolt and rumble of the wooden-wheeled vehicle.

Until seventy years ago the transport of goods beyond the rail and canal networks depended on horses and wooden wheels—the carrier's cart, the delivery van, the four-wheeled wagon loaded with coal or bricks—these were the commercial road traffic. Early in the present century a little of the load was transferred to steam traction engines and the fine old 'steamers' of Messrs Foden and others could be encountered chuffing their way along quiet country roads. Soon the motor car would begin to replace the gig and trap, the carriage and brougham, but mechanisation came slowly and unevenly at first. In 1913 the farm where the writer was born still sent hay to London in wagonloads and a continuous stream of fodder flowed into the city to maintain a large population of working horses.

Between the wars the displacement of the horse from road traffic continued, but the wagon, with many other horsedrawn implements, continued in use on the farm. By the 1930s the pneumatic tyre appeared on two-wheeled carts, but the Depression discouraged investment in anything new and, in fact, the wooden-wheeled vehicle was quite widely used in farm cartage until some twenty-five years ago.

The sound of the iron-tyred wooden wheel came out of the remote past, rose to a crescendo in the nineteenth century, and died away in our own time. It lasted longer in the countryside than the town and it was the villages that saw the last of the craftsmen who sustained it.

Of all the vehicles which rolled through the centuries on the products of the wheelwright's craft, the most representative of the countryside, and in many ways the most interesting because of its regional variations, is the farm wagon. Now that the tractor-trailer, the grain truck and the muckspreader have finally replaced the wagon and the two-wheeled tumbril, one must look in museums for their finest examples. Fortunately, many have been salvaged and preserved, but others may still lie, ruinous and abandoned, in ancient cartsheds and overgrown rickyards. The observant traveller, did he know what to look for, might have a hand in saving them, and these relics of the last phase of horse-powered farming are as worthy of rescue as the early traction engines.

The farm wagon

By this date design and construction were at their peak. Within the limits of the materials used (wood and iron), nothing better made or more efficient in operation could be envisaged. Wagonbuilding was widely distributed through the counties. The making of bodies and underframes was within the competence of skilled carpenters and joiners—more numerous then than now—though the decorative bodywork of many wagons boasts an artistic exuberance that went beyond mere skill. But a wagon was only as good as its wheels and it is the wheelwright who deserves to rank with the great eighteenth-century furnituremakers in his mastery of timber.

Types of wagon

The four-wheel or 'harvest' wagon was the largest product of the wheelwright's yard. Its design varied in different parts of the country and the regions remained faithful to their own distinctive patterns right up to the time when building ceased. Regional traditions were maintained even in such matters as colour and the style of lettering on front and tailboard.

The regional features were usually long-established. The Lincolnshire wagon, for instance, with its deep, narrow body, strengthened at the sides by many 'spindles'—a kind of exterior framing—was based on ideas brought over by the Dutch when they drained the Fens. Like the East Anglian wagon it was expected to operate on a flat terrain and could risk having large wheels and a high centre of gravity. In hilly areas, the West Country and the Cotswolds, wheels were smaller and the stability of the loaded wagon was as important as its capacity.

Winter rest for the wagon (*John Tarlton*)

The lateral distance between a wagon's wheels, the equivalent of a railway gauge, was in the past a thing very difficult to change once locally established. This aspect of design varied from place to place and was rigidly adhered to in its own region. It helped to keep wagonbuilding as a local industry and was one reason why the long-distance transport of heavy goods failed to expand before the coming of the canals.

The trouble was that only on main highways could wagons move outside their own area, and even these were frequently impassable to them. All too often the wagon had to move not on roads but in ruts. Long after MacAdam, secondary roads and village tracks were unmetalled; the ruts gouged out in winter failed to disappear in summer, they merely solidified and the wagonwheels continued to trundle along in them. Year by year they grew a little deeper and more solidly packed at the bottom and a wagon with wheels wrongly spaced to fit them not only had to contend with a rougher surface but ran the risk of getting two wheels in and two out. Then, with a high load, it might capsize.

So the wagon must be made to 'take the rout' as they put it, and woe betide the waggoner—jolly as those of his calling were popularly supposed to be—who found himself on a country road with a 62in rut-gauge and leading a wagon with a 70in track.

This fact is worth recalling, not only to explain why wheelwrights stuck so closely to the basic measurements taught them by their predecessors, but as another illustration of the autonomy and self-sufficiency that prevailed in different parts of Britain. Local usage in trades and professions persisted despite the unifying influence of industrialism and modern communications. The wheelwrights kept stubbornly to the old formulas long after the need to do so had passed, for a tradition long established survives by inertia. It is when we ask why these particular traditions in the spacing of wagonwheels should have become established that we find in it another reminder of the local economic independence in which our forefathers lived.

The wagon, bred in the village yard, might outlive its owner, travel thousands of miles and carry thousands of tons on and off the farm where it was based, yet rarely leave its own parish. It would take corn to the mill and bring back flour and miller's offals for the stock, carry piles of faggots for the baker's oven, coppice-wood for the hurdlemaker and straw for the thatcher. It would fetch lime from the kiln and marl from the marl-pit. It would cart stone from the nearby quarry and timber from the sawpit to the carpenter's shop and the yard where it was made. On Mayday, garlanded with flowers, it would be filled with children bound for the local revels. Sombre in black drapings it would take the master on his last journey to the lych gate. It performed a whole range of functions in the community distinct from its primary role of farm cartage. And because of the nature of

Oxfordshire wagon (*MERL*)

Lincolnshire wagon (*MERL*)

that community it could do so without ever travelling to distant places or on strange roads.

Building the wagon

The finished work is always more interesting when the maker's problems have been appreciated.

Details of the bodywork were dictated by local standards, as were overall dimensions, length varying 8–10ft in different areas. The way the floorboards are laid is also sometimes characteristic of a particular region—Lincolnshire wagons are generally cross-boarded, while the Oxford or Woodstock type has the boards running lengthways. In the great corn-growing regions, the thought of carrying the harvest and of transporting corn in sacks seemed to rule out consideration of the wagon's other possible uses, but elsewhere the builders expected it to be used for loose cargoes which had to be unloaded with a shovel. With the boards running in the same direction as the shovelling the job was finished more easily and cleanly.

The sides of the body, which had to withstand outward pressures, were sometimes strengthened by the aforementioned exterior struts or spindles, but more often by iron 'standards', L-shaped fittings bolted to the floor and the inner face of the sides. Where the body was shallower the sides needed less support, but then they posed a problem with the large rear wheels coming up to, or even above, the top of the sides. At haytime and harvest a good loader would build his load out beyond the sides and this had to be kept clear of the wheels. One solution was the 'hooped rave', the wheelguard which characterises the designs of the south and west. It partly accounts for the splendid, curving, ship-like lines of the Oxford, Wiltshire, Dorset, Somerset and Devon wagons.

The body timbers were often beautifully planed and chamfered, and this had a purpose beyond that of appearance. The experienced wheelwright would often spend days on it, smoothing away every unnecessary pound of timber, bevelling and reducing wherever he knew this could be done with safety. Only by rigorous paring and the expert choice of timber could he keep weight to a minimum. A decorative motif would emerge from all this chamfering and bevelling, but it must have a utilitarian reason. George Sturt, in his classic *The Wheelwright's Shop*, tells of a farmer who stipulated that his new wagon should have no 'postles' on it. He was not going to pay for decorative woodwork like the carved apostles at which he gazed weekly in church. They were hard bargainers, the farmers, even in their Golden Age of the mid-nineteenth century. Sometimes they wanted

Wheelwright at work in Herefordshire in 1937 (*MERL*)

wagons delivered unpainted, so that there should be no concealing of knots in the timber. Knowing that one must deal with such customers surely did much to maintain standards of workmanship.

The under-frame of the wagon carried the body and into this were built the axles. The front and rear axles were coupled by a long timber called the 'pole', and through this the strain of the forward pull was transmitted to the rear wheels, and not concentrated on the fore-end of the wagon. The front wheels were mounted on the 'fore-carriage' which swivelled in a horizontal plane to facilitate turning. The degree to which the fore-carriage could turn, known as the 'lock' long before motor vehicles were thought of, was continually improved. Early wagons were said to have needed half a field in which to turn, but by 1900, with good horses, a wagon could be turned in its own length.

The wheel Consider for a moment the problems it presents. It must be made from many separate pieces of timber assembled so that the rim is a true circle and the hub its true centre. It must be as light as possible, yet strong enough to bear a downward thrust of up to a ton while running on wildly uneven surfaces. The timber used in its construction must be well seasoned so as not to swell in the wet or shrink in the burning sun, for in the first case the wheel would burst within the constraint of the iron tyre, and in the second it would fall apart. And then there is another problem, peculiar to the horsedrawn heavy vehicle, which some unknown genius solved by the invention of the 'dish'.

A walking horse has a slight rolling, sideways motion, and this sets up a rhythmic swing from side to side in whatever he is pulling. Anyone who has travelled standing up in a wagon will recollect this gentle swaying, no matter how level the ground, though probably without realising its potential effects on the wheels from the incessant outward shove at the hubs, first on one side and then on the other, a lateral thrust with the weight of the load behind it. If now you think of the wheel as a disc being heavily and continuously thumped at the centre you can imagine it beginning to bulge outwards. And finally, like an umbrella inverted by a gale, it will collapse.

So, if you inspect the wheel, you will find it is not built in one plane but is shaped like a very shallow saucer or, more exactly, a dish; it is shaped as a very flat cone with its point closest to the body of the wagon; the danger of a collapse outwards has been met by a built-in bulge the other way. The spokes are not at right-angles to the axle but are set in the hub so that they slant outwards.

Repairing the front wheel of a Cotswold wagon. Shaving one of the felloes—the segments of rim which form a perfect circle (1955) (*Fox*)

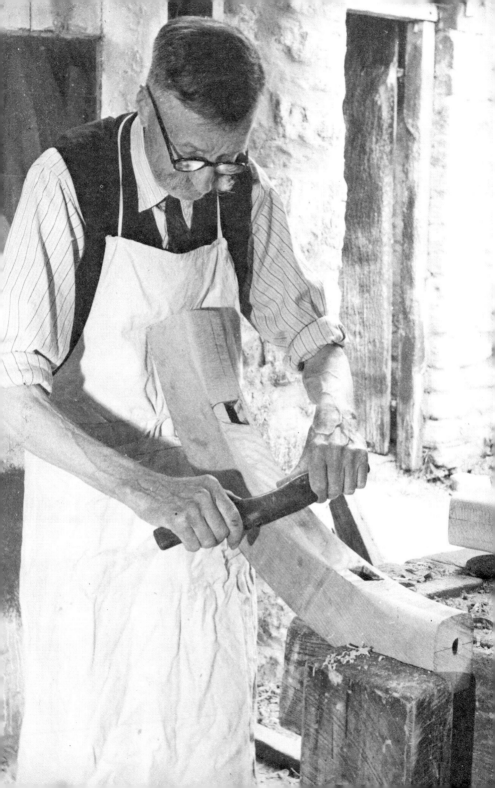

Wheelmaking started with the nave, shaped from long-seasoned elm and about a foot in length and the same in diameter. Around its circumference the mortises for the spokes were chiselled out, always an even number such as twelve or fourteen, so that each of the felloes or rim segments could be attached to two spokes. The mortising required great skill, for not only must the spoke be equi-distant and in line, but each must fit into the nave at the same angle. The smallest inaccuracy in cutting the mortises would be disastrous if not discovered, for once driven home the spokes were almost immovable. A special gauge was used to ensure that the square holes all had the same tiny slope to their sides so that the spokes should lean fractionally to create the dish shape.

Oak was used for the spokes, shaped and trimmed with the spokeshave to combine strength with minimum weight. The square tenon to be mortised into the nave—square so that it should not twist—was known as the 'foot'. It was so shaped and measured that it could not be merely tapped into its mortise, but must be driven in by a strong man using a sledgehammer, iron-hard oak into unyielding elm, not to be moved or adjusted.

The outer ends of the spokes, after their tremendous battering, were now also shaped into tenons for insertion into the rim. This was built up from curved sections, the felloes, usually of ash or beech and shaped from a pattern or template to form a circle of the right diameter when assembled. Each felloe had two mortises to take the spoke tenons and, like those in the nave, they had to be cut at a precise angle.

The wheel, perhaps the height of a man when standing upright, was now ready for the final dramatic act of tyring. Occasionally tyres were of separate strips of iron, known as 'strakes', but the hoop tyre, a continuous iron circle, was preferred. The wheel was laid flat on the tyring platform and its exact circumference measured with a 'traveller', a sort of mini-cyclometer which enabled the smith to calculate the length of iron bar from which he would forge the tyre. The bar was cut, heated, rolled flat, made into a hoop, and the ends welded. If the calculations were right it would be just too small to encircle the wheel when cold.

Now it was heated again and three men would lift it from the forge with long-handled tongs called 'dogs' and run with it, glowing fiercely, to the tyring platform. There it was laid on the wheel and hammered down over the rim. Clouds of acrid smoke would pour from the scorching timber, to be replaced by clouds of steam as the tyre, now in place, was cooled with cans of water before it set fire to the rim.

This was the moment of truth for the smith and of some anxiety for the wheelwright. For the rear wheels of a wagon the difference between the inside circumference of the tyre when cold, and the outer circumference of the rim, had to be $1\frac{7}{8}$in. Then the tyre would expand just enough when hot

Red-hot tyre being fitted while the wheel is clamped in an iron bed (*John Tarlton*)

and shrink by the right amount as it cooled. Too large and the tyre would be loose; too small and the terrible embrace of the cooling iron would distort or even snap the oaken spokes. But this rarely happened and the wheelwright usually had the satisfaction of seeing his work squeezed into a perfect and durable whole.

Where to see them

Though their wheels have ceased to turn, fine collections of them are to be seen in many parts of the country.

Bristol   Blaise Castle House Folk Museum
Kent   Wye College, Near Ashford (summer only)
Lincolnshire   Museum of Lincolnshire Life, Burton Road, Lincoln
Oxford   City and County Museum, Fletcher's House, Woodstock
Sussex   Horsham Museum and Michelham Priory, near Hailsham

Wiltshire   The George Inn, Sandy Lane, Chippenham
York   The Castle Museum

Many other collections are open to the public, but probably the finest and most comprehensive of all is to be found at the Museum of English Rural Life at the University of Reading.

Harnessmaking and harness ornament

A harnessmaker's shop was once found in almost every village large enough to have a smithy, and is often remembered today in the name of 'Saddlers' or 'The Saddlery' attached to a private house or cottage.

In a community dependent on horses and, earlier, on oxen as well for transport in general and for motive power on the farm, the making and repair of harness was an absolutely vital industry. The craft of saddlery, like that of farriery, cannot be turned over to factory production. Not, at least, in the case of quality products, as the present price of a set of pony harness clearly shows. The making of riding harness is now the part of the saddler's work that ensures his survival, but right up to the 1930s he was more concerned with the commercial than the recreational side of the trade and, except in hunting, there was little demand for riding equipment.

Draught harness

We cannot hope to survey all the different aspects of saddlery, but the harnessing of draught animals is worth considering for a few moments since it was in this field that the village relied most upon its saddler, as it did upon its smith, to keep the wheels turning. Harnessmaking, like wheelwrighting, is also a good example of a craft developing by trial and error over thousands of years until something near perfection is reached.

The first domesticated horses were in fact ponies of about 13 hands high (a hand equals 4in). It is probable that they were at first too small to be ridden and increased in size only with selective breeding and the better feeding that came with domestication. Quite early on, however, about 1500 BC, they were being used to draw light war chariots in the Middle East. The two-wheeled vehicles had a pole about 7ft long projecting from the front and a pair of ponies were harnessed to this, one on either side, probably with a leather breast harness attached by traces to the body of the chariot. Thus the use of the pole pre-dated that of the pair shafts, introduced when single-horse vehicles became practicable. The pole remained in use for road vehicles drawn by more than one horse, including, of course, the most highly developed of them, the stagecoach.

For heavy draught work like ploughing and hauling wagons, the ox or bullock has a much longer history than the horse. It was almost universally

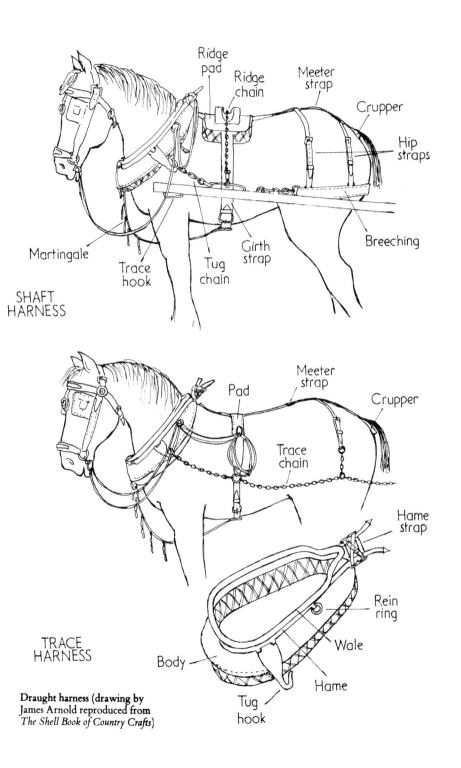

Ridge pad

Ridge chain

Meeter strap

Crupper

Hip straps

Breeching

Girth strap

Tug chain

Trace hook

Martingale

SHAFT HARNESS

Meeter strap

Crupper

Pad

Trace chain

Hame strap

Rein ring

Wale

Hame

Body

Tug hook

TRACE HARNESS

Draught harness (drawing by James Arnold reproduced from *The Shell Book of Country Crafts***)**

used for these purposes in the Middle Ages, and in the middle of Queen Victoria's reign the horse *v* ox argument was still raging. In 1965 there were still some 600,000 working oxen on the Continent, mainly in Italy, Spain and Portugal. The arguments in favour of oxen are referred to elsewhere but one minor point is relevant here. Ox harness was very simple and cheap, the medieval peasant could concoct it himself from pieces of wood and some leather thongs, and it is still basically unaltered.

Harnessmaking evolved into a major craft precisely because horses were such a tricky problem. They had no horns or other protuberances to which things could be tied. They were relatively fast-moving, sensitive and easily injured or upset. Effective control came with the bridle and bit, and saddle and stirrups completed the basic riding harness. The pack-saddle, which transferred a commercial load to the horse's back and left his master to walk, also became important along the many trade routes which were no more than trails and bridleways.

The method of attaching a vehicle to the horse or, rather, of fitting the horse with something to which the vehicle could be attached, reached its final form when the Romans invented the collar. Prior to that, the breast harness had been used, a broad strap across the horse's chest to which the traces could be hooked. Such a harness is adjustable and within reasonable limits one set will fit any sized horse. It is still in use and over most of the world it has been preferred because it makes no very heavy demands on the harnessmaker's skill. In Britain, however, we took over the more efficient but technically more demanding horse collar from the Romans and have kept it as a fundamental part of draught harness ever since.

Some historians have claimed that the horse collar ranks second only to the wheel among basic inventions. This is a gross exaggeration since horses are used quite effectively without it, but a well fitted collar does enable a horse to exert its full tractive power by leaning its weight against a comfortably padded surface. Individually fitted collars were common on well run farms in the last century and a collar would be altered if it had to pass from one horse to another. In the crack coaching teams, each horse had its own harness and, especially, its own collar. The harnessmaker served a long apprenticeship, and at the end of it his ability was measured as much by the quality of his collars as by that of his riding saddles.

Long-disused collars may still be found hanging in barns and stables, usually with their straw stuffing housing families of mice. Better preserved specimens will be found in many museums, examples of the skilled, if unspectacular, leather work that was once taken for granted.

Making the collar The collar is roughly egg-shaped, the narrow end fitting the horse's neck, the broad lower part butting against his chest and

Horse collar. The perfectly fitting collar was the greatest test of the saddler's art and essential to efficient working (*MERL*)

shoulders. The horse's head is, of course, wider at the top than further down, so the collar has to be slipped over it upside down and then turned round to rest in the correct position. If it is badly made it may chafe and cause sores before the damage is noticed. So the harnessmaker's reputation was at stake with every collar he made.

The shape of the collar is determined by the leather part, which is tightly stuffed and faced with a soft material, traditionally serge, where it is in contact with the neck and shoulders. This is the 'body' of the collar. The front leather part is called the 'wale', and between the two a groove or depression encircle the collar. This groove is occupied by the remaining element of the collar, the 'hames'.

The hames—generally 'anes' in the Home Counties and East Anglia—form a metal clasp going right round the collar. Made in two curved sections, they are joined by a hinge or a short chain at the base and are drawn together by straps at the top. Curved to fit the collar, they lie in the groove and are prevented from slipping back by the solid mass of the body. They carry the tug hooks to which the traces or chains are hitched and the rings through which the reins are passed. The forward thrust of the horse is transmitted through the collar to a strong metal fitting which takes the strain of the pull without the horse itself ever coming into contact with a hard surface. The hames were at one time made of wood, but wrought iron or brass replaced it, the latter being preferred where high standards of spit-and-polish were maintained in the turn-out.

Strap-work, materials and tools Draught harness does not end with the making of a good collar. A full set of shaft harness has some twenty different straps, and the village saddler had to be capable of producing them all from sheets of intractable leather straight from the tanners.

The bridle consisted of the headpiece, cheekpiece, blinkers, browband and noseband. In the centre of the horse's back the saddlepad was held in place by the girth, and over it passed the backband which supported the shafts. The saddlepad was also kept in position by the fillet strap leading back to the crupper. Several long straps comprised the breeching which allowed the horse to exert a braking effect when going downhill and to reverse the pull on the shafts when backing. The reins and possibly the traces are also of leather.

All this varied leatherwork must be easily adjustable, of the right strength for the particular purpose, and properly sewn. A broken strap might be no more than a nuisance, but it could just possibly be a disaster.

The sheets of leather usually came from local tanneries, which in the past were fairly numerous. Although cow hides were used for harness work many saddlers preferred horse hides—which might seem a somewhat

The saddler at work (*MERL*)

macabre choice for horse harness. But with a population of working horses running into millions, as it did in the nineteenth century, this particular raw material was inevitably plentiful. The leather arrived in a stiff, board-like state and was rendered pliable by being repeatedly rubbed with tallow and mutton fat before coming into use—a somewhat messy and smelly business. Draught harness was dyed black and riding harness brown.

Riding saddles Until about AD 300 riders had only a soft pad saddle, held in place by a girth and not equipped with stirrups. The modern saddle is supposed to have originated with the Mongol horsemen who repeatedly swarmed into Europe from Central Asia and whose culture and warfare were largely based on their understanding of horses.

Horse brass (*MERL*)

In an ordinary present-day saddle the tree is made of beech, curved to fit over the horse's back from just behind the withers. The underside is padded with the pads resting on either side of the spine. The harnessmaker in Britain has never made his own saddle trees, the production of which is a craft in itself. It is a very localised craft, too, being concentrated in the Walsall district. Practically all the saddler's tools and equipment also come from this Midlands area, as do the strange ornaments we have come to know as 'horse brasses' and which in the trade have always been called 'Walsalls'.

The pads of the cheapest riding saddles are covered with serge, like the bodies of collars and the saddlepads of draught harness, but more luxurious saddles are padded with linen or calfskin. The layers built up on top of the

Horse brass (*MERL*)

tree are the flap, the skirt and the seat. The first two are usually of calf, but the proper material for the seat is pigskin.

Fashions in saddles have varied a lot through the centuries and although the general-purpose type is now a universal design, the modern saddler turns out a number of variations. Special saddles are required by the mounted police and cavalry regiments, and the latter, with the Royal Horse Artillery units, contribute to the demand for what has now become ceremonial harness. The harnessmaker was once as important as the farrier among Army tradesmen and the lack of enough skilled men to keep up the supply of collars for the Army's horses in World War I led to a temporary return to the simpler breast harness for artillery and transport horses.

Horse brasses

Harness ornaments, to give brasses their proper title, are among the few horse relics collectable by the private individual. They have a perennial fascination as reminders of the greatest phase of horse history, the nineteenth century, and their subject matter and manufacture are worthy of study. Many of those seen nailed to the beams of country pubs are of modern origin, but antique specimens may still be found in out-of-the-way junk shops and even among the sundries and harness oddments at farm sales. Nor should the modern artefacts be despised since they meticulously preserve the traditional designs.

The actual making of horse brasses was not, of course, a country craft. They came from Walsall like most of the harnessmaker's equipment. A century ago they were bought in vast numbers to decorate the harness of plough and wagon teams, dray horses, and even roundsmen's cobs. In this utilitarian age one cannot imagine a tractor driver worrying overmuch about the appearance of his machine, but the smartness of his turn-out was one of the few satisfactions in the hard and restricted life of the Victorian carter or horseman. Brasses became an essential part of the harness and when Housman's dead ploughman asks, 'Does the harness jingle as when I was man alive?', it was no doubt the familiar tinkle of the brasses that he meant.

And the ornaments were more than purely decorative, they were lucky. They began, centuries ago, as protective amulets, and horsemen sometimes reinforced their powers with homemade charms. As late as 1859, a Norfolk ploughman was found to be safeguarding his horse from the evil eye by suspending from its neck the thumb of an old glove containing a neatly written copy of the Lord's Prayer. A throwback to the piety of the Middle Ages and, further still, to the phylacteries of Judaism.

The earliest brasses one is likely to find date from the eighteenth century and are inferior in every way to those produced later. They were cut out of sheet metal with a hammer and punch, designs are simple and the hammer marks are sometimes discernible—though not in themselves a guarantee of authenticity. The metal used was latten, the complex alloy of copper, zinc, lead and tin used in much the same manner for making memorial brasses.

In the nineteenth century, as farming became more prosperous and the size of a farm was reckoned more often in the number of working horses it employed than in its actual acreage, the output of harness ornaments increased tremendously. It seemed almost as though the ever-growing status of the Shires and Suffolk Punches was proclaimed in the elaboration of their dress. Victorian brasses were mass-produced, yet against all probability they were good both in design and execution.

These later brasses were not cut and hammered out of sheet metal but cast

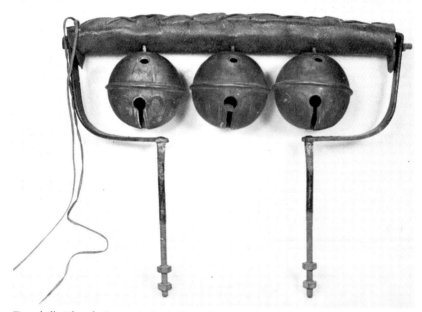

Team bells. These had a practical as well as a decorative purpose—to give warning of approach in narrow lanes (*MERL*)

in moulds. The method allowed a more sophisticated treatment of the design and a surprising amount of detail, another facet, perhaps, of the wealth of talent in engraving obvious in Victorian book and periodical illustration.

Essentially, the brass became a woodcut. The design was carved in a close-grained wood, usually pear, and then impressed on a mould of damp sand. After removal from the mould the surface texture of the metal was sometimes modified by treatment with acid or more often lacquered to reduce tarnishing and corrosion. In fact, the Victorian harness ornament was a quality product, which accounts for the fact that so many have survived in good condition.

Collections

Many country museums and folk museums with displays of horsedrawn vehicles have comprehensive collections of harness and specimens of brasses. What is probably the finest collection of brasses in existence will be found at the Hull Transport Museum.

Thatching

Before decimalisation it was commonly said that it cost ten shillings to send a thatcher up a ladder and a pound to get him down. The equivalent costs

233

today are no doubt much higher, for time has brought the poor relation of roofing materials to be a symbol of affluence.

Up to the eighteenth century, when tiles and slates came into wider use, thatch was a universal roof. It was as common in town as in the country and contributed to the frequent horrors of fire among the huddled alleyways of timber houses. Primitive fire-fighting equipment, sometimes kept in the parish church, usually included hooks and grappling irons for dragging down blazing thatch before the rest of the structure caught alight. The church itself, of course, might also be thatched, though normally only in a rural parish.

As alternative roof coverings became available, thatch was gradually relegated to the cottage and the farm building. By the mid-nineteenth century, only livestock, labourers and the poorest farmers slept under the protection of straw. The reversal in fashion came with the buying up and restoration of country cottages by townsfolk, a development that coincided with a growing shortage of materials and of craftsmen to use them.

Thatching materials

In Britain, these have included heather, broom and birch twigs, but the craft evolved mainly around the use of wheat straw and the so-called Norfolk reeds.

Although dwellings with thatched roofs were to be found in all parts of the country they were, and still are, more common south of the Humber– Mersey line than north of it. In corngrowing areas of eastern and south-central England and the Midlands, it was natural for thatch to predominate, but it held its own too in the most unlikely places until well into the last century. Country houses were frequently thatched in the southern half of Wales until the development of railways brought a new, cheap, but heavy substitute from the slate quarries not so far away.

Suitable wheat straw was available locally over much of England from the Middle Ages until the 1950s. Then, when the preservation of thatched roofs was becoming fashionable, the supply almost ceased.

This was an inevitable consequence of the revolution in harvesting methods. From Bronze Age times until our own the sequence of operations had not changed, though mechanical power gradually replaced hand labour. Corn was cut by sickle or binder, carted and stacked, threshed by flail or machine. Threshing was spread over many months and although, following the introduction of the stationary baler, some straw would be baled, there was always loose straw in reasonably good condition to be had.

Dorset, 1954. Two surviving crafts in operation: the smith works while re-thatching is in progress (*John Topham*)

The local thatcher might well cast an eye on growing crops and harvesting conditions as he went around and put in an order for so many loads of straw when the produce of particular farms became available.

The combine-harvester, telescoping the reaping and threshing processes into one, put an end to this. The combine cuts higher than the binder, leaving a longer stubble and shorter straw. The farmer treats the straw as a by-product, useful for litter and possibly as a supplementary stock-feed. To deal with it as economically as possible, the mobile baler follows the combine and compresses it into neat rectangular blocks, easily carted and stored. If it is infested with weeds a match is put to it and a wall of flame marches across the field. In neither case is there anything for the thatcher.

The renewed demand for thatch and the fact that it has become what country people call a 'millionaire's roof' has now done something to create new supplies of usable straw. A number of enterprising farmers have turned the clock back, reaping part of their wheat crops with the binder and threshing it with a 'drum'. The machines may be ancient relics that had rusted in dark corners or been sold for scrap at an auction, but in this case they are not being preserved for reasons of nostalgia. If, travelling a country road at harvest time, you should see a field patterned with rows of shocks instead of the familiar tracks of the combine, the farmer is not a drop-out from the march of progress. He is cashing in on the demand for straw, and loads of it will soon be fitted snugly over an old cottage or a proud new house, anywhere from Cornwall to Scotland—even, it is said, in Hampstead. A plastic substitute for straw thatch has been patented, but perhaps the less said about this, the better.

Production of Norfolk reeds has been increasing. Reed thatch is very durable, having a life of some fifty years compared with about fifteen for straw. The reed used is the tallest of our native grasses, *Phragmiles communis*, and it grows in marsh and shallow water in East Anglia, Kent, Hampshire and other places. The name of Norfolk was applied to the reed only because that county was the first in which it was used for thatching. More reed beds are now being regularly cut than for a long time past: the harvesting is not easy work but the produce, neatly bound in long, straight bundles, is valuable although rising costs explain the use of other roofing materials.

The thatcher at work

The supply of thatchers was affected by changes in farming methods as inevitably as the supply of straw. When the corn harvest was stored in the sheaf it was kept either in a Dutch barn or in stacks. The latter, usually round in the Midlands and the North, more often large and rectangular in the Home Counties, had to be thatched. Many farm buildings were thatched. In Buckinghamshire and parts of Wessex, the boundary walls of

A Hampshire thatcher drives in a hazel spar to hold the new thatch (*John Tarlton*)

farmyards were sometimes built of blocks of straw and puddled clay, like the 'claybat' cottages of Essex, and they too had to be thatched to stop them disintegrating in rain and frost. So that one way and another every arable farm had at least one worker familiar with the rudiments of thatching. Some of these farm craftsmen attained high standards in their occasional thatching. The big Hertfordshire stacks, for instance, with their rounded apse-like ends decorated with elaborate finials worked in straw, were minor masterpieces created for a few short months and destroyed at threshing time. From such men the professional house thatchers were continually recruited.

Overleaf: Reed cutting on the Norfolk Broads in the 1950s. There is still a demand for Norfolk reeds for thatching (*Topical Press*)

Thatching a corn rick in Dorset in the 1950s (*John Topham*)

Working a ship's wheel on a re-thatched roof in Cornwall. Skill in decoration varies widely among thatchers but the experts like to leave some distinctive 'trademark' (*Central Press*)

With the cessation of farm thatching this labour pool dried up, and the craft was only saved from extinction by the rewards offered to young entrants by the proud owners of thatched roofs. Training and apprenticeship were revived, the Association of Master Thatchers was formed, and today nearly a thousand skilled thatchers ply their trade in Britain.

To the layman watching the process for the first time, one of the most astonishing things is indeed the amount of straw that a good thatcher packs on to a roof. Beginning as a mountainous mass it slowly shrinks into a small pile of short and broken straws discarded during yelming, and an area of thatch that seems quite inadequate to contain it.

Equally daunting is the volume of old straw to be carted away and burned at a safe distance when an ancient deep thatch, perhaps the accumulated layers of a century or more, is stripped. Dusty and brittle, honeycombed with the nests of field mice and sparrows, the straw will contain scores of hairpin-shaped sprindles. Brittle as the straw and easily snapped, they will be identical with the pile of new ones lying hard by the straw heap. Things have not changed much since hands long stilled twisted and sharpened them, although the thatcher is now a man of substance and comes to work in a car.

To climb the thatcher's ladder and get a close-up view of work in progress is to realise the skill that goes into the apparently simple ornamentation of the completed roof. The regularity of the design is plain enough when one stands back and surveys the whole, and the thatcher will often be seen doing just that, but only experience and something of the artist's vision can tell him that the picture is right when he is, so to speak, close to the brushwork.

Another example of his exact visual judgement comes in the trimming of the eaves. A lot of straw is left hanging until one part of the roof is finished, a long unkempt fringe obscuring the windows. As part of the final trim this is cut back to the proper level and the cut must be perfectly horizontal from front to back and follow accurately the line dictated by wall and window. The tool employed is usually an old scythe blade, wavy-edged and razor-keen from incessant sharpening. It looks an unhandy tool for an operation in which any miscalculation would do irreparable damage, but the eaves always emerge straight and clean-cut.

Of the claybat or daub-and-wattle cottage they say, 'The house'll stand while the roof lasts', and this is true. Built of poles cut from a nearby coppice and clay dug from any convenient spot, thousands of such cottages have yet survived for centuries under their warm hats of straw or reed. Without the continuous exercise of the thatcher's skill they would long since have mouldered back into the land from which they were raised.

Well-thatched corn stacks. In pre-combine days, every arable farm needed a competent thatcher on its staff (*MERL*)

7 Crafts of the Coppice

The word 'coppice' is a variant of 'copse' and comes from the French *couper*, to cut, but whereas copse has come to mean any small patch of woodland, coppice has acquired the meaning of a special type of tree cultivation.

It was long ago discovered that many tree species, when cut down to ground level, neither died nor threw up another single trunk or bole. Instead they produced a mass of shoots which grew into straight stems, increasing annually in height and thickness. These stems could be harvested regularly, every year in some cases, according to the size required, and the 'stool' or 'crown' would go on producing for thirty or forty years.

Coppice wood in the past was raw material for hurdles and hayrakes, brooms and thatching spars, lobster pots and coracles, baskets and shepherds' crooks and many other essentials. For some purposes it is still used. The most usual trees for coppicing are ash, willow, birch, hazel, alder and sweet chestnut.

Making besoms

There never was a simpler looking implement than the birch broom—a long bundle of twigs, tightly bound at the top, and with a trimmed pole for a handle. Fortunately for those gardeners who like it, the birch broom is still made, and is indeed a useful tool, very light and made even easier to use by its springiness. The resilience of the birch twigs lifts wet leaves off a lawn when a rotary brush tends to flatten them and wire tines catch maddeningly in the turf. The massage of a slightly worn-down besom is also good anti-moss therapy for lawns, and the tool is wonderfully effective for sweeping fresh snow.

Despite the simplicity of both, there is nothing haphazard about the process. The 'spray' used is the long straight growth from coppice birch, preferably from crowns about seven years old. The growth is cut early in winter, tied in bundles and stacked for seasoning. The bundles in each layer are laid at right angles to those in the layer beneath, so that there are spaces to permit the free circulation of air. The whole rectangular heap is built with a ridged roof, like a haystack, and finished off with closely packed bundles running from ridge to eaves and acting as thatch as they once did on Highland cottages. Any reader feeling the urge to make his own besom will realise from this that it cannot be done with twigs cut from a mature tree. He will have to start by felling a few trees and cultivating a coppice plantation.

Turning chair legs in the Buckinghamshire beechwoods. The local furniture industry grew up around the skilled work of the 'bodgers' who used the primitive pole lathe powered by a bent sapling (*Mirror Features*)

One of the few besom-makers left in 1960 (*PA–Reuter*)

The seasoned bundles are withdrawn from the stack in spring and the spray trimmed and cut to length with a light bill. The twigs finish at different lengths, ends that are too thick or too thin being removed. Where broom-making was a considerable local industry, piles of these trimmings were collected and sold to the village baker as fuel for his ovens. This may sound very ancient history, but the writer's own village, 40 miles from London, was supplied with bread from brick ovens heated by faggots until World War II.

The broom-maker, with a quick, shuffling movement, arranges a bundle of the correct size so that the longest twigs are in the centre, thus giving the end of the broom a slightly convex shape. Compressing the handle end of the broom ready for binding is done by pressure of hand and knee or, more usually, by mechanical means. In that case, the operator sits astride a 'broom-horse' and clamps down a crude wooden vice on the bundle by pressure on a foot pedal. Binding was traditionally done with thin strips of hazel or ash, or even lengths of briar or bramble trimmed of their thorns. The knot used in securing the binding is the same as that employed in hand-tying sheaves of corn with a straw band or 'bond'—one which requires some practice but has the advantage of never slipping or relaxing its grip. Nowadays, wire is generally used, and sometimes gives way before the broomhead is worn out.

Ash poles are preferred for handles and are trimmed to remove any possible splinters but not to eliminate all irregularities. The slight bumpiness of the besom handle usually gives a better grip than the smoothness of the machined product. The end to be inserted into the broomhead is pared down to a long taper, the tip is pushed into the very tightly packed twigs, and the other end of the handle thumped on the ground to drive it finally into place. In a well-made broom it is held as tightly as in a close-fitting socket, though for extra security a wooden peg is sometimes driven through a hole drilled in the handle.

At the beginning of the present century there were some sixty full-time besom-makers in the Hindhead district of Surrey, where the heathlands and natural birch plantations guaranteed a supply of raw materials. So well established was the industry that they were known as the 'broom squires', a title which transferred to practitioners of the craft in other places. The broom squires did not live and work in the woods like some timber craftsmen, birch is rarely part of a fully developed mixed woodland and the coppices were often managed by woodmen who sold the bundled material to the broom-makers. It was truly a cottage industry, advertised by the carefully stacked bundles outside the cottage. When besoms were in general use, output was considerable and a skilled worker was said to be able to complete a broomhead every two-and-a-half minutes.

Sheep hurdles: the man cuts mortise holes in an upright while his wife finishes a hurdle (*Fox*)

Hurdle-making

Hurdles are a form of movable fencing in 6ft lengths. Their major use has always been in the 'folding' of sheep, the penning of the Down breeds on arable fields so that they can graze root and green crops sown specially for them. Such fields have no permanent stock-proof fencing and the fold confines the flock to one section at a time, being moved when the forage crop is thoroughly cleared up.

Wooden hurdles are light to handle and it was reckoned that one shepherd, with the help of his dog and a man with a horse and cart for transport, could dismantle and re-erect the fencing for 100 sheep as often as was necessary. Hurdles also seem to have other recommendations. The gentleman farmer of the mid-nineteenth century was told that '. . . they are universally known to be temporary, and are easily and cheaply set down and taken up, and do not break or mar the home-views or near-scenery of the adjacent mansion'. This referred to their use in parkland for both sheep and cattle, and hurdlemakers of those days were prepared to furnish

Wattle hurdles being made in 1960. Originally meant for penning sheep and sheltering lambs, the wattle hurdle has a new lease of life as garden fencing (*Sport and General*)

ornamental products for the occupants of the mansion who could not be expected to gaze upon the same common hurdles as the shepherd in the turnip field. Most of the wattle hurdles made today are used as fencing in country gardens.

Many portable substitutes in wire and metal have been evolved, and controlled strip-grazing with the daily-moved electric fence has extended the principle of the folded flock. But wooden hurdles are still made, and the writer knew of two hurdlemakers who were practising in adjacent Essex villages in the 1950s, long after the local blacksmith had shut up shop.

Gate hurdles The two end posts of the hurdle are split from fairly substantial ash poles which will have taken about twenty years to grow. Six mortises are cut through each end post to take the slightly tapered ends of the cross bars. The bars are not equally spaced but are furthest apart at the top and closer towards the bottom where sheep and lambs are likely to cause trouble by reaching through after some inaccessible morsel. A vertical brace runs from top to bottom in the middle of the hurdle, and two diagonal braces from the bottom corners meet at the top of this vertical brace. Using the minimum quantity of timber the hurdle made is absolutely rigid, and until it decays can never collapse or get out of shape.

A lot of skill goes into splitting the poles and selecting for the end posts those just big enough to take the six mortises without being dangerously weakened.

Wattle hurdles Whether any are now made for enclosing sheep is doubtful, but any that are will be about 42in high and have a small hole exactly in the centre. The purpose of this is to enable a number of hurdles to be threaded along a pole and carried easily by two men—anyone who has tried carrying just one in a high wind will appreciate the idea. Garden ones are, of course, apt to be a lot taller than the field variety.

Wattles are a woven product, needing no tools to make except a saw and a sharp bill, and in theory they are simplicity itself. In fact a reader with access to some good size hazel bushes might well try his hand at making a few.

Good, straight rods are needed for the stakes, nine or eleven for each hurdle, up to an inch in diameter. The two at the ends should be stouter than the others, and all should be sharpened at one end and 6in longer than the intended height of the hurdle. Traditionally, the end stakes are known as 'shores' and those between them as 'sails'—names for which no explanation is forthcoming. The lengths of hazel for weaving, the 'runners', may be of varying thickness down to lead pencil size; thick ones may be split if the operator has the requisite skill.

Fixing the willow strips of a trug basket (*Norman Wymer*)

The Sussex trug

This all-purpose garden basket is now often made of brightly coloured moulded plastic, but the wooden article is still obtainable and capable of outlasting its modern counterpart.

No-one seems to know why the trug is so named or why Sussex should be its native county. The name may be of Saxon origin—Sussex was a great Saxon stronghold—or it may be a version of 'trough' from the basket's shape, though really the trug is boat-shaped, and is clinker built in a reversed fashion with each board overlapping the one above it.

Trugmaking has always been a workshop job rather than a cottage industry, employing a group of craftsmen and a certain amount of equipment. It is not strictly a coppice craft either, the boards which form the body of the trug being cut from fair-sized willows of about fifteen years' growth. Frames and handles, however, are made from cleft coppice-grown ash or sweet chestnut.

The very thin boards are cut from the willow with a small-toothed circular saw of the type used in preparing veneers. They are shaped and pared down to be thinner near the rim than at the bottom of the basket, then they are shut in a steaming chest until pliable before being bent over a frame. In this condition they can be persuaded to take almost any shape.

The size of the trug is determined by the frame which forms the rim. There were formerly three sizes, garden, market garden and agricultural, but the last two are no longer wanted. The lengths of ash or chestnut for the frames are steamed like the boards, bent into a rectangle of the proper size and left to set. The boards will have been shaped so that they fit exactly inside the frame, and can be nailed to it at the ends. Either seven or nine boards are used, one along the centre and three or four on each side. A look at a trug, even one that has seen years of service, will confirm how precisely the boards are curved to fit together without gaps or bulges. The thing seems to be almost in one piece, ensuring that the wear and tear is evenly distributed.

The handle is made from the same material as the frame and completely encircles the trug underneath. Thus, at the point of greatest load, where the basket is deepest, the pressure is directly on the handle and not the boards. Garden models have wooden 'stands' underneath so that they rest level when set down, but these are usually omitted in the larger sizes.

Walking sticks

Time was when a country gentleman would have felt improperly dressed had he gone out without what Dr Watson would have called 'a stout ash-plant'. His city counterpart would have carried a more elegant version made from imported cane. An immense range of walking sticks was on sale up to 1914, and no doubt many countrymen made their own—drovers, especially, always sported a weird do-it-yourself assortment.

For a stout, durable, country stick ash has always been preferred. It is cut at two to three years old and few other woods are as good at that age. Sweet chestnut is an alternative, and in theory any growth that is straight, strong, and can be formed into a natural hand-grip at one end, is suitable for this kind of stick.

The ordinary crook handle is the most convenient. It can be hooked over the arm, leaving both hands free, and is a valuable aid in blackberrying and nut gathering. The crook is formed by steaming the stick in the same way as the trug components and bending the thicker end into shape, or by softening the end in a bucket of wet sand kept warm for some hours. When really pliable it is bent into any desired curve up to a complete U-turn and tied in that position until it hardens. The bending must be done cautiously to avoid cracking.

It is also possible to bend over the end of a growing stem of ash and wait for this contortion to become a natural handle in a year or so's time.

A method of producing quite different types of handle has long been practised by Welsh stickmakers. In this, a growth of coppiced ash is hacked up with a chunk of rootstock left on the end of it. This piece of hard wood is carved and polished into whatever shape its initial form suggests to the craftsman. It may be a smooth symmetrical knob or a vicious-looking projection like a parrot's bill, but it often gives a highly individualistic finish to the stick.

Professional foresters sometimes fashion curious oddments in spare moments, and the writer knew one such who used to make 'thumbsticks'. A thumbstick is an attenuated version of a pilgrim's staff, longer than a normal walking stick and terminating in a short fork into which the thumb is

Walking-stick maker (*Mirror Features*)

Assembling a rake head and handle (*Norman Wymer*)

Norfolk basketmaker (*Leslie F. Thompson*)

hooked. These particular examples were made of many apparently unpromising woods, including blackthorn, beautifully smoothed and polished.

Hayrakes

The hayrake is an example of an agricultural tool which right up to the end of its long history was made entirely of wood except for a couple of screws. For at least a thousand years the basic design must have been unaltered and the annual production of rakes was considerable until quite recent times. Even between the wars, when so much of haymaking was already mechanised, they would appear about April in every country ironmonger's and agricultural merchant's, shining with the freshness of new wood and a reminder of the approach of haytime.

At that time, of course, they were not being used on anything like the scale they had been fifty years earlier, when whole gangs of male and female workers swarmed in the hayfields, but even in the 1930s wages were very low and capital for machinery limited by years of depression. One could turn a swathe left by the mower almost as quickly as one could walk along it, casting the rake forward and pulling it back with every sidelong step, rolling the swathe over to expose its green underside. And when the hay had to be cocked at the threat of rain, a lad with a rake could follow the men pushing it into heaps along the windrows and leave the tidy job that meant so much to the old-time farmworker. Wooden rakes are still used on crofts and hillfarms and in large gardens.

Basketry

The native material for all kinds of woven baskets is willow. Craft shops sell many handmade baskets, and there is a continuous demand for crab and lobster pots, eel traps, creels and other things demanding heavy-duty canework. The amateur in this field has gone over almost entirely to imported centre cane, prepared in standardised thicknesses and in pieces of greater length than can be obtained from willow, which is also more difficult to work with.

The willow coppice producing the slender rods for weaving is known as an osier bed, though in Essex it is inexplicably known as a 'hope'. The rods themselves are called osiers and sometimes withies, though a withy is strictly speaking an osier used instead of string for tying. Willow is so pliable that it was used like this by nurserymen and market gardeners until quite recently.

All willow is stripped of bark before use, the rods being pulled through a simple contrivance called a stripping brake which scrapes the skin off cleanly. The old folk dance 'Strip the Willow' must take its title from this process, though there seems no obvious link. As to the uses of willow canework, this is no place to get involved in the ramifications of basketry. The making of wicker containers is almost as old as chipping of flints and has gone on developing since the first men learnt to weave and plait twigs. The ancient terminology of the craft, the processes of upsetting, randing and waling, will be familiar to many readers even though their practical experience may be limited to a short spell of occupational therapy in hospital. Professional basketmakers carry on a long unbroken tradition, and to some extent still depend on supplies of English willow. The bundles of prepared osiers, incidentally, are known as 'bolts', the name also used for rolls of cloth.

Coracles

The coracle is a small keel-less boat and, like the canoe, goes back a long way in history. The Britons were using it when the Romans came and the lineal descendants of the Britons, the people of Wales, are still the admitted experts in its construction. Its correct name, *corugl*, is Welsh.

Use of the coracle once extended far beyond Wales to lakes and rivers in many parts of Britain. It was a fisherman's craft on the Spey, the Dee and the Severn. Its extremely shallow draught suited it to the lagoons and reed-grown swamps of the Fenland where it was used by Queen Boadicea's tribe, the Iceni, and ten centuries later by Hereward the Wake and his followers.

In shape, the coracle is a shallow oval bowl, the form of the oval varying with the river area of its origin. Those of the Welsh rivers, Teifi and Towy, have a genuinely boat-like appearance, roughly egg-shaped. The Severn type is more nearly circular, and that of the Dee an almost perfect oval. Dimensions vary, for each coracle is custom-built for its user and takes account of his size and weight. The length is generally about 6ft and the beam some 40in. The depth is only 12–15in. It is of course a one-man craft and the thwart is amidships or slightly aft of that. Not only is the boat so lacking in rigidity that its shape may change appreciably under the weight of its occupant, it is so light as to be easily carried on the back. It is inverted over the head with a band, fastened at the ends of the thwart, passing across the chest, so that the boatman trudges along looking from the rear like a tortoise walking on its hind legs. Coracles are not moored at the bank but taken home. In the past they were used not only for fishing but for essential journeys that involved crossing a river lacking both bridges and fords. Easy portage was vital for this purpose.

A coracle covered with tarred canvas. This flimsy craft is still occasionally used by anglers (*Council for Small Industries in Rural Areas*)

Our reason for slipping the coracle in among the coppice crafts is that, basically, it is just a large willow basket with a waterproof skin. The framework is made of broad willow slats cleft from stout poles, usually six running lengthwise and eight or nine crosswise. They are interwoven in an under-and-over pattern and held in place by their own tension. No nails or other fastenings are used at the points where they cross lest there should be a projection which might wear its way through the covering.

The structure of the coracle is finally strengthened by two diagonal strips across the floor and by the insertion of the seat, making it less likely to collapse. Now comes the outer covering of tarred canvas, which in Hereward's time would have been of hide or skin. It is still secured in the same way, being wrapped over the gunwale and tightly bound. The craft is now ready for use and, despite its apparent flimsiness, will hold a fisherman and a substantial catch. At one time it was used extensively for salmon-netting, the net being stretched between two coracles for trawling the salmon run. This method fell into disfavour with the authorities and coracle fishing is now mainly of the dry fly variety. It was also once used quite a lot during the annual sheep-dipping, but modern more sophisticated methods have made it unnecessary for shepherds to take to the water in this way.

Propulsion is by paddle, the boatman using the canoeist's 'figure-of-eight' stroke. Owing to the distribution of weight the stern tends to lift out of the water and, despite the absence of any sort of streamlining, the extremely shallow draught makes it possible for the practiced paddler to skim along at a fair rate of knots.

The solemakers

Of all the coppice craftsmen none was more truly a woodlander than the maker of alderwood soles for clogs. He worked the alder plantations all over northern England, and it is said that he still exists in North Wales. These men moved from place to place, living rough in turf-roofed huts like those of the charcoal burners, supplying the local clog manufacturers and moving on again when the demand was satisfied or the alder coppices exhausted for the season.

Their virtual disappearance was due not so much to abandonment of the clog as to the transfer of its production entirely to the factory. Wooden-soled footwear has not vanished even now, and in more sophisticated forms the clog has made something of a comeback. It has a very long history and was worn by country folk long before it began clattering over the cobblestones of northern milltowns. In the Low Countries and France it was almost universal peasant wear, being slipped off on entering the house as the modern farmer slips off his wellingtons. Hillfarmers in North Wales had worn clogs for generations, and their adoption by the workers of the new Lancashire manufacturing towns was a natural extension. They are still found on French peasant holdings and in their traditional home, Holland.

Poles 6 or 7in thick are used for making soles, cut at ground level and sawn into short lengths by two men working with a wide-bladed bow saw. Each log is split down the middle and the resultant clefts are split again to give pieces rather larger than the ultimate sole will be when shaped. Only a rough shaping is done by the coppice workers, but it is done expertly and speedily with various implements, of which the most important is a 'stock knife'. This resembles the peg knife used in trimming the teeth on the hayrake and is a sort of guillotine. It has a stout blade with a long handle projecting from one end and a small ring at the other. The ring is engaged with a hook on a bench or 'horse', so that the blade is tethered but can be moved up and down by the handle and also—unlike a guillotine—slanted in any direction. The cleft blocks are shaped in outline by the stock knife and further trimmed with lighter tools. The day's output of soles, which may be considerable with a good team working continuously, is piled up in the shape of an old straw skep beehive, with a criss-cross arrangement and plenty of air-spaces throughout the pile, to season.

The last phase comes with delivery to the manufacturers for final shaping and attachment of leather uppers. The traditional French *sabots* and Dutch *klompen* (evocative name) are of wood throughout, uppers and all, and a much greater test of the woodworker's skill than the British clog. But one fears that, except at folk festivals, they are now never seen.

Charcoal burning

Charcoal is partially burnt wood, charred under conditions which prevent it bursting into flame. If you pack some wood chips into a closed tin with a small hole in the lid and heat it over a fire or gas ring, the wood will first lose any moisture it contains, and then the combustible gases will be driven off and can be burnt as a somewhat erratic jet above the hole. The stuff remaining will be black, quite light in weight and, if used as fuel, will burn with very little flame and a red-hot glow. In the forced draught of a forge or furnace the heat intensifies and the charcoal becomes white-hot.

The early iron-masters discovered this and used it for smelting the ore and forging the iron into tools and weapons. By Roman times it was the accepted fuel for the purpose. The ironworks of England were for centuries located in Sussex and fed with charcoal from the forests of the Weald. The commercial importance of charcoal in medieval and Tudor times was enormous, as great as that of coal in the nineteenth century or oil today. It forged the cannon that harried the Armada and the balls they fired, and was an essential ingredient of the gunpowder—which, typically of such occasions, happened to be in short supply.

Charcoal kilns near Thetford, Norfolk. Charcoal burning has been a woodland craft for more than a thousand years and despite new techniques it is as important as ever (*Forestry Commission*)

Charcoal burning in the Forest of Dean early this century (*Forestry Commission*)

Chestnut stakes for young fruit trees being made in Kent. Many Kentish farms still have plantations of this valuable coppice wood used to make garden paling as well as in more traditional crafts (*Press Association*)

For the young, scattered industries of Britain charcoal was a vital material, declining in importance only when coal began to replace it and the iron foundries moved from the south to Ironbridge and Sheffield. Charcoal was used in the smelting of all metals, in the making of glass, the glazing of pottery and to a limited extent for domestic heating. Its value in a furnace where high temperatures are required is obvious when you consider that the only alternative in pre-coal days was wood. One has only to imagine the consequences of applying the blacksmith's bellows to a hearth stoked with wood—the production of a roaring but not very hot flame—to see why a different type of fuel was essential for an intense, steady heat. The soft coal which was the first to be mined suffered from the same defect as wood under forced draught conditions and, until the hard 'steam coal' was mined, the early locomotives were fired with coke.

Charcoal remained a useful fuel long after coal came into use. Small foundries and smelting works, supplied from local ore deposits, sometimes had no accessible coal, but great reserves of woodland which could be tapped during the seventeenth and much of the eighteenth centuries. In them the charcoal industry flourished.

The burner's craft Charcoal still has a host of industrial uses, in ferrous alloys, synthetic fibre production, as a deodorant and gas absorbent, and in many minor chemical roles. It is mainly produced in kilns or in retorts which enable the volatile gases driven off in the process to be condensed as acetic acid, wood alcohol and creosote. The basic principle of burning the wood under conditions which prevent complete combustion by limiting the supply of oxygen is the same as with the centuries-old traditional methods.

The old-fashioned charcoal burner lives with the job, spending the summer burning-season camped in the woods. It is commonsense to work on the spot rather than move the wood, for 25 cwt of wood is eventually carted away as only 5cwt of charcoal, even though its bulk is almost the same.

The process begins with cutting the wood into convenient lengths of 2–4ft. It may be coppice wood grown for the purpose, or split material from larger branches. It is usually seasoned for a few months.

Experienced burners produced charcoal of very uniform quality despite their apparently primitive methods. The billets of wood were expected to retain their shape, coming out black, glossy, comparatively clean to handle, but brittle and only a fraction of their original weight. It is a very pure form of carbon, the skeletal framework, as it were, of the tree's cell structure. Everything else has been burnt away, only a honeycomb of tiny carbon boxes remains. It is this cellular structure, exposing a mass of interior surfaces to the air, that gives charcoal its power of removing smells, absorbing gases, and acting as a purifying and filtration agent.

8 The Country Garden

Medieval and Tudor gardens

The Saxons grew their limited range of vegetables in a 'wort yard' and probably also cultivated fruit trees, medicinal herbs and even flowers. But the first systematic gardeners were the monks.

The buildings of a monastery were normally grouped around a quadrangle which was likely to be the monastery's burial ground. The real garden, supplying food crops, culinary and medicinal herbs, and flowers for the altars, was usually close to the infirmary. It was not intended to be ornamental and in appearance was probably nearer to our conception of a market garden.

The reconstructed Great Garden at Pitmedden House, Aberdeen. A magnificent example of the eighteenth-century box-edged parterre (*National Trust for Scotland*)

The idea of really *designing* a garden came with new conceptions of architecture from Renaissance Italy. New varieties of edible and decorative plants came from Europe, the East, and eventually from the Americas. The science of botany came into being, and in the year of Elizabeth I's accession the first gardening book in English was published by Thomas Hill. In 1597 Gerard published his famous *Herbal*, and his first catalogue of plants in cultivation. The kitchen garden was by then quite well stocked, and quite humble gardens were producing gooseberries, strawberries and raspberries. Among flowers the carnation, antirrhinum, wallflower, lily, sweet pea, even the French marigold from Mexico, were either established or coming into cultivation.

The most typical aspect of late Tudor gardening, however, was the attention given to layout, and of all the labour-intensive gardening fashions ever devised, the knot garden was the most extravagant. The basic conception was a rectangular bed on which a design was formed by close-clipped hedges of a dwarf shrub, usually box, but sometimes rosemary. The more complex or 'enknotted' the pattern the more highly thought of it was. The spaces between were filled with low-growing plants, coloured pebbles, or a mixture of both.

From 1600 to 1800

By the mid-seventeenth century, and certainly after the Restoration, the smaller manor houses, parsonages, and even farmhouses were often set in excellent gardens. The first half of this century saw the importation of many new plants and foreign ideas. Many gardening books appeared and tree planting over the next two centuries was to shape much of the country scene we know today.

The chief exponent of the French style of landscape gardening was André le Nôtre, gardener to the Sun King, Louis XIV, and the theme of his gardens was perfect symmetry. Versailles, Fontainebleau and St Cloud, with their many lesser replicas, established le Nôtre as the first gardener of Europe and France and as the arbiter of garden fashion. Some of the original masterpieces have survived more or less intact.

In Britain the ideas of le Nôtre were most effectively used and adapted by George London and Henry Wise, who went into partnership in 1687 and founded a complete garden service based on London's Brompton Park nurseries. For the first time it became possible to hire a firm who would design and construct your garden, supply the necessary plants and trees, and give a continuing advisory service.

The basis of modern horticulture was being laid in other ways. Men like John Tradescant introduced plants from tropical and subtropical regions, and experiments in protected cultivation increased. The predecessor

Sheffield Park Gardens, Sussex. A landscape garden of 142 acres, started in the eighteenth century and finished in the twentieth. Famous for its immense variety of trees and shrubs (*National Trust*)

Manor house garden (*National Trust*)

of the greenhouse was the orangery, of which many examples are extant.

During the reign of William and Mary, Dutch influence began to affect the layout of gardens with more lavish use of water and evergreen shrubs. More bulbs and flowering plants were being used, including, of course, the tulip. In some ways Dutch William encouraged formal gardening. He liked topiary, which was carried to extreme lengths, every sort of bird, beast and geometrical design appearing in clipped evergreens.

In the space of a hundred years English landscape gardening became world-famous. The architect William Kent is credited with being the first to associate the new naturalistic style with the fine Palladian houses he designed. To him is attributed the establishing of the 'ha-ha'—a deep trench separating garden lawns and adjoining parkland. On the garden side the face of the trench was vertical and covered with a brick retaining wall, the other side sloped gently up and was covered with grass. Thus cattle grazing in the park could go down into the ha-ha but were unable to come up into the garden, while viewed from the garden side this very effective barrier was quite invisible. It must be remembered that, apart from using the scythe, the only other ways of maintaining a short sward was by grazing.

Everything that smacked of enclosure or obstructed the view was banished from the vicinity of the house. Even a walled kitchen garden might be sited a quarter of a mile away. Any boundaries needing to be defined on the distant fringes of the parkland would be marked by the plantings of woodland which merged into the more general view. The geometrical pictures of le Notre were discarded.

Many gifted amateurs set about landscaping their estates, rooting up the parterres, planting trees, and giving serpentine shores to their rectangular water gardens. But the movement received its greatest impetus from a professional, Lancelot Brown.

Of all our great gardeners 'Capability' Brown has the best known name, perhaps because so many of us visit stately homes and he seems to have been associated with most of them. He did indeed carry out major plans on over 150 estates, and no doubt advised the owners of others. His nickname derived from his invariable comment that a site was 'capable of improvement'.

Unlike London and Wise, Brown had no nursery of his own, and no permanent labour force. He bought trees through the trade and sub-contracted the constructional work and, given the chance, the scale of his operations was vast. At Fisherwick, in Staffordshire, he planted 100,000 trees, mixed hardwoods and conifers. Whole villages were levelled and rebuilt elsewhere because they spoilt a view. At Blenheim Palace he dammed the river Glyme to provide a sheet of water large enough to justify Vanburgh's magnificent bridge.

The Victorians and after
By the time of Victoria's accession gardening was being influenced by the new scientific spirit that was apparent in agriculture. The flow of exotics from overseas was becoming a flood; the construction and heating of greenhouses made rapid strides and it was realised that given light and warmth almost any species could be cultivated under glass. Nurserymen, seedsmen and professional gardeners proliferated, the kitchen, fruit and flower gardens were re-established as part of the general layout, and to them was added an ever-increasing range of glasshouses.

It became fashionable to take an interest in cultural details—in 'scientific' gardening. The movement was spurred on its way by a Scot, J. C. Loudon, and given the crown of approval in mid-century by Joseph Paxton. Loudon believed the garden should not look natural or picturesque, its prime function being the effective display of plants. Paxton was less of a gardener than Loudon, his major contribution to the Victorian scene being the building of glasshouses. The biggest of them all, the Crystal Palace, brought him a knighthood, but long before the Great Exhibition he had been building them for the Duke of Devonshire at Chatsworth where, in 1836, he began the construction of a greenhouse 277ft long and 133ft wide. It lasted until 1920 and was one of the things that made Chatsworth internationally famous.

Formal gardens came back. The parterre was reinstated in a new form capable of endless permutations of design and colour—carpet bedding. Expanses of colour in 'floral patterns', relieved and punctuated by specimen plants, urns, sundials, jardinieres and other horticultural equivalents of drawing-room knick-knacks, were universal. The greenhouses kept up the supply of plants, and labour was no problem. Gardeners in the 1870s worked a ten-hour day and a six-day week, with unpaid work like watering and boiler stoking on Sundays. A good journeyman gardener received sixteen shillings a week with certain perquisites. There was no more incentive to save labour in the Victorian garden than in the Victorian household, and the over-elaborate consequences were much the same.

The inevitable reaction came towards the end of the century, with Sir William Robinson's concept of the wild garden. Robinson, an Irishman by birth, wrote a long and still fascinating book, *The English Flower Garden*, first published in 1883, in which he deplored the Italian Renaissance imitations crammed with exotic plants, and wanted gardens to be based on hardy species and our own natural flora. He described flower-garden planting as being '. . . made up of a few kinds of flowers which people were proud to put out in thousands and tens of thousands, and with them, patterns, more or less elaborate, were carried out in every garden save the very poorest cottage garden'.

Typical old cottage garden. Thomas Hardy's birthplace near Dorchester (*MERL*)

Robinson at first even rejected the whole idea of 'designing' a garden. He advocated a wild garden in the sense of establishing plants which would co-exist in harmonious groups and leaving them to get on with it. This extreme view had to be abandoned, but Robinson's insistence on the beauty of hardy plants, shrubs and trees, growing as nature intended them to, yet in a carefully chosen setting, has had a lasting impact.

The cottage gardens had of course escaped all the swings of garden fashion. There was never any question of emulating the big house, the rectory, or the new villa. It would be walled or hedged, slightly shaded by a few fruit trees and, although mainly given over to vegetables, the paths would be fringed with a happy jumble of perennial flowers. Climbing roses and honeysuckle would mask walls and fences, and the general effect would be one of satisfying colour, scent and growth, totally unplanned but with a natural unity.

Gardening on the grand scale for the private estate came to an end in 1939. It became economically impossible, and only the intervention of the National Trust and the National Trust for Scotland has preserved for us so many examples of its past glories.

A number of great gardens were laid out during this last phase, some of which are only now reaching perfection. They show the influence of Robinson and also of the artist Gertrude Jekyll who turned to the making of gardens in the 1880s. She popularised the herbaceous border and convinced Robinson that at least a modicum of design in the relationship of plants to one another was necessary to bring out form and colour.

Gardens of the late nineteenth and early twentieth centuries conform to no dictated pattern. They possess great individuality, their shapes and planting being guided more than ever before by climate, soil and terrain. It was better to take advantage of what nature offered than to use the bulldozer of preconceived ideas. Everything was acceptable in the right place, from the wildest woodland to the most perfect formality; the pendulum of fashion oscillated gently about a central point. Among these later examples is Bodnant, a magnificent 100 acres of the Conway valley in North Wales, where the work, begun by his family before the end of the last century, was given to the National Trust by the late Lord Aberconway in 1949.

9 History in Customs

In scores of country towns and remote villages throughout **Great Britain,** the past and sometimes the very distant past, obtrudes into the modern world. The customs and traditions of our ancestors cling tenaciously to life, or perhaps we cling to them, knowing that an occasional backward glance can do no harm. Celebrations of faith and deliverance, echoes of folk-beliefs in the propitiation of the gods of nature, usages derived from our ancient laws and institutions, all these are still to be found.

True, some of our customs have lapsed and been revived in an ambience of self-conscious folksiness, but others have endured without a break for the best part of a millennium. Even the deliberate revivals are usually connected to the past by some continuous thread, however slender. The modern Morris Dance movement, for example, exists because a few poor men from Headington set out to earn a few coppers by going through the centuries-old steps before Cecil Sharp—almost the only man in the kingdom who could recognise this long-cherished remnant of medieval rustic merrymaking.

Religious observance is at the heart of the liveliest customs. Sometimes it is purely Christian, sometimes starkly pagan, more often the sort of amalgam natural to people who disliked hard logic and preferred to give a thought to the old gods while formally worshipping the new. The early Church, as we shall see, recognised the desire of simple people to retain this extra insurance policy against uncontrollable natural forces and grafted many of its own great festivals on to existing pagan ones. The real intentions of the latter are now somewhat beyond our imagination. We can scarcely even guess why the men of Ashbourne in Derbyshire should usher in the austerities of Lent with a ferocious football match spread over miles of terrain and lasting into the dark of a winter's night. Or why the people of Hallaton in Leicestershire celebrate the joy of Easter by eating hare pie and striving fiercely in a boundary tussle involving their neighbours from Melbourne and three small beer kegs. No doubt reasons existed for associating such activities with the major feasts and fasts of the Church, but they are not to be found in the tenets of Christianity.

The origins of some customs may be explained and dated with accuracy, but even those with a precise birthday and a legally defined purpose seem to build up an accretion of legends like the polyps of a coral reef. It is known when the Tichborne Dole was founded, but who could authenticate the terrible story of the dying Isabella Tichborne's last act of charity? Certainly the bell, Black Tom of Soothill, has tolled the Devil's Knell from

Dewsbury Church every Christmas Eve, reminding all good Christian men of their redemption and Satan of his doom, for centuries past, but was the original Thomas de Soothill really doing penance for the crime of murder when he gave the bell?

So many of these odd ceremonies are still to be found that we can do no more than list an assorted handful of them. All seasons and most parts of Britain have customs worth seeing and studying. Readers who would like to work out an itinerary of the more exotic goings-on should get a copy of *The Customs of Britain* from The British Tourist Authority. This comprehensive dossier is kept up to date and is unlikely to include customs recently defunct.

The turn of the year

Scottish Hogmanay procedures such as first-footing need no description here, but January has other customs related to the time of year and a few that have no apparent seasonal significance. New Year customs tend to be confused with Christmas ones and the dates of others are not what they should be because they seem never to have adjusted to the adoption of the Gregorian Calendar in 1752. That traumatic event, when people retired on the evening of 2 September and awoke on the morning of 14 September, was simply ignored by some of our folk festivals which have been mistimed ever since.

On 6 January the Haxey Hood Game is played at Haxey, Lincolnshire, as it probably has been since at least the thirteenth century. The story behind it is that one Lady Mowbray was riding home from church on Christmas Day when a high wind blew away her scarlet hood. No less than twelve labourers retrieved it for her and in reward for their gallantry she bestowed the rent of a piece of land in the village—still known as Hoodlands—to finance an annual game in which twelve men dressed in scarlet competed for the prize of a hood. The game, which has been aptly described as a kind of debased rugby football, has suffered many changes. It is now a struggle for twelve pieces of canvas and a piece of leather, all known as 'hoods', between members of the crowd and slightly sinister figures known as 'Boggons'. The latter wear a certain amount of fancy dress including something scarlet and have certainly been part of the proceedings for a very long time. So has the Fool, whose duty has been to recite the story of Lady Mowbray, after which the strips of paper which decorate his costume were formerly set alight, an amiable custom known as 'smoking the Fool'.

Also on 6 January is the Feast of the Epiphany and the festivities of Twelfth Night, since it is the last of the Twelve Days of Christmas. The Holy Thorn of Glastonbury blooms at this time because it goes by the old calendar and this is old Christmas Day. The people of Carhampton,

Somerset, go wassailing their apple trees, toasting them in cider and firing shotguns into the branches to discourage the evil spirits, on Twelfth Night. But they too kept to the old calendar and so do their wassailing on 17 January.

The first Monday after Twelfth Day is traditionally Plough Monday, a festival with a chequered history which died of unpopularity. Or nearly died—in the village of Goathland, Yorkshire, the Plough Stots Dance is still performed on Plough Monday. 'Stot' is an old name for bullock and a reminder of the days when oxen pulled the plough.

Mayday and summer

The maypole and its attendant rituals still survive even if they are no longer a spontaneous and rowdy expression of delight at the thought that summer would soon be bursting out all over. The tall pole, garlanded with flowers and encircled with ribbons and streamers and dancing youth, has somehow survived the winds of change and denunciation. It is older than our most venerable institutions, it is the Sacred Tree, representing the instinctive worship of procreation and growth. The Church never managed to assimilate it as it did other pagan practices and, except by the Puritans, it was generally tolerated.

Our existing May ceremonies are not all associated with the maypole. The first place off the mark is at Padstow, Cornwall, with its distinctive 'Obby 'Oss celebration, beginning with the singing of the May Song just after midnight on 30 April. The song is the usual cheerful nonsense about everyone uniting in the merry month of May, but the main proceedings which begin at 10.30am are not typical Mayday stuff. The Hobby Horse itself is a sinister apparition, a tent-like affair with a grotesque head, completely concealing the man inside. It moves through the decorated town, followed by cheering and singing crowds and men dressed as pirates, bobbing and gyrating and stopping outside houses to address their occupants by name. At last it is ritually slaughtered and dies realistically in the roadway.

Two May ceremonies worth noticing take place at Flore, Northamptonshire, and Gawthorpe, Yorkshire, on the first Saturday in the month. The Flore proceedings include carrying the May Garland in procession, almost the only survival of an almost universal custom. So important was it that the First of May was often known as Garland Day.

The Gawthorpe Feast is remarkable for being a largely equestrian event. The maypole procession from Gawthorpe village to Ossett Market Place is headed by the May Queen and her six maids of honour, all mounted, and followed by perhaps a hundred riders and decorated floats. A traditional usage adapting itself to the equally traditional Yorkshire love of the horse.

With the Helston (Cornwall) Furry Dance on 8 May we are really moving into summer. Whatever its intentions the Furry Dance has survived its worldwide renown and remains a genuine and spectacular folk festival.

A considerable number of customs are concentrated around Ascension Day and Whitsuntide in late May and early June. The three days before Ascension Day are Rogation Days, when the crops were blessed by clergy walking in procession about their parishes. A few years ago these rogation services seemed to have died out completely but recently a number of parishes have revived them and found that they evoke a response.

The rogation ceremonies in the past were often associated with the custom of Beating the Bounds—a custom which is carried on in a few places though its raison d'être has long since vanished. In the days when few people could read or write, when maps were practically non-existent, and the parish was an important administrative unit, it was vital for the parish boundaries to be clear in the minds of a certain number of villagers.

Shrovetide and Easter

Candlemas (2 February) commemorates the presentation of the Infant Christ in the Temple. Henry VIII proclaimed that lighted candles be carried 'in memorie of Christe, the spiritual lyghte, when Simeon dyd prophecye, as it is redde in the church that daye'. Candlemas was once generally observed in country parishes and had a place in rustic weather forecasting; a spring-like Candlemas was a bad omen for the critical months ahead:

> If Candlemas Day be fair and bright
> Winter shall have another flight.

This belief crossed the Atlantic to the eastern states of America where 2 February is remembered as Ground Hog Day. It is said that this little animal emerges from hibernation then but immediately retires for another month or so if it sees its own shadow—if, in other words, the sun is shining. In this country at least there appears to be some slight basis for the belief, a mild bright spell in early February often being followed by a cold late spring.

The day after Candlemas, 3 February, is the Feast of St Blaise, the patron saint of woolcombers and sufferers from throat ailments. Within a week of St Blaise's Day the very curious custom of Hurling the Silver Ball is enacted at St Ives, Cornwall. It is nominally connected with the Feast of St Ia, the remarkable lady who fled from persecution in Ireland, miraculously crossed the Irish Sea on a leaf, gave St Ives its name and converted all that part of Cornwall to Christianity.

Shrove Tuesday, the day when Christians traditionally confessed and were shriven of their sins before the solemn fast of Lent, has always been a dull affair in this country. It is a natural day for a last burst of merrymaking but we have no carnival or Mardi Gras. Nothing but pancakes and football. Why pancakes should be important in the pre-Lenten feast is not clear, except, perhaps, because the natural laying season for hens is then approaching.

Most of today's pancake races are modern institutions, but there is evidence that those at Olney, Buckinghamshire, have been run since 1445. Competitors must be over sixteen years of age, wear aprons and have their heads covered. The race ends at the Parish Church, where the winner is kissed by the ringer of the Pancake Bell, and is followed by the Shriving Service.

Association football, the townsman's greatest spectator sport, developed from a village game which was once a general Shrove Tuesday amusement. That is generally conceded. At least two good Shrovetide matches may still be seen. One is at Alnwick, Northumberland, between teams of about 150 each, representing the parishes of St Michael and St Paul. A more vigorous and perhaps more typical game takes place at Ashbourne, Derbyshire, between the Up'ards and Down'ards. The contestants traditionally live on opposite sides of Henmore Brook, but anyone rash enough may join in.

This time of the year sees other observances quite unconnected with Lent. On 14 February, just before midnight, the ancient ceremony of Blessing the Salmon Nets is performed at Pedwell Fishery, Northam-on-Tweed. This is an old centre of salmon fishing and the service is held in the last few moments before the season opens. The boats put out promptly at midnight, and if the first nets to be 'shot' bring in a salmon it is presented to the vicar. The congregation at this service is advised to wrap up warmly, wear wellingtons, and carry torches.

St Valentine's Day has a history of varied customs. One inevitably speculates on the connection between Valentine, priest and martyr, beheaded on 14 February AD 269, and the practice of exchanging lovers' greetings. There is none; the Valentine really dates back to the Roman Feast of the Lupercalia which also fell about mid-February. Part of this uninhibited festival involved the drawing of women's names from a box, and a similar idea was perpetuated in Christian Europe and attached to a Christian saint's day.

By the early nineteenth century St Valentine had become the excuse for a more open form of blackmail. Children bedecked with ribbons paraded the villages chanting:

> Good morrow, Valentine.
> Please to give me a Valentine
> And I'll be yours and you'll be mine . . .

Easter, like that other great Christian feast, Christmas, is interlaced with pagan themes. The early Christians linked their own rejoicing in the

Resurrection with the seasonal celebrations of new life, of birth and growth. They even named this supreme festival after Eostra, the Saxon goddess of dawn and springtime. All the traditional adjuncts of Easter, the lambs, the flowers, the wearing of new clothes, reflect the awareness of a new beginning. The ubiquitous egg, of course, has been a fertility symbol from earliest times before the Church appropriated it for Easter. A prayer for the blessing of eggs in church was introduced under Pope Paul V, beginning 'Bless, O Lord, we beseech Thee, this Thy creature of eggs . . .'. Ceremonial Easter eggs were originally just hard-boiled eggs dyed in various colours, and their use was very widespread. The household records of Edward I refer to the purchase of 450 coloured eggs for Easter distribution. They cost him one shilling and sixpence.

The few remaining Pace-egg ceremonies are worth noting as the survivals of once general village entertainments. The name 'Pace', like the use of 'paschal' in relation to Easter, is a link with yet another religion—Judaism. It refers to the 'Pasch', the Jewish Passover and we meet it again in the Pasque Flower, the lovely purple spring-flowering *Anemone pulsatilla*.

Pace-egging was pursued by village children in some counties, Cheshire, for instance, up to the beginning of World War II. Like St Valentine's Day it was really a collecting exercise, at first for eggs and later for

Schoolboys perform the Pace-Egg Ceremony in Midgley, Yorkshire (*Fox*)

money. Niggardly people were told that their hens would lay addled eggs.

Pace-egg plays were mummers' plays which just happened to be performed at Easter. All mummers' plays deal with the same basic issues of life, death and resurrection and have roughly the same motley cast. A series of these plays is performed in the Upper Calder Valley, Yorkshire, going on throughout Good Friday in five towns and villages.

Egg-rolling was another Eastertide activity as popular as it was apparently pointless. With local variations it consisted of solemnly rolling hard-boiled eggs down any convenient slope. The universal explanation was that it symbolised the rolling away of the stone at the entrance of Christ's tomb, but one suspects that this may have been the Church's rationalisation of a custom which even the participants could not explain.

The persistence of rough-and-tumble sports like bottle kicking and Shrovetide football is rather odd in these sophisticated days. The events are rated as tourist attractions, but the participants and their communities are certainly not out for financial reward. It must be another example of the way in which we accept the fact that something has always been done as a completely valid reason for continuing to do it.

Doles and fairs

Private charity, whether in the form of individual benefactions and bequests or through the agencies of the Church, was once an important factor in the relief of poverty. Many charitable bequests, no longer of material significance in the days of the Welfare State, are still made in accordance with the terms of their founders' wills. It is difficult to see how some of them could legally be stopped and part of their interest lies in the exact documentary evidence of their age and continuity.

Of this great network of succour almost the last relic is the Wayfarers' Dole, given at the Hospital of St Cross, Winchester, Hampshire. This is part of a larger charity founded in 1133 by Henry de Blois and later reformed by William of Wykeham; it still dispenses bread and ale to the traveller. If you knock at the door of the Porter's lodge and ask for the Dole you will, provided the day's supply is not exhausted, be given bread on a carved wooden platter and ale in a horn bearing the arms of the Knights Hospitallers of St John. You cannot claim the ration on Sunday, but there are no questions asked and no restriction on who shall receive it, though it has been suggested that if you were truly down and out the allowance would be increased.

The famous Biddenden Dole, by which bread and cheese is distributed at the Old Workhouse, Biddenden, Kent, on Easter Monday, has origins that are both macabre and doubtful. It is said to date from 1100, but this is unproven. Then there are the stories surrounding the twin sisters, Eliza and

Maypole dancing at Abinger Common, Surrey. The innocent descendant of a pagan ritual and the 'stinckying idoll' denounced by the puritans (*Central Press*)

Mary Chaulkhurst, who left a legacy of twenty acres, still known as the Bread and Cheese Lands, to finance this annual treat for the poor of the parish. They are said to have been born joined at the hip and shoulder and to have died within six hours of each other at the age of thirty-four. According to tradition the one to survive longest was urged to allow herself to be separated from her sister's body, but this she refused, saying they would die as they had lived, together.

In Hampshire the Dole is a gift of flour to the parishioners of Tichborne and Cheriton. The general public is admitted to the ceremony in the grounds of Tichborne House, where the flour is blessed and sanctified with holy water before distribution on Lady Day (25 March) and prayers are said for the soul of Lady Isabella Tichborne, the founder of the charity.

If private benefaction was important in the field of welfare, fairs were equally so in the field of commerce. It may be difficult to realise, wandering round the average stereotyped pleasure fair with its 'rides' and side shows, that all fairs were originally trading occasions with entertainment only a very secondary feature. Country fairs, especially horse fairs, were mainly commercial events well into the last century when the steam merry-go-round was beginning to give them an exciting new image.

Their entertainment value has kept a surprising number of fairs alive, and many of them are very old indeed. Their history is almost a history of the

Fair Day at Wallingford-on-the-Thames, probably at the turn of the century (*MERL*)

Fair Day, Bude, 1905. At this time many small fairs were still held for trade purposes, being little more than periodic or occasional markets (*MERL*)

country's internal trade, for most fairs were based on charters of licences to assemble in a particular place at a particular time—often a saint's day—to buy and sell and generally transact business.

The value of the fair as a shop or, rather, as a supermarket, resulted from the isolation of country communities and their enforced self-sufficiency which was so obvious a feature of our past until the canals and improved roads of the late eighteenth and early nineteenth centuries allowed freer movement of goods and people. Until then there was no distribution network as we understand it, a merchant or manufacturer relying on sales within a limited area. Many scattered villages and small towns would be willing to buy his wares but it was uneconomic to cart his goods along appalling roads for mere handfuls of customers. A fair had the advantage of concentrating in one place potential buyers from miles around, and the merchant's problems were reduced to a single transport operation. On the other side, farmers would bring their produce for sale and buyers from the larger population centres would find worthwhile quantities ready for negotiation.

Fairs in the past brought together people who would not otherwise have met and whose relationship, had they done so, could have been mutually hostile. A clue to this situation may be seen at Barnstaple, Devon, whose fair opens with considerable ceremony on the Wednesday nearest to 17 September. A large stuffed white glove garlanded with flowers is suspended from a window of the Guildhall on the opening day as a sign of welcome—the hand of friendship to visitors. This is not a purely local custom, the sign of the hand was once generally displayed at fairs as a pledge that outsiders could trade there.

The use of wooden hands or mammoth gloves to denote this sudden outbreak of free trading was kept up at many fairs long after it ceased to have practical significance. At Exeter Lammas Fair a stuffed glove was carried on a decorated pole in the opening procession, and during the Summer and Autumn Fairs at Chester a painted wooden hand hung on St Peter's Church up to the 1860s. But it may be that Barnstaple is now the only fair to remind us of the 'restrictive practices' of the past.

Among the survivals Barnet Horse Fair in Hertfordshire still actually has some horses; its proximity to London once made it a great horsetrading event but the old fairground is now a suburban housing estate. Nottingham Goose Fair begins on the first Thursday in October and maintains a record going back to 1155, but is now a pleasure event entirely lacking in geese. Widecombe-in-the-Moor, Devon, reminds us of Bill Brewer, Jan Stewer, *et al.* on the second Tuesday in September by having its fair presided over by a master of ceremonies in a smock and carrying a shepherd's crook. Perhaps more authentically it has good sheepdog trials and Dartmoor pony

A performing bear with gypsies was sometimes a fair attraction (*MERL*)

classes. And, incidentally, Uncle Tom Cobley would have had no need to
hitch a lift on Tom Pearce's unfortunate beast. He was a well-to-do farmer
who lived to the age of ninety-six and was buried in 1794, according to the
church register at Spreyton, near Okehampton.

The Egremont Crab Fair in Cumberland, on the Saturday nearest to 20
September, is the venue of the Gurning Championships, a distinction which
it claims to have held since 1266. The reader will of course know that
gurning is the sport of pulling hideous faces.

The choice of September and October for holding fairs was dictated by
the cycle of country life. There was a pause between the end of one farming
year and the beginning of another, time for a break and an outing. There
were crops to market such as corn and hops, fat cattle from grass, and geese
from the stubbles, before the winter came. There were supplies and
equipment to be bought with the proceeds of sales and all the transactions
associated with changes of occupation at Michaelmas.

There are exceptions to this preference for autumn in the matter of fairs.
At King's Lynn, Norfolk, the Mart is proclaimed on 14 February by the
mayor and lasts for up to twelve days. This event was once among the
greatest religious and commercial gatherings in East Anglia and has
probably been held for 800 years, though its legal establishment goes back
only to Henry VIII. Other major fairs take place during the spring and
summer, but far fewer than in the autumn. It was, however, almost
obligatory to hold one type of fair in the autumn, at the start of the farming

year. This was the Mop Fair, the predecessor of the employment exchange. Farmworkers and domestic servants were engaged on yearly contracts and the Mop Fair was a shop window for those seeking employment. Hiring by the year continued into Victorian times and any sort of gathering always provided an opportunity for potential employers and workers to meet. But the formal hiring fairs became obsolete and today's Mop Fairs differ from others only in their titles and their history.

One such fair is held at Tewkesbury, Gloucestershire, on or about 10 October, but it appears to have nothing to distinguish it now from other pleasure fairs. At Stratford-on-Avon, however, a very odd custom has survived. It has both a Mop Fair and a Runaway Mop Fair. The first was probably flourishing long before Shakespeare's time and was important to a large district. It is held on 12 October, and is followed by the Runaway Fair a few weeks later, intended to give a second chance to the worker who had repented of his bargain.

The pleasure fair and its travelling showmen came to mean a lot to the country people who had few amusements but self-made ones. It was an exciting event in a very static way of life for many small communities up to World War I. But pleasure was never the primary purpose of a fair and even the most ordinary collection of dodgems and chairoplanes may be the last word in a fascinating story of mercantile history.

Wells, rushes, and summertime

The curious cult of well-dressing is mainly practised around Ascension Day though examples of it occur throughout the summer. The wells are blessed and then decorated with greenery and flowers. The ceremonies are almost entirely confined to the county of Derbyshire, and one explanation often given is that the area was a centre of worship of the Roman god, Fontus, the spirit of wells and springs.

The best known ceremonies are at Tissington, Wirksworth, Ashford-in-the-Water and Tideswell in May and June, and Buxton, Bonsall, Stoney Middleton and Eyam in July and August. Dates and fuller details should be sought from the Peaks Park Planning Board at Bakewell.

The Tissington well-dressing is quite famous. The five wells are decorated with large floral mosaics of moss, leaves and thousands of flower petals on a moist surface, usually forming pictures of Biblical scenes. Local craftsmen have been producing these floral designs for generations and no other well-dressers seem to have quite the same expertise.

The ceremony is said to date back to 1350 and to be a thanks offering for Tissington's immunity to the Black Death, which ravaged the surrounding countryside. The villagers ascribed their escape to the purity of their water supply, another example of a local reason being found for a general custom.

Well-dressing at Tissington, Derbyshire, 1899. This strange art form is still practised, and although apparently Christian in origin its roots may be in Roman Britain (*MERL*)

Another village where well-dressing goes on, Eyam, certainly has no such deliverance to celebrate though it does remember a unique story of collective courage. In the summer of 1665 the plague was brought to Eyam and, after a pause during the winter, broke out with renewed virulence in 1666. The Rector, William Mompesson, seeing that surrounding districts were still unaffected, persuaded the people of Eyam not to flee from the village and so spread the infection, but to quarantine themselves. They stayed within the parish, going out only to collect food which was left for them at a distance. The disease ran its course and ceased after October 1666, but by then five people out of six in a community of three hundred souls had died, including Mompesson's wife. Beyond the parish boundaries there was not a single death from the plague.

By the end of June we begin to discover rush-strewing ceremonies in a few country churches—though in these days of effective land drainage it may be hay- or grass-strewing instead. They are interesting examples of the way in which severely practical activities manage to get themselves preserved as formalised traditions, in this case transforming spring cleaning into a church service.

We have seen that medieval churches usually had floors of beaten earth and that congregations—except for the weakest who went to the stone benches against the wall—stood. The floor was kept covered with rushes and by the winter's end, with the seasonal shortage of such material, and after months of trampling by muddy boots, the state of this covering is better imagined than described. As soon as new rushes could be cut and dried the church was cleaned out—'mucked out' is possibly more accurate—and a clean, sweet-smelling carpet was laid.

Some of the surviving ceremonies take place around Whitsun, which may or may not coincide with the Spring Bank Holiday, and others at the end of June. They go under various titles, some are quite elaborate and others charmingly simple with small children bearing their offerings of rushes. The following are still held.

Whit Saturday—hay-strewing, Shenington (Oxfordshire); 29 June—rush-strewing, Barrowden (Rutland) and Warcop (Westmorland); Sunday nearest to 29 June—hay-strewing, Braunstone (Leicestershire); last Sunday in June—grass-strewing, Wingrave (Buckinghamshire); Sunday after 29 June—rush sermon, Farnborough (Kent) and hay-scattering, Langham (Rutland). There is a rush-bearing service at Grasmere (Westmorland) on the Saturday nearest to 5 August, and this is one of the most famous and impressive of them all, involving a procession in which traditional designs woven in rushes are carried.

Finally, the custom is observed in two utterly different churches with literary associations. One is in St Mary Redcliffe, Bristol, where the 'marvellous boy', the ill-starred Thomas Chatterton, claimed to have found in the muniment room the poems so incredibly written by himself. Rush-bearing at St Mary's, said to be the most splendid parish church in England, is a civic ceremony dating from 1493, when a former mayor of the city, William Spensor, left money for an annual sermon to be preached before all succeeding mayors at the rush-bearing on Whit Sunday. Today the lord mayor is present to hear the sermon, the aisles are strewn with freshly gathered rushes and posies of flowers are placed in every seat.

The parish church at Haworth, Yorkshire, where the Reverend Patrick Brontë once officiated and the most extraordinary literary family in our history worshipped, is in bleak contrast to the splendours of St Mary Redcliffe. Its Rush-bearing Ceremony is an ancient one and was allowed to lapse for some twenty-five years. Now it has been revived in its simplest form with the children scattering their offerings of rushes before the beginning of service on the third Sunday in July.

Functions and festivals of all sorts come thick and fast in the midsummer season. The summer solstice is celebrated at Stonehenge (though the ceremony is a modern invention); midsummer bonfires are still lit in

Cornwall; the Beltane Festival lasts a week at Peebles, and the Manx Parliament meets on Tynwald Hill. In West Linton, Peebleshire, the Whipmans' Week celebrates the once vital role of carters and ploughmen in the rural community, there is a Fyshinge Feast at Burrator, Devon, and a Love Feast at Alport Castle, Derbyshire.

By now the Morris dancers, who began their strenuous activities at Easter, will be in full trip and jingle, the troupes, or 'clubs' performing on many a village green. In Thaxted, Essex, the Morris men hold their own special festival in a town that provides a perfect setting, beginning with a procession from the great fourteenth-century church.

We have no space to give even a list of the strange observances which the summer traveller in Britain may discover, let alone describe them. Their titles echo like the voices of past generations that yet live; The Payment of the Rose, The Cakes and Ale Ceremony, The Grand Wardmote of the Woodmen of Arden. . . . Two more, however, which come before the days of harvest and autumn, must be mentioned.

One of them is at West Witton, Yorkshire, on 24 August. It is known as the Burning of Bartle and is one of the very few cases in England in which an individual is remembered by the burning of his effigy. Indeed, Guy Fawkes is probably the only other example, although there are some in Northern Ireland too. Bartle was said to have been an outlaw who specialised in making off with the villagers' pigs. One day they were chasing him down the fellside when he fell and broke his neck. The delighted locals cremated him in Grassgill Lane. There they still burn his effigy, carrying it through the village after dark and pausing at intervals to recite the story of his iniquities.

And, at the end of summer, 4 September to be exact, the Horn Dance is enacted at Abbots Bromley, Staffordshire. This most strenuous performance is supposed to celebrate the granting of hunting rights to the village in the reign of Henry III, but it recalls hunting dances from a very much earlier time. The dancers clearly represent the quarry and not the hunters and the ritual has some resemblance to the hunting dances of many primitive peoples in which the victim is a participant. One extraordinary feature of the Horn Dance is that the horns are in fact six reindeer skulls complete with antlers, polished and blackened with age and carefully preserved in the parish church for use on this one day. Reindeer have never existed in Britain and where these fine specimens came from is a complete mystery. Maybe the Norsemen brought them, and if so they probably brought the dance as well.

From harvest to Christmas

Past customs related to the completion of harvest are mentioned elsewhere

The Abbots Bromley Horn Dance. Physically exhausting and one of the more
mysterious of surviving customs (*MERL*)

in the book; they were usually matters for each individual farm and not the
sort of public celebration dealt with in this chapter. The Harvest Festival as
we know it is a quite modern institution devised by that powerful eccentric,
the Reverend Stephen Hawker of Morwenstow. His belief in a general
desire to give thanks for the fruits of the earth was fully justified and harvest
thanksgiving services tend to draw larger congregations in country areas
than any others.

One or two really ancient public ceremonies connected with harvest are
to be found in the corn counties. The First Fruits Ceremony at Richmond,
Yorkshire, is a case in point. Here the first local farmer to bring a decent
sample of new season's wheat to the market cross receives a bottle of wine
from the mayor. It is then customary for this to be drunk on the spot by
those present and for the farmer to receive another bottle to take home.
This is clearly not a celebration of a safely completed harvest—that is still a
long way off—but a modification of the ritual of offering first fruits in
sacrifice, though the only actual sacrifice here seems to be the farmer's first
bottle of wine.

A more overtly religious ceremony, one of the few of its kind remaining,
takes place at Painswick, Gloucestershire, on the Sunday nearest to 19

September, when local children join in Clipping the Church. 'Clipping' in this context derives from a Saxon word meaning to enclose or embrace and the children walk round the parish church singing the Clipping Hymn and then join hands and form a continuous circle round the building to demonstrate their loving embrace of Mother Church.

Autumn is a great time for the paying of dues and quit rents, for the assembling of Courts Baron and Courts Leet, the election of Sheriffs, Bailiffs, Ale-tasters and other officials, and the confirming of ancient manorial rights. Some of these things still have the force of law, others continue because of our attachment to old customs. In this connection it should be remembered that the Common Law of England is itself nothing but a great body of accepted custom.

A summary of these legal and civic junketings would require more space than we can spare, but a single example gives something of their peculiar flavour. An early riser may go before dawn on 11 November to Knightlow Cross on Dunsmore Heath, Warwickshire, to see the Wroth Silver Ceremony. The place is the site of an ancient tumulus, the occasion is the payment of dues by the parishes of the Knightlow Hundred to the lord of the manor, the Duke of Buccleuch. Wroth silver is of Anglo-Saxon derivation and the term probably means road money. The title of the toll, either a contribution to the upkeep of such roads as existed or to the control of wandering cattle, is an indication of its antiquity.

Nowadays the steward of the lord of the manor calls the roll of parishes and the representative of each throws his contribution into the stone bowl at the foot of the cross. Everyone then repairs to the Dun Cow Inn at Stretton-on-Dunsmore for breakfast. A parish not paying up in full could face a fine of one pound for every penny lacking or—a costly penalty today—the forfeiture of a white bull with red ears.

In November we also have a custom that deserves mention for what it is not. It is celebrated on the fifth and has absolutely no connection with Guy Fawkes. To see it you must go to the village of Shebbear, Devon, for the ritual of Turning the Devil's Boulder. It lies under an old oak tree and on Guy Fawkes' Night a peal is rung on the church bells and this large lump of rock, allegedly dropped by the Evil One, is solemnly turned. It has been claimed that this is one of the oldest annual ceremonies in the whole county and local belief is that misfortune will befall the village if it is not observed.

With December the apparently dying sun sinks to its lowest point and the great conglomerate festival of Christmas, a fusion of so many religious beliefs and customs, sets about cheering man's body with warmth and light and food, and lifting his spirit in the concept of salvation and the world reborn.

Christmas customs are too well known to need description, but the most casual examination of them reveals the differing strands that time and the Church's fight for survival in a pagan world have woven round the central core of Christ's birth.

Among local Christmas customs there are still some mummers' plays to be seen. One is at Crookham, Hampshire, on Boxing Day and is fairly traditional in cast and action. Two villains, Bold Roamer and Bold Slasher, are slain by King George and later resurrected by the Doctor. King George then fights and defeats the Turkish Knight, and ends up by killing Father Christmas, who is not resurrected. This last episode is believed to be unique to the Crookham play and is even more inexplicable than the rest. Mummers' plays have been performed since the twelfth century and probably long before, on village greens and in the halls of the great.

Sources of Information

Sources of information

For those who like to have definite objectives in exploring the countryside there are many ways of finding out what any particular district has to offer.

The British Tourist Authority, 64 St James' Street, London SW1A 1YX. For Information Sheets on current events, which describe the celebrations, traditional customs, ceremonies, fairs and similar goings-on which take place somewhere or other in every month of the year. Also publishes periodical *In Britain*, describing noteworthy places and events in town and country.

The Forestry Commission, 25 Savile Row, London W1X 2AY. For details of National Forest Parks and general information on public access to forests. Publishes books on forestry for the general reader and illustrated booklets on wildlife of the forests.

The Inland Waterways Association, 114 Regents Park Road, London NW1. For data on canal restoration and canal routes open to traffic. Publishes *The Inland Waterways Guide*, full of detailed information and maps.

The National Farmers Union—consult the local or county branch in any district (address in the telephone book) for information on agricultural shows in the region, farms and research stations holding 'open days' for visitors and, possibly, farmhouse holidays or working holidays for would-be fruitpickers.

The National Parks Commission, 1 Cambridge Gate, Regents Park, London NW1. The Commission has overall responsibility for the National Parks, the extended footpaths such as the Pennine Way and the South Downs Way, and for efforts to protect certain areas of outstanding natural beauty. Reports on its work are published regularly by HMSO and may be obtained through booksellers.

The National Trust, 42 Queen Anne's Gate, London SW1 H 9AS. The catalogue *Properties of the National Trust* is available to members and non-members. It contains up-to-date descriptions with times and conditions of access to those properties open to the public. These include not only historic houses and famous gardens but nature reserves, windmills, watermills, farms, deer parks and churches.

The Nature Conservancy, 19 Belgrave Square, London SW1. Is responsible for more than 100 nature reserves inland and on the coast. The most important organisation engaged in the preservation of animal and plant wildlife and its habitats. Reports on its work and information on reserves suitable for particular studies are obtainable.

The Rare Breeds Survival Trust, Cotswold Farm Park, Guiting Power, Gloucestershire. Open to visitors for much of the year, this growing collection of famous breeds from the past of British agriculture is unique. Here, under ideal farm conditions, may be seen breeds of horses, cattle, sheep, pigs and poultry which once stocked the farms of Britain.

The Royal Agricultural Society, Stoneleigh, Warwickshire. This is the permanent site of the Royal Show, held annually in July, and many other events of interest to both farmers and non-specialist visitors. The 'Royal' is worth at least one visit in a lifetime, but although a most impressive spectacle one may learn more about farming from shows of a more manageable size. These range from large events like the Great Yorkshire Show and the East of England Show, Peterborough, to the average county affair, which still caters for every sort of rural interest.

The Society for the Protection of Ancient Buildings, 55 Great Ormond Street, London WC1. Especially for lists of windmills and watermills in working order.

Museums

Museums

The many Folk Museums and Open-air Museums now in existence have done a great job in salvaging and displaying country relics of every sort, from buildings and machines to hand tools and kitchen utensils. A comprehensive guide to museums is published by ABC Travel Guides, London Road, Dunstable LU6 3EB.

Many rural crafts are very much alive and exhibitions of the work of modern craftsmen are featured at shows and other functions. For general information on contemporary rural crafts, contact the Council for Small Industries in Rural Areas (COSIRA), 39 Camp Road, Wimbledon Common, London SW19 4UP.

Many aspects of country life in the past are featured in the following collections: Angus Folk Museum, Kirk Wynd, Glamis, Angus, Scotland; Avoncroft Museum of Buildings, Redditch Road, Bromsgrove, Hereford & Worcester; Bicton Countryside Museum, Bicton Gardens, East Budleigh, Devon; Blaine Castle House Folk Museum, Bristol; Bridewell Museum, Norwich, Norfolk; Castle Museum, York; Farmland Museum, High Street, Haddenham, Cambridgeshire; Hampshire County Council Museum, Chilcombe House, Bar End, Winchester, Hampshire; Horsham Museum, The Causeway, Horsham, Sussex; Hull Transport Museum, High Street, Hull. For a unique collection of horse brasses: Jackson Collection, Old Kiln Museum, Reeds Road, Tilford, Farnham, Surrey; Mary Arden's House, Wilmcote, near Stratford-on-Avon; Museum of English Rural Life, University of Reading, Whiteknights, Reading (a major collection containing one of the finest displays of wagons); Nortons Farm Museum, Sedlescombe, Battle, Sussex (vintage farm machinery in a farm setting; a private museum); Oxford City and County Museum, Fletcher's House, Woodstock, Oxfordshire; Rutland Museum, Catmoss Street, Oakham, Leicestershire; Weald and Downland Museum, Fingleton, Chichester, Sussex; Welsh Folk Museum (National Museum of Wales), St Fagans, Cardiff (among other noteworthy exhibits it contains the machinery of the great water-powered Esgair Moel woollen mill); West Yorkshire Folk Museum, Shibden Hall, Halifax, Yorkshire; White House, Stedman Homestead, Aston Munslow, Shropshire.

A Farming Glossary

A farming glossary

All trades have their technical vocabularies and farming is no exception. The layman is at times puzzled by farming terms and sometimes fails to understand them properly. Old usages change and new words and expressions come with new techniques. A selection of those in everyday use is given below.

Arable   Land for ploughing and tillage, which the Romans called *arabilia*. The drier eastern side of Britain has more arable land than the moister western half where there is a higher proportion of permanent grass.

Artificial insemination   Many more calves are now born to AI than to natural service. The Milk Marketing Board maintains a network of AI centres throughout the country, relieving dairy farmers of the expense of keeping a bull and enabling them to improve their herds by the use of sires which they could not afford to own.

Bale   An oblong or cylindrical bundle of hay or straw, mechanically compressed and tied with twine or wire. The bale has replaced the *truss*, which was cut from a stack and tied by hand. Balers were formerly stationary and the material baled had to be fed into them, but the modern baler is mobile, picking up the material from the ground.

Binder   Abbreviation of 'reaper-and-binder'. A machine which cuts grain crops and binds the sheaves. Now superseded by the combine-harvester, though still to be found on some small farms and where the farmer produces straw for thatching, straw from the combine being unsuitable for this purpose. Prior to the introduction of the binder, sheaves of corn were tied with straw bands, often called *bonds* made from the crop itself.

Break-crop   A crop introduced into the rotation to break a sequence of corn crops. Frequently peas or beans or a root crop such as sugar beet or potatoes.

Broadcast   To sow by scattering seed on the surface and harrowing it in. Corn was sown in this way from the earliest times until the invention of the drill in the eighteenth century. The practice has sometimes been revived in times of emergency—when much land was waterlogged after the severe winter of 1947, broadcast sowing from light aircraft was attempted.

Cad   The smallest pig in a litter, a runt. Almost every part of the country will be found to have a different name for this unfortunate animal.

Cast   Condition in which an animal lying on its back is unable to regain its feet. May happen to any quadruped with fatal consequences if no help is given, therefore a serious possibility in sheep flocks spread over wide terrain. Another word with many regional equivalents; in Scotland and the north of England a cast sheep may be described as *wigwelted*.

Cereals   Food grains for human and animal consumption. Botanically, the cereals, named after Ceres, the goddess of harvest, are grasses. Principal cereal crops in Britain are wheat, barley and oats, the largest acreage being of barley and the smallest of oats. Rye is also grown for the manufacture of crispbread, and in the southern half of England an increasing though still small area is being sown to new varieties of maize. All cereals are referred to in Britain as 'corn', in the United States the word applies to maize only, the generic term for other cereals being 'grain'.

Clamp A long, ridge-shaped mound of potatoes or other roots stored for winter use. Also known as a *pie*. Once a very familiar sight, especially in potato-growing districts, but rare now that potatoes are stored in insulated buildings. The clamp was built with steeply sloping sides and covered with thick layers of straw and soil. The contents remain dry and safe from frost but the clamp cannot be opened in severe weather and the preparation of potatoes for market has to be done in the open. For these reasons barn storage is now preferred to clamps.

Dibble To plant a seed or seedling in a hole made by a dibber. Before World War I large acreages of beans were sown in this way, each seed being sown and covered by hand. Plants such as brassicas were generally set with the dibber until the 1930s, transplanting machines were then introduced which set plants very rapidly and watered them in.

Drill The small trench in which seed is sown, also a machine for sowing in rows. The invention of the drill was a fundamental advance in crop husbandry and its construction has become steadily more sophisticated. *Direct drilling*, the sowing of seed on land cleaned by a herbicide but not ploughed or cultivated. *Combine drill*, one which deposits fertiliser simultaneously with the seed. *Precision drill*, very advanced type designed to sow each seed at an optimum distance from its neighbours.

Fallow Arable land left uncropped during the growing season to restore fertility and facilitate destruction of perennial weeds by repeated cultivations. Left uncropped for an entire season it is a 'bare fallow', if an early crop is taken and the land fallowed from late summer it is a 'bastard fallow'. In Essex and East Anglia the word is frequently pronounced 'follow'. Fallowing is now rarely practised except when sowing schedules are completely disrupted by very bad spring weather.

Fertiliser Inorganic plant foods based on the essential elements nitrogen, phosphorus and potassium (referred to collectively as NPK) and certain trace elements. Fertilisers are at present necessary to maintain yields high enough to prevent global starvation, but their widespread use has stimulated a reaction from advocates of 'organic' husbandry who believe in using only animal manures and compost. Farmworkers' names for fertilisers include 'artificials', 'bag-muck' and 'compass'. The last is a most curious usage in this context, being an old variant of 'compost'.

Grain-dryer Equipment for drying grain by the circulation of warm air. Corn threshed by the combine harvester usually has a moisture content too high for safe storage and the drying plant is a necessary adjunct of the combine involving large capital expenditure. In the past, corn was cut, stooked and allowed to finish drying naturally in the stack before threshing.

Hay Types of hay differ according to their source. *Meadow hay* is the product of permanent grassland and contains a variable mixture of grasses, herbs and white clover. *Seeds hay* or *mixture* is made from a temporary ley and may be either a mixture of grasses and clovers or consist of a single variety. Where red clover is used it may be mown for hay when about to bloom and then allowed to produce a second crop of bloom followed by seed. The seed is combined and the rest of the growth may be saved as an inferior kind of hay called *stover*.

Herbicide   A weedkiller, especially a selective one which destroys or inhibits weeds without damage to the crop. A great many herbicides are now available for specific purposes and their adoption over the last 30 years has possibly done more than mechanisation to reduce the labour requirements of the arable farm. Contact herbicides, which destroy vegetation but leave no toxic residue in the soil, have made possible the clearance and planting of land without ploughing.

Lactation   Period for which a milking animal remains in production after the birth of its young, applied mainly to dairy cows. A standard lactation under the National Milk Records scheme extends over a maximum of 305 days and is the accepted basis for measuring a cow's performance. In practise, a cow may 'dry off' in less than 305 days, or she may continue in milk after that time, but the criterion is based on the assumption that for maximum profitability a cow should calve once a year with a rest period of two or three months between the end of one lactation and the birth of the next calf. Yield varies greatly during the lactation, reaching a maximum about three weeks after calving and then slowly declining. The highest yield usually occurs in a cow's third lactation but this of course varies with individuals.

Land   For convenience in ploughing, a field is divided into strips called lands, which are joined up as the work progresses. It is completed by ploughing round the margins, the *headlands*. The systems of grooves on the face of a millstone are also called lands, presumably by association with furrows.

Leguminous plants   Peas, beans and members of the clover family. They have a special place in crop rotations since the nitrifying bacteria in their root nodules leave the land richer in nitrogen.

Ley   Temporary crop of grasses or clovers, as opposed to permanent pasture. The seed is usually sown in a young cereal crop in spring. This shelters the early growth of the ley and is known as a *nurse crop*.

Milking parlour   Building in which cows are milked but not housed. To be distinguished from the *cowshed, byre* or *shippon* in which the animals are housed in winter as well as milked.

Mole drain   Small tunnel in clay subsoil formed by a tool pulled through it by crawler tractor, formerly by steam ploughing engines. The tunnels remain open for some years, carrying away surplus water to a piped lead or a ditch. A *tile-drain* consists of short pipes, now usually made of concrete but originally of baked clay, like tiles. The latest type of land drainage pipe is of continuous perforated plastic.

Plough   The ordinary mould-board plough needs no description; the names of some of its parts, however, are of interest in that over the centuries they have been adopted as surnames. *Slade* is the base of the plough which slides in the furrow, *pratt* the iron hook for attaching the plough chain, and *rice* is believed to be a contraction of the old name for the mould-board plough, *turnwrest*.

Rotation Sequence of cropping designed to maintain fertility and reduce the build-up of pests and diseases in the soil. A typical medieval rotation was fallow, wheat, peas or oats, fallow; thus the land was uncropped in two seasons out of four. In the eighteenth century the Norfolk or four-course rotation was adopted by progressive farmers who demonstrated its ability to bring fertility to poor, light land. It consisted basically of cereals, grass or clover, cereals, and turnips. The fact that two of the courses were essentially fodder crops enabled more livestock to be kept and increased the supply of animal manure. With modifications, the Norfolk rotation was in general use throughout the nineteenth century and was sometimes made obligatory in tenancy agreements. With the intensive use of fertilisers, conventional rotations have been increasingly disregarded and there has been continuous cropping with cereals, though there are signs of a return to more traditional cropping schemes.

Silage Chopped green matter preserved for fodder by compression and the exclusion of air. Regarded as an alternative to hay. Materials used may be grass or clover, mown several times in a season, or a bulky crop such as maize grown for its foliage. Silage is sometimes fed to cattle on self-service lines by giving them access to it under controlled conditions at regular mealtimes.

Strip-grazing System of controlled grazing in which an electric fence is moved across the grazing area giving cattle access to a fresh strip when the previous one has been thoroughly eaten down. The method is applicable to forage crops like kale in addition to pasture. The single strand of electrified wire is very effective in controlling cattle, who soon learn exactly how far they can reach under and beyond it without getting a shock, but it is ineffective with sheep who are heavily insulated by their fleece.

Top fruit Fruit grown on trees, the main commercial varieties being apples, pears, plums and cherries. Apples are the most important and the quality of English apples has been recognised for centuries. The best dessert apples are produced in areas of low rainfall in south and south-east England, culinary varieties are widely distributed and cider apples are mainly associated with the west. Plum acreages have declined—plum jam is no longer popular—and production is largely concentrated in Cambridgeshire and West Midlands districts such as the Vale of Evesham. Cherries have come from Kent since Tudor times, but production is, sadly, decreasing as old orchards are grubbed and not replanted. There is at present no dwarfing stock for cherries as there is for apples, a cherry orchard takes 15 years to come into profit and the tall trees are leading to prohibitive costs in management and picking. One of our finest summer fruits is already disappearing from the shops.

Further Reading

1 *The Face of the Land*

The handful of books mentioned below deal more with the forces, natural, human and elemental, that have made the land than with straightforward topographical description.

Cutler, W. H. R. *The Enclosure and Redistribution of Our Land* (Clarendon Press). Now 'dated', it remains a most convincing account of the fundamental changes brought about by the enclosures.

Darby, H. C. *The Medieval Fenland* (David & Charles, 1974) A full-scale study of the strange amphibian region and the early stages of its transformation.

Defoe, D. *A Tour Through the Whole Island of Great Britain* (Dent, 1927).

Forestry in the British Scene (The Forestry Commission, 1968) An inexpensive book of splendid photographs and informative captions.

Gould, Jack. *Discovering the Forests of Central England* (Shire Publications, 1972) Crammed with essential information about some of the most famous forests in the country. Maps and details of accessibility.

Hawkes, Jacquetta. *A Land* (Hodder & Stoughton, 1951) Anyone who has not read this book has missed an experience. The writer brings to the task of geological interpretation such a sensitivity and depth of insight that we begin to see our environment for the first time.

Higgs, Clyde. *A Visual History of Modern Britain: The Land* (Studio Vista, 1969) A record of change in word and picture. Read it together with Baker and Harley's *Man Made the Land* (David & Charles, 1973).

Hoskins, W. G. *The Making of the English Landscape* (Penguin, 1970) A standard work, lively and comprehensive, dealing with the evolution of both town and countryside. Also by Professor Hoskins, *English Landscapes* (BBC Publications, 1973).

Lambert, J. M. *The Making of the Broads* (Murray, 1960) Fascinating look at the Middle Ages and the inadvertent creation of a waterscape.

Massingham, H. J. *The English Downland* (Batsford, 1943) More in the 'guide book' tradition, but Massingham on the countryside was no ordinary writer and this is the product of a lifelong love affair with the downland.

Trueman, A. E. *Geology and Scenery* (Penguin, 1949) A very clear exposition of the different types of scenery produced by the random clash of forces.

2 *Village and Cottage*

Village Personal records of village life are too numerous to list, and the reader will already be familiar with many of them. The following deal with the broader aspects of the subject.

Beresford, M. W. *The Lost Villages of England* (Lutterworth, 1954) Read it for entertainment and take it with you when exploring.

Frankenberg, Ronald. *Communities in Britain* (Penguin, 1970) For a detailed look at villages still what the author described as 'truly rural'.

Hoskins, W. G. *The Making of the English Landscape* (Penguin, 1970) For the evolution of the village and its place in the scheme of things.

Jennings, Paul. *The Living Village* (Hodder & Stoughton, 1968) The modern village, based on village scrapbooks and presented with humour and understanding.

Nohl, Johannes. *The Black Death* (Allen & Unwin, 1973) An account, not confined to Britain, of the greatest depopulation of historical times. Compiled from contemporary documents.

Sharp, Thomas. *The Anatomy of the Village* (Penguin, 1946) Examination of what makes a village community and keeps it going.

Placenames

Beresford, M. W. *The Lost Villages of England* (Lutterworth, 1954)

Field, John. *Discovering Placenames* (Shire Publications, 1971) Paperback introduction to the subject, guaranteed to whet anyone's appetite for more.

Grigson, Geoffrey. *The Shell Country Book* (Dent, 1968) The chapter on place-names is as good as everything else in this book.

Pulbrook, E. *English Country Life and Work* (Batsford, 1923)

The Concise Oxford Dictionary of Placenames compiled by E. Ekwall, is the standard reference work. The English Placename Society's county survey has now reached nearly fifty volumes and full information may be obtained from the Society's headquarters at University College, Gower Street, London WC1.

Cottage

Batsford, Harry and Fry, Charles. *The English Cottage* (Batsford, 1938) Several times revised, this splendidly illustrated book is a guide to practically every type of cottage found in England and, in the case of stone buildings, many in Scotland and Wales.

Reid, Richard. *The Shell Book of Cottages* (Michael Joseph, 1977)

3 *Farming*

A short selection of books costing 35p upwards, all the more expensive ones being freely available in public libraries. Historically, the choice is weighted in favour of the nineteenth century, which saw the great transition from old to new methods and the birth of modern farming.

Bonnet, H. *The Saga of the Steam Plough* (David & Charles, 1972) Story of the only successful application of steam power to the problems of cultivation and of the most majestic of the traction engine breed.

Collins, E. T. *Sickle to Combine* (University of Reading, 1974) The history of the cereal harvest from earliest times. Illustrated from contemporary sources.

Ernle. *English Farming Past and Present* (Longman, 1941) Lord Ernle's standard work ran through many editions and it is worth getting the most recent. A massive history that contrives never to lose sight of the individual.

Evans, George Ewart. *The Horse in the Furrow* and *Ask the Fellows Who Make the Hay* (Faber, 1969, 1967). For direct, personal accounts of many aspects of farming and rural life in the recent past and what it meant to be a fellow-worker with the heavy horse, these two are unbeatable.

Groves, R. *Sharpen the Sickle* (National Union of Agricultural Workers, 1949) The story, simply and often movingly told, of the farmworker's hesitant attempts to gain social justice.

Hasbach, W. A. *History of the Agricultural Labourer* (Cass, 1956) Professor Hasbach's book was written in 1898, the modern edition appearing in 1956. He had an almost contemporary view of the consequences of an over-abundant labour supply in nineteenth-century rural England and was among the first to blame them on the mistaken Poor Law policies at the beginning of the century.

Jewell, C. A. (ed) *Victorian Farming* (Barry Shurlock, 1975) Extracts from practical writers of the period dealing with farming operations, season by season. The illustrations, mostly contemporary prints detailing practically every process, tool and implement, are a joy.

Orwin, C. and Whetham, E. *History of English Agriculture 1846–1914* (David & Charles, 1971) From the peak years of the Golden Age to the end of the Great Depression.

Trow Smith, R. *A History of British Livestock Husbandry*, Vol I to 1700 and Vol II 1700–1900 (Routledge & Kegan Paul, 1959) This absorbing story ends at the turn of the century, since when there have been changes in livestock farming as great as all those of the past.

Vince, John. *Old British Livestock* and *Vintage Farm Machines* (Shire Publications, 1974, 1973). Few writers have so well mastered the art of condensation without loss of readability. These two slim paperbacks, fully illustrated, with many photographs, are an easy introduction to farming's recent past.

Watson, James Scott and Hobbs, May Elliot. *Great Farmers* (Faber, first published 1937, second edition 1951) The human side of pioneering in a business which has not always welcomed pioneers. Some rugged individualism and a little eccentricity.

4 The Country Church

The Parish Church

Betjeman, John. *Collins Guide to English Parish Churches* (Collins, 1958) In his introduction to this book Sir John Betjeman says that the parish churches are more varied than the landscapes, and the succeeding chapters confirm this. Outstanding churches of each county are described by separate authors with a rare blend of knowledge and affection. Lavishly illustrated.

Cox, J.C. and Ford, C.B. *The Parish Churches of England* (Batsford, first published 1935, second edition 1950) One of the *English Heritage* series and very good.

Harries, John. *Discovering Churches* (Shire Publications, 1972) In 104 small pages this book deals interestingly with the history of churches and their architecture and ends with a gazetteer of those most worth visiting in every county from Orkney to Cornwall.

Lindsay, I. G. *The Scottish Parish Kirk* (Edinburgh University Press) More than a survey of buildings, a story of deeply held faiths and troubled times.

Penguin Dictionary of Architecture (1970)Compiled by Messrs Fleming, Honour and Pevsner, this comprehensive paperback is a great comfort when visiting churches, stately homes, or other edifices where one is likely to be loaded with information couched in terms that only architects should be expected to understand.

Churchyards

Brown, R. L. *A Book of Epitaphs* (David & Charles, 1969) A wide-ranging and authentic collection—though some are quite a strain on one's credulity.

Lindley, Kenneth. *Of Graves and Epitaphs* (Hutchinson, 1965) By an author well known to readers on country subjects.

Wright, Geoffrey N. *Discovering Epitaphs* (Shire Publications, 1972) Admirable short history of memorials and inscriptions. Ends with a gazetteer of churchyards of more than usual interest.

5 Communications

Roads

Anderson, M. D. *History by the Highway* (Faber, 1967) A travel book in the best sense, dealing with the road itself and the country, village and town through which it runs.

Berry, Bernard. *A Lost Roman Road* (Allen & Unwin, 1963) For an insight into the methods of Roman civil engineering and the fascination of archaeological detection.

Bryant, Arthur. *The Age of Elegance* (Collins, 1950) An account, perhaps slightly idealised but full of life and colour, of the great days of coaching.

Scott-Giles, C. W. (ed) *The Road Goes On* (Epworth Press, 1946) First published in 1946, this anthology is well worth getting from the library. Should be compulsory reading for those who complain about the tribulations of travel in our own time.

Canals

Hadfield, Charles. *British Canals: An Illustrated History* (David & Charles, 1969) paperback. Very readable study of the rise and decline of canals and of their financial and economic background. Charles Hadfield is also responsible for many of the fourteen or so books, published by David & Charles, which together form a complete regional survey of the canals of Britain. Details and individual titles from the publishers.

Mcknight, Hugh. *The Shell Book of Inland Waterways* (David & Charles, 1975)

Metcalfe, Leon and Vince, John. *Discovering Canals* (Shire Publications, 1970) Another of these handy paperbacks, informative and well illustrated. The section on outstanding constructional features and the routes to them is most valuable.

Rolt, L. T. C. *Narrow Boat* (Eyre & Spottiswoode, 1944) Story of a 400-mile journey on the Midlands waterways, superbly told and packed with history and evocative description. Its publication in 1944 introduced many people to the lore and even the existence of canals for the first time and had much to do with the modern restoration movement.

The Inland Waterways Guide (1973) is published by the Inland Waterways Association, 114 Regents Park Road, London NW1 8UO. It is the essential source of up-to-date information on everything to do with canals and navigable rivers.

Railways
Railway historians have been blessed with an immense legacy of documentation and every mile of track ever laid in Britain must have been written about. For the coverage of the subject in relation to its social and economic background the nine volumes of *A Regional History of the Railways of Great Britain* (David & Charles) have the advantage of being readable by the total non-specialist. Compact and recommended are:
Barman, C. *Early English Railways* (Penguin, 1950).
Robins, Michael. *The Railway Age* (Routledge & Kegan Paul, 1963 and Penguin, 1965).

6 Six Basic Crafts

Windmills
Freese, Stanley. *Windmills and Millwrighting* (David & Charles, 1971) One of those rare books which give a full technical treatment to the subject and make it all so easy by the use of personal experience and observation.
Skilton, C. P. *British Windmills and Watermills* (Collins, 1948) Full of description and information.
Wailes, Rex. *The English Windmill* (Routledge & Kegan Paul, 1954) A fairly recent book by an acknowledged expert. A fine, broad picture of history and development.
Vince, John. *Discovering Windmills* (Shire Publications, 1973) A concentrated introduction to the subject plus a pretty full county list of mills. Take this little book with you on long country runs.
   Properties of the National Trust (the National Trust, 1973) Lists all their mills with details of public access and descriptive literature.

Watermills
The reader cannot do better than spend a few pence on *Discovering Watermills* by John Vince (Shire Publications, 1970). Not only does this paperback contain a county-by-county list of extant watermills, it also has a very comprehensive bibliography and a timely reminder that the first edition of OS sheets (David & Charles) are invaluable in tracing the sites of vanished mills.

The Village Smithy
Evans, George Ewart. *The Horse in the Furrow* (Faber, 1960) A standard book on everything to do with the heavy horse. Evocative and very readable.
Niall, I. *Country Blacksmith* (Heinemann, 1960) For unusual material, including some on the shoeing of oxen.
Tylden, G. *Horses and Saddlery* (J. A. Allen, 1965) Horse equipment in the British Army.
Webber, R. *The Village Blacksmith* (David & Charles, 1971) An historical survey, informative, amusing, and splendidly illustrated.

The Wheel of the Wagon
Sturt, George. *The Wheelwright's Shop* (Cambridge University Press, 1903) paperback. This is the story of a wheelwright's business in the 1890s, a superbly written evocation of time, place, men and work.

Jenkins, Geraint. *The English Farm Wagon* (David & Charles, 1972) Reprinted many times, the book is probably the most detailed study of the subject available. Text and illustrations combine to make it wonderfully readable.

Arnold, James. *The Farm Wagons of England and Wales* (John Baker, 1968) This limited edition will appeal as much to the bibliophile as to the wagon enthusiast, should he be able to get hold of a copy. The author's coloured plates make it a unique pictorial record.

Vince, John. *Discovering Carts and Wagons* (Shire Publications, 1970) Like others in the *Discovering* series the book is inexpensive, slips into the pocket and is packed with information and illustrations.

Harnessmaking

Evans, George Ewart. *The Horse in the Furrow* (Faber, 1960) A standard work on everything to do with the heavy horse.

Hartfield, George. *Horse Brasses* (Abelard Schumann, 1965) Very comprehensive and full of odd bits of horse lore.

Tylden, G. *Discovering Harness and Saddlery* (Shire Publications, 1971) Another of Shire's invaluable paperbacks by a recognised expert. And by the same author: *Horses and Saddlery* (J. A. Allen, 1966) Especially saddlery in the British Army. Sometimes disquieting.

Vince, John. *Discovering Horse Brasses* (Shire Publications, 1972) Excellent introduction and well illustrated.

Also recommended are the relevant parts of Goodall's *Horses of the World* (David & Charles, 1973) and *The Shell Book of Country Crafts* by James Arnold (John Baker, 1970).

Thatching

Very little devoted solely to the subject is available. Technical material is published by the Council for Small Industries in Rural Areas. The general reader will find plenty of information in *The Shell Book of Country Crafts* (John Baker, 1970) and in *The English Cottage* by Harry Batsford and Charles Fry (Batsford, 1938), to name only two out of the many books which deal with the thatcher's work.

8 *The Country Garden*

Anthony, John. *Discovering Period Gardens* (Shire Publications, 1972) A valuable short paperback surveying garden history from the earliest times to the present day. Useful guide to gardens with period features in all parts of the country.

Dutton, Ralph. *The English Garden* (Batsford, 1937) One of the *English Heritage* series. Not a recent book, but a compact, readable illustrated survey of the whole subject.

Fish, Margery. *Cottage Garden Flowers* (David & Charles, 1970) Practical rather than historical, but showing deep insight into the origins and nature of the cottage flower garden.

Hadfield, Miles. *A History of British Gardening* (Spring Books, 1969) A very full treatment of the subject, laced with absorbing biographical detail. For the average gardener-reader it could hardly be bettered, the only minor fault in a long book being its very confusing index.

Hellyer, Arthur. *The Shell Guide to Gardens* (Heinemann, 1977).

Acknowledgements

The author wishes to thank the many individuals and organisations responsible for providing information and photographs. Especially Reading University Museum of English Rural Life, *The Field* Photographic Library, *The Farmers Weekly*, The Forestry Commission and The National Trust.

Index

Abbots Bromley, Staffordshire, 282, 283
Abinger Common, Surrey, *275*
Abinger Hammer, Sussex, 201
Alfreton watermill, *202*
Alnwick, Northumberland, 272
Andrew Mac, as inn name, 52
Arch, Joseph, 85
Ashbourne, Derbyshire, 268, 273
Ashby-de-la-Zouch, 55
Aspley Guise, 55
Avebury, Wiltshire, *39*

Bakewell, Robert, 76
Barnet Horse Fair, 277
Barnstaple, Devon, 277
Barrowden, Rutland, 281
basket making, 249-50, 253-4, *249, 252*
Bastard, John, architect, 169
Bath, 160-1
Bell, Reverend Patrick, 95
Bernwood Forest, Aylesbury, 30
Berrick Salome, 55
Bicton, Devon, 187
Biddenden, Kent, 274
Black Death, 42, 160, *43*
blacksmiths, 205-12, *206-9, 234*
Blandford, Dorset, 160
Blenheim Palace, 264
Bletchley, 30
Blisworth, *190*
Blue Boar, as inn name, 52
Bodmin Moor, 13, 23
Bodnant, North Wales, 267
Bourton-on-the-Water, 41
Braunstone, Leicestershire, 281
Brent Pelham, 56
Bridgewater, Duke of, 187
Brightling, Sussex, 168
Brimham Rocks, Ripon, *10*
Brindley, James, 187, 189, 189-90
Bristol, 281
Brixworth, Northamptonshire, 158
Broadway Hill, Cotswolds, 187
Bronze Age, 15, 178

broom making, 243-7, *244*
Brown, 'Capability', 30, 264
Brudenell, Sir Robert, 42-3
Bryce, Joseph, 94-5
Bude, *276*
Burning of Bartle, West Witton, 282
butter making, 123-4, *125*

Cader Idris, 13
Caldon canal, *189, 192*
Cambrian Age, 11-12
Canals, 187-92, *188-90, 192, 194*
Cannock Chase, 30
Carboniferous Age, 13, 17
Carhampton, Somerset, 269-70
carrier's cart, Oxfordshire, *47*
Celtic placenames, 57-60
Celts, 86, 152, 163
chair making, *244*
Chalk Downs, 15, 19, 23-5, 178
charcoal burning, 257-8, 260, *258*
Chatsworth House, 265
Cheddar caves, 15
cheesemaking, 124-6, *125*
Chester, 277
Chillenden, Kent, *198*
Chilterns, 24
churches, 148-76, *149*ff
Cirencester, 153
Clare, John, 26
Classical architecture, 160
Clavering, Essex, 38
clog making, 256-7
Cobbett, William, 48
Coke of Holkham, 76, 91
coracles, 254-6, *255*
Cornish placenames, 57-8
Corn Production Acts, repeal of, 81
Cornwall, 12, 13, 23, 147, *186, 240*
Cotswolds, 24, 41, 55, 145-7, 153, 167, 187, *71, 221*
cottage, styles of, 60-7, 69, *61, 66*
Court of Purbeck Marblers, 13
Crookham, Hampshire, 285
crosses, 163
Crossthwaite, *206-7*

Crystal Palace, 265
customs, old, 268-85
Cutler's Green, Essex, 153-4

dairying, 116-23, 150-1, *72, 117-19,
    120, 122-3*
Dartmoor, 13, 19, 22-3, *14, 184*
decorated architecture, 159-60
deserted village, 41-4, *43*
Devizes, Wiltshire, 169-70
Dewsbury, 269
Downs, the, 15, 19, 23-5, 178
Drayton Basset, 174
dry-stone walling, 142-7, *143, 145-6*
Dunsmore Heath, Warwickshire, 284
Dunstable Downs, 15
Durham Cathedral, 158

Earls Barton, Northamptonshire, 157
Early English architecture, 159
East Anglia, 27, 65, 167, *103*
East Grinstead, Sussex, 168
egg-rolling, 274
Egremont Crab Fair, 278
Ely Cathedral, 150-1
epitaphs, 168-71
Epping Forest, 30
Essex, 153-6, *155, 157*
Exeter Lammas Fair, 277
Exmoor, 23
Eyam, Derbyshire, 280

fairs, 274-9, *276, 278*
farming, 70-147, *71*ff
Farnborough, Kent, 281
Fens, 17, 19-20, 32-3
First Fruits Ceremony, Richmond,
    283
Fisherwick, Staffordshire, 264
Fletcher, Alexander, of Balmoral,
    209
Flore, Northamptonshire, 270
Flowton, Suffolk, *164*
forestry, 28-31, *20, 29*

gardens, 261-7, *261, 263, 266*
Gawthorpe, Yorkshire, 270
geology, 9-17
Glastonbury Thorn, 269
Goathland, Yorkshire, 270
Gothic architecture, 159

Gothic revival, 161
Grand Junction canal, 189-90
Grand Union canal, *190, 194*
Grasmere, Westmorland, 281
gravestones, 167-71
Great Malvern, Worcestershire, 163
Greenstead-juxta-Ongar, Essex, 156
    157
Grimes Graves, Norfolk, 162

Hales, Norfolk, *158*
Hallaton, Leicestershire, 268
Hardenhuish, Wiltshire, 160-1
harnessmakers, 224-33, *225*ff
harvesting, corn, 92-9, *96-7, 106*
Hawker, Reverend Stephen, 283
Haworth, Yorkshire, 281
Haxey, Lincolnshire, 269
haymaking, 108-16, 253, *title page,
    107, 109, 110-11, 113*
Headington, Oxford, 268
Heathcote, Sir Gilbert, 44
hedges, 25-8, 138-42, *139, 140-1*
Helston Furry Dance, 271
High Easter, Essex, 167
Hindhead, Surrey, 245
Holme Fen, 33
Horn Dance, Abbots Bromley, 282,
    283
Houghton Conquest, 55
hurdle making, 247-8, *246, 247*

Ice Ages, 15-17
Icknield Way, 178
Ingarsby, Leicestershire, 42
Iron Age, 178-9
Isle of Ely, 32

Jacob sheep, 127, *131*
Jekyll, Gertrude, 267
Jurassic Age, 13, 178

Kent, William, 264
Kentish plough, 86
Kentish Rag limestone, 161
Kilpeck, Herefordshire, 159
Kingsbridge, Devon, 169
King's Lynn, 278
Kingston Bagpuize, 55
Kirkby Lonsdale, 158

'Lady Isabella' wheel, 203
Lake District, 12, 22
Langham, Rutland, 281
Langstrothdale, Yorkshire, *16*
Laxey, Isle of Man, 203
Layer Marney, 55
Lincolnshire wagon, 214, 218, *217*
Llangollen canal, 190
London basin, 15-16
London, George, 262
lost villages, 41-4, *43*
Loudon, J.C, 265
Lower Ditchford, Gloucestershire, *43*
Lower Slaughter, 55, *146*
Long Melford, Suffolk, *154*
lych gates, 165

McAdam, John Loudon, 182
McCormick reapers, 95
Macclesfield canal, 188
Madeley, Hereford, 168
Malvern Hills, 13, *11*
Marton, Yorkshire, 170
Maxey mill, *204*
maypole dancing, *275*
Midgley, Yorkshire, *273*
mills, 196-205, *197, 198, 200, 202, 204*
Milton Abbas, 43
Milton Combe, *49*
Miserden, Gloucestershire, 168
Mompesson, William, 280
Mop Fairs, 279
museums, 213, 223-4, 233, 288

National Trust, 266-7, *261, 263*
Neolithic peoples, 23, 178
New Forest, 30
Norfolk, 101, *158, 197, 252*
Norfolk Broads, 33, *238-9*
Normans, 28, 32, 34, 152, 158-9, *158*
Normanton, Rutland, 44
Northam-on-Tweed, 272
Nôtre, André le, 262, 264
Nottingham Goose Fair, 277

Oldbury, Kent, 178-9
Old Dalby, Leicestershire, 170
Olney, Buckinghamshire, 272
Ordovician Age, 12-13

Oxfordshire wagon, 218, *217*

Pace-egg ceremonies, 273, *273*
Padstow 'Obby 'Oss, 270
Painswick, Gloucestershire, 167
   283-4, *164*
Palladian style, 160
Pantry Bridge, Wiltshire, 185
Paxton, Joseph, 265
Peak District, 23, *18*
Pembrokeshire, 13
Pennines, 13, 145
Perpendicular style, 159, 160
Pickworth, Rutland, 42
pigs, 135-8, *135, 137*
Pilgrims' Way, 178
Pitmedden House, Aberdeen, *261*
placenames, 54-60
ploughing, 86-90, *72, 87*
plough stots dance, Yorkshire, 270
Pontcysyllte aqueduct, 190
public houses, 48-52, *49, 50-1, 188, 240*
Purbeck marble, 13

railways, 192-5, *193, 194*
rake making, *252*
'Rebecca's Daughters', 182
Richmond, Yorkshire, 283
roads, 177-87, *180-1, 184, 186*
Robinson, Sir William, 265-6, 267
Rockingham Forest, Stamford, 30
Romans, 32, 34, 41, 52, 86, 126-7, 179, 181-3, 187, 226, 257, *180, 280*
Rotherfield, Sussex, 168
Royal Mail coaches, 192

Saffron Walden, 65, 154, 156
St Ives, Cornwall, 271
Saxons, 34, 38, 62, 71, 73, 86-7, 96-7, 152, 156-8, 163, 261, *157*
seed-sowing, 90-2, *82, 83*
sheep, 126-35, *128, 132, 134, 154, 246-7*
Sheffield Park Gardens, Sussex, *267*
Shenington, Oxfordshire, 281
Slaughterford, Gloucestershire, 55
Slaughterford, Wiltshire, 55
Slaughterwick, Surrey, 55
Smeaton, John, 189

Somerset 'green lanes', 178
Sompting, Sussex, 158
Speenhamland system, 84-5
Stanegate, Northumberland, 187
Stansted Mountfitchet, 55
Stockton & Darlington Railway, 192
Stoke Bruerne, Northamptonshire, *188*
Stoke Poges, 55
Stone Age, 23, 33, 178
Stone Allerton, Somerset, *208*
Stratford-on-Avon, 279
Stratton, Cornwall, *51*
Sussex trug, 249

Telford, Thomas, 182, 190, 192
Tewkesbury, 279
thatching, 233-42, *234, 237, 238, 239, 240, 242*
Thaxted, Essex, 282, *258*
threshing, 99-104, *100 101, 103*
Tichborne, Hampshire, 275
Tichborne Dole, 268
Tissington, Derbyshire, 279-80, *280*
tithes, 171-76, *172-3, 175*
Tradescant, John, 262
Tull, Jethro, 91
Turnpike Trusts, 181-2, 187

Upper Slaughter, 55

Vermuyden, Cornelius, 19, 32
village shop, 45-8, *44, 45*
villages, types of, 34-5, 38-41

Wadhurst, Sussex, 168
wagons, 214-24, *215*ff
walking-stick making, 250-3, *251*
Wallingford-on-the-Thames, *276*
Warcop, Westmorland, 281
watch boxes, in churchyards, 165
Wayfarers' Dole, 274
Wendens Ambo, 56
West Witton, Yorkshire, 282
wheelwrights, 213-24, *213*ff
White Boar, as inn name, 52
Wicken Fen, 19, 33
Widecombe Fair, 277-8
Winchester, 274
Windsor, Berkshire, 40-1
Wingrave, Buckinghamshire, 281
Wise, Henry, gardener, 262
Witney, Oxfordshire, 153
Wood, John, architect, 160-1
Woodwalton Fen, 33

Yorkshire, geological, 15, 16, *16*